Touring Spain and Portugal

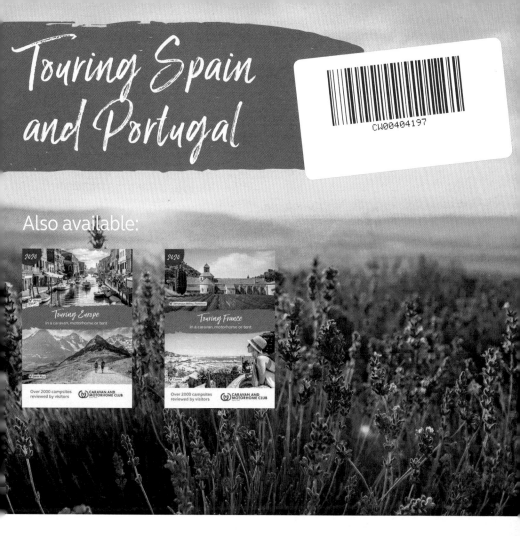

Also available:

Touring Europe — in a caravan, motorhome or tent. Over 2000 campsites reviewed by visitors. CARAVAN AND MOTORHOME CLUB

Touring France — in a caravan, motorhome or tent. Over 2000 campsites reviewed by visitors. CARAVAN AND MOTORHOME CLUB

© The Caravan Club Limited 2020
Published by The Caravan and Motorhome Club Limited
East Grinstead House, East Grinstead
West Sussex RH19 1UA

General Enquiries: 01342 326944
Travel Service Reservations: 01342 316101
Red Pennant Overseas Holiday Insurance: 01342 336633
Website: camc.com

Editor: Kate Walters
Publishing service provided by Fyooz Ltd
Printed by Stephens & George Ltd
Merthyr Tydfil
ISBN: 978-1-9993236-4-6

Maps and distance charts generated from Collins Bartholomew Digital Database
Maps ©Collins Bartholomew Ltd 2020, reproduced by permission of HarperCollins Publishers.

Discover our Worldwide Holidays

10 new tours in 2020/21

Moraine Lake, Canada

Experience unforgettable sights and create everlasting memories by choosing from our wide range of escorted and independent Worldwide Holidays.

Covering New Zealand, Australia, Southern Africa, USA and Canada including two new escorted tours.

Visit: **camc.com/worldwide**
Or call: **01342 779 349**

CARAVAN AND
MOTORHOME CLUB
SINCE 1907

Welcome...

...to another year of touring across Europe!

Wherever and however you travel, people who camp (whether in a caravan, motorhome, campervan or tent) share a sense of adventure and freedom that you don't get from other types of holidays.

However as we enter 2020 we are still in a period of uncertainty regarding the UK's position in the European Union and what will happen when we leave. While it is unlikely that Brexit will stop us from touring the EU, you might need to plan further ahead and do more research before you travel.

At the time of this book going to press much of what will change once the UK leaves the EU is unknown, and therefore it is very difficult to advise on issues such as border controls, customs, visa requirements and pet passports. Therefore you're strongly advised to check this information before you travel, especially if the UK has already left or will leave the EU while you're travelling. Check camc.com/overseas for our most up-to-date advice.

So as you start another year of touring adventures, I would like to thank you for continuing to buy and contribute to these guides. If you can, please spare five minutes to fill in one of the site report forms at the back of this book or visit camc.com/europereport to let us know what you think about the sites you've stayed on this year. Happy touring!

Kate Walters

Kate Walters, Editor

Contents

Campsites

Site listings

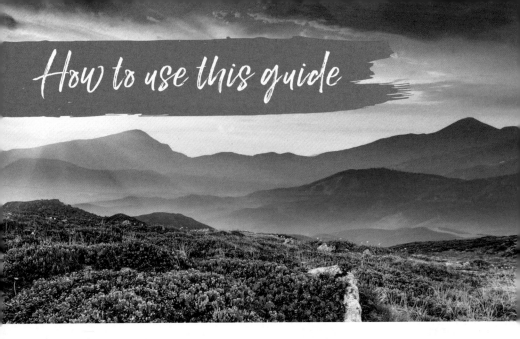

How to use this guide

The Handbook

This includes general information about touring in Europe, such as legal requirements, advice and regulations.

Country Introductions

Following on from the Handbook chapters you will find the Country Introductions containing information, regulations and advice specific to each country. You should read the Country Introduction in conjunction with the Handbook chapters before you set off on your holiday.

Campsite Entries

After the country introduction you will find the campsite entries listed alphabetically under their nearest town or village. Where there are several campsites shown in and around the same town they will be listed in clockwise order from the north.

To find a campsite all you need to do is look for the town or village of where you would like to stay, or use the maps at the back of the book to find a town where sites are listed.

For an explanation of the site entries and a guide to symbols please see the following pages. You'll also find a guide to site entries on the fold out on the rear cover.

Campsite Fees

Campsite entries show high season fees per night for an outfit plus two adults. Prices given may not include electricity or showers, unless indicated. Outside of the main holiday season many sites offer discounts on the prices shown and some sites may also offer a reduction for longer stays.

Campsite fees may vary to the prices stated in the site entries, especially if the site has not been reported on for a few years. You are advised to always check fees when booking, or at least before pitching, as those shown in site entries should be used as a guide only.

Site Maps

Each town and village listed alphabetically in the site entry pages has a map grid reference number, e.g. 3B4. The map grid reference number is shown on each site entry.

The maps can be found at the end of each country section. The reference number will show you where each town or village is located, and the site entry will tell you how far the site is from that town. Place names are shown on the maps in two colours:

Red where we list a site which is open all year (or for at least eleven months of the year)

Black where we only list seasonal sites which close in winter.

These maps are intended for general campsite location purposes only; a detailed road map or atlas is essential for route planning and touring.

The scale of the map means that it isn't possible to show every town or village where a campsite is listed, so some sites in small villages may be listed under a nearby larger town instead.

Satellite Navigation

Most campsite entries now show a GPS (sat nav) reference. There are several different formats of writing co-ordinates, and in this guide we use decimal degrees, for example 48.85661 (latitude north) and 2.35222 (longitude east).

Minus readings, shown as -1.23456, indicate that the longitude is west of the Greenwich meridian. This will only apply to sites in the west of France, most of Spain and all of Portugal as the majority of Europe are east of the Greenwich meridian.

Manufacturers of sat navs all use different formats of co-ordinates so you may need to convert the co-ordinates before using them with your device. There are plenty of online conversion tools which enable you to do this quickly and easily - just type 'co-ordinate converter' into your search engine.

Please be aware if you are using a sat nav device some routes may take you on roads that are narrow and/or are not suitable for caravans or large outfits.

The GPS co-ordinates given in this guide are provided by members and checked wherever possible, however we cannot guarantee their accuracy due to the rural nature of most sites. The Caravan and Motorhome Club cannot accept responsibility for any inaccuracies, errors or omissions or for their effects.

Site Report Forms

With the exception of campsites in The Club's Overseas Site Booking Service (SBS) network, The Caravan and Motorhome Club does not inspect sites listed in this guide. Virtually all of the sites listed in Touring Europe are from site reports submitted by users of these guides.

Sites which are not reported on for five years are deleted from the guide, so even if you visit a site and find nothing has changed we'd still appreciate an update to make sure that the site isn't archived.

You will find site report forms towards the back of the book, or you can submit them at camc.com/europereport - use the abbreviated site report form if you are reporting no changes, or only minor changes, to a site entry. The full report form should be used for new sites or if sites have changed a lot.

Please submit reports as soon as possible. Information received by mid August will be used wherever possible in the next edition of Touring Europe. Reports received after that date are still very welcome and will appear in the following edition. The editor is unable to respond individually to site reports submitted due to the large quantity that we receive.

Tips for Completing Site Reports

- If possible fill in a site report form while at the campsite. Once back at home it can be difficult to remember details of individual sites, especially if you visited several during your trip.

- When giving directions to a site, remember to include the direction of travel, e.g. 'from north on D137, turn left onto D794 signposted Combourg' or 'on N83 from Poligny turn right at petrol station in village'. Wherever possible give road numbers, junction numbers and/or kilometre post numbers, where you exit from motorways or main roads. It is also helpful to mention useful landmarks such as bridges, roundabouts, traffic lights or prominent buildings.

We very much appreciate the time and trouble you take submitting reports on campsites that you have visited; without your valuable contributions it would be impossible to update this guide.

Acknowledgements

Thanks go to the AIT/FIA Information Centre (OTA), the Alliance Internationale de Tourisme (AIT), the Fédération International de Camping et de Caravanning (FICC) and to the national clubs and tourist offices of those countries who have assisted with this publication.

Every effort is made to ensure that information provided in this publication is accurate. The Caravan and Motorhome Club Ltd has not checked these details by inspection or other investigation and cannot accept responsibility for the accuracy of these reports as provided by members and non-members, or for errors, omissions or their effects. In addition The Caravan and Motorhome Club Ltd cannot be held accountable for the quality, safety or operation of the sites concerned, or for the fact that conditions, facilities, management or prices may have changed since the last recorded visit. Any recommendations, additional comments or opinions have been contributed by people staying on the site and are not those of The Caravan and Motorhome Club.

The inclusion of advertisements or other inserted material does not imply any form of approval or recognition, nor can The Caravan and Motorhome Club Ltd undertake any responsibility for checking the accuracy of advertising material.

Explanation of a Campsite Entry

Site map grid reference

Distance and direction of the site from the centre of the listing town in kilometres (or metres), together with the aspect of the site (urban, rural or coastal).

GPS co-ordinates – latitude and longitude in decimal degrees. Minus figures indicate that the site is west of the Greenwich meridian

The town under which the campsite is listed, as shown on the relevant Sites Location Map at the end of each country's site entry pages

Campsite name

Campsite address.

HARO *1B4* (0.5km N Urban) *42.57824, -2.85421*
Camping de Haro, Avda Miranda 1, 26200 Haro
(La Rioja) 941-31 27 37; campingdeharo@fer.es;
www.campingdeharo.com

Site information shown by symbols, a guide to which can be found on the next page or inside the rear cover. Where further information is available (e.g. a price for dogs or if a toilet block is heated) is shown after the symbol.

Site contact details, including telephone number, email address and website address where available.

Fr N or S on N124 take exit sp A68 Vitoria/Logrono & Haro. In 500m at rndabt take 1st exit, under rlwy bdge, cont to site on R immed bef rv bdge. Fr AP68 exit junc 9 to town; at 2nd rndabt turn L onto LR111 (sp Logroño). Immed after rv bdge turn sharp L & foll site sp. Avoid cont into town cent. 2*, Med, hdg, mkd, pt shd, EHU (6A) inc; gas; bbq; 70% statics; phone; bus 800m; Eng spkn; adv bkg acc; ccard acc; site clsd 9 Dec-13 Jan; car wash; CKE. *"Clean, tidy, well run, lovely site - peaceful LS; friendly owner; some sm pitches & diff turns; excel facs; statics busy at w/ends; conv Rioja 'bodegas' & Bilbao & Santander ferries; recep clsd 1300-1500 no entry then due to security barrier; excel & conv NH for Santander/Bilbao; lge o'night area with electric; big, busy, vg site; easy walk to lovely town; san facs constantly cleaned!"*
€30.00, 27 Jan-10 Dec, E02.   2017

Directions to the site are shown in bold text.

Comments and opinions of tourers who have visited the site shown in italic text

Additional site information, including pitch information and electric information. For details of the abbreviations used please see the following pages.

The year in which the site was last reported on by a visitor. Sites are archived if we don't receive a report for 5 years so please consider sending in a report if you visit a site with an older date shown.

Guide price for 2 adults, an outfit and a pitch in high season.

Booking reference for a site the Club's Overseas Travel Service work with, i.e. bookable via the Club.

Opening dates for the site, may give specific dates or the general months of opening. If no dates are present the site will be open all year, as shown by the symbol in the symbols section.

Guide to symbols

Symbol	Explanation
12	The site is open all year. Some sites may decide to close if they are not busy so call ahead out of season.
	Dogs are allowed on site, usually at an extra cost (shown if known). Please see the description or member comments for any restrictions.
	Toilets available. If followed by (cont) they will be continental style toilets.
WD	Chemical toilet disposal.
	Showers available.
	Family bathroom or baby and toddler room on site. Facilities may vary.
	Toilet and/or shower facilities available for disabled guests on site. Facilities may vary.
	Laundry facilities available. Facilities and costs may vary.
	Electric hook ups are available. See the description for details of the amperage, costs and any further information.
MSP	Motorhome service point. Low level waste discharge point for motor caravans; fresh water tap and rinse facilities should also be available
	Quiet site - set in a peaceful location although at busy times you may still experience noise from other site users.

Symbol	Explanation
	Wi-Fi available, usually at an extra cost.
	Bar on site or nearby if followed by nr.
	Restaurant on site or nearby if followed by nr.
	Snack bar, cafe or takeaway on site.
	Shop on site or nearby if followed by nr.
	Playground or play area on site. Age restrictions may apply.
	Entertainment on site - this may either be evening entertainment or organised daytime activities or excursions.
	Pool on site. Where known the listing will specify if heated (htd), covered (covrd).
	Paddling pool for younger children on site
	Beach nearby, followed by the distance and information about the type of beach where known.

Site Description Abbreviations

Each site entry assumes the following unless stated otherwise:

Level ground, open grass pitches, drinking water on site, clean wc unless otherwise stated (own sanitation required if wc not listed), site is suitable for any length of stay within the dates shown.

aspect
    urban – within a city or town, or on its outskirts
    rural – within or on edge of a village or in open countryside
    coastal – within one kilometre of the coast

size of site
    sm – max 50 pitches
    med – 51 to 150 pitches
    lge – 151 to 500 pitches
    v lge – 501+ pitches

pitches
    hdg pitch – hedged pitches
    mkd pitch – marked or numbered pitches
    hdstg – some hard standing or gravel

levels
    sl – sloping site
    pt sl – sloping in parts
    terr – terraced site

shade
    shd – plenty of shade
    pt shd – part shaded
    unshd – no shade

Site Facilities

adv bkg -
    acc – advance booking accepted
    rec – advance booking recommended
    req - advance booking required

beach - symbol followed by:
    1km – distance to beach
    sand beach – sandy beach
    shql beach – shingle beach

bus/metro/tram
    Public transport within 5km

chem disp
    Dedicated chemical toilet disposal facilities;
    chem disp (wc) – no dedicated point; disposal via wc only

CKE
    Camping Key Europe accepted

CL-type
    Very small, privately-owned, informal and usually basic, farm or country site similar to those in the Caravan and Motorhome Club's network of Certificated Locations

el pnts - symbol followed by
    Mains electric hook-ups available for a fee;
    inc – cost included in site fee quoted
    10A – amperage provided
    conn fee – one-off charge for connection to metered electricity supply
    rev pol – reversed polarity may be present (see Electricity and Gas section

Eng spkn
    English spoken by campsite reception staff

gas
    Supplies of bottled gas available on site or nearby

Mairie
    Town hall (France); will usually make municipal campsite reservations

NH
    Suitable as a night halt

open 1 Apr-15 Oct
    Where no specific dates are given, opening dates are assumed to be inclusive, ie Apr-Oct – beginning April to end October (NB: opening dates may vary from those shown; check before travelling, particularly when travelling out of the main holiday season)

phone
    Public payphone on or adjacent to site

pool - symbol followed by:
    Indoor – indoor pool
    htd – heated pool
    covrd – indoor pool or one with retractable cover

red CCI/CCS
    Reduction in fees on production of a Camping Card International or Camping Card Scandinavia

BBQ
barbecues allowed (may be restricted to a separate, designated area)

serviced pitch
Electric hook-ups and mains water inlet and grey water waste outlet to pitch;
all – to all pitches
50% – percentage of pitches

shwrs - symbol followed by:
inc – cost included in site fee quoted

ssn
Season;
high ssn – peak holiday season
low ssn – out of peak season

50% statics
Percentage of static caravans/mobile homes/chalets/fixed tents/cabins or long term seasonal pitches on site, including those run by tour operators

sw
Swimming nearby;
1km – nearest swimming
lake – in lake
rv – in river

TV
TV rm – separate TV room (often also a games room)
TV (pitch) – cable or satellite connections to pitches

Other Abbreviations

AIT	Alliance Internationale de Tourisme
a'bahn	Autobahn
a'pista	Autopista
a'route	Autoroute
a'strada	Autostrada
adj	Adjacent, nearby
alt	Alternative
app	Approach, on approaching
arr	Arrival, arriving
avail	Available
Ave	Avenue
bdge	Bridge
bef	Before
bet	Between
Blvd	Boulevard
C	Century, eg 16thC
c'van	Caravan
CC	Caravan and Motorhome Club
ccard acc	Credit and/or debit cards accepted (check with site for specific details)
cent	Centre or central
clsd	Closed
conn	Connection
cont	Continue or continental (wc)
conv	Convenient
covrd	Covered
dep	Departure
diff	Difficult, with difficulty
dir	Direction
dist	Distance
dual c'way	Dual carriageway
E	East
ent	Entrance/entry to
espec	Especially
ess	Essential
excel	Excellent
facs	Facilities
FIA	Fédération Internationale de l'Automobile
FICC	Fédération Internationale de Camping & de Caravaning
FFCC	Fédération Française de Camping et de Caravaning
FKK/FNF	Naturist federation, ie naturist site
foll	Follow

fr	From
g'ge	Garage
gd	Good
grnd(s)	Ground(s)
hr(s)	Hour(s)
immac	Immaculate
immed	Immediate(ly)
inc	Included/inclusive
indus est	Industrial estate
INF	Naturist federation, ie naturist site
int'l	International
irreg	Irregular
junc	Junction
km	Kilometre
L	Left
LH	Left-hand
LS	Low season
ltd	Limited
mkd	Marked
mkt	Market
mob	Mobile (phone)
m'van	Motor caravan
m'way	Motorway
N	North
narr	Narrow
nr, nrby	Near, nearby
opp	Opposite
o'fits	Outfits
o'look(ing)	Overlook(ing)
o'night	Overnight
o'skts	Outskirts
PO	Post office
poss	Possible, possibly
pt	Part
R	Right
rd	Road or street
rec	Recommend/ed
recep	Reception
red	Reduced, reduction (for)
reg	Regular
req	Required
RH	Right-hand
rlwy	Railway line
rm	Room
rndabt	Roundabout
rte	Route
RV	Recreational vehicle, ie large motor caravan
rv/rvside	River/riverside

S	South
san facs	Sanitary facilities ie wc, showers, etc
snr citizens	Senior citizens
sep	Separate
sh	Short
sp	Sign post, signposted
sq	Square
ssn	Season
stn	Station
strt	Straight, straight ahead
sw	Swimming
thro	Through
TO	Tourist Office
tour ops	Tour operators
traff lts	Traffic lights
twd	Toward(s)
unrel	Unreliable
vg	Very good
vill	Village
W	West
w/end	Weekend
x-ing	Crossing
x-rds	Cross roads

Documents

Camping Key Europe

Camping Key Europe (CKE) is a useful touring companion. Not only does it serve as ID at campsites, meaning that you don't have to leave your passport at reception, it also entitles you to discounts at over 2200 sites.

CKE also offers third-party liability insurance for families including up to three children, which provides cover for loss or damage that occurs while on site. For more information on the scheme and all its benefits visit www.campingkey.com.

You can purchase the CKE from the Club by calling 01342 336633, or it is provided free for Red Pennant Overseas Holiday Insurance customers taking out 'Motoring' cover.

If you are using a CKE or CCI card as ID at a site, make sure that you collect your card when checking out. Also check that you have been given your own card instead of someone else's.

Driving Licence

A full (not provisional), valid driving licence should be carried at all times when driving abroad. You must produce it when asked to do so by the police and other authorities, or you may be liable for an immediate fine and confiscation of your vehicle(s).

If your driving licence is due to expire while you are away it can be renewed up to three months before expiry - contact the DVLA if you need to renew more than three months ahead.

Rules regarding driving with a provisional licences vary across Europe, so you may not be entitled to drive in some EU countries unless you have a full licence.

All EU countries recognise the photocard driving licence introduced in the UK in 1990, subject to the minimum age requirements (normally 18 years for a vehicle with a maximum weight of 3,500 kg carrying no more than 8 people).

Old-style green paper licences or Northern Irish licences issued before 1991 should be updated before travelling as they may not be recognised by local authorities.

Passport

In many EU countries everyone is required to carry photographic ID at all times. Enter next-of-kin details in the back of your passport and keep a separate photocopy. It's also a good idea to leave a photocopy of it with a relative or friend at home.

You can also scan or take a photo of your passport to keep saved on your smart phone or in a cloud storage service so you are able to access it while you're away.

The following information applies to British passport holders only. For information on passports issued by other countries you should contact the local embassy.

Applying for a Passport

Each person travelling out of the UK (including babies) must hold a valid passport - it is no longer possible to include children on a parent's passport. A standard British passport is valid for ten years, or 5 years for under 16s.

All newly issued UK passports are now biometric, also known as e-passports, which contain a microchip with information which can be used to authenticate the holder's identity.

Full information and application forms are available from main post offices or from the Identity & Passport Service's website, www.gov.uk where you can complete an online application. Allow at least six weeks for first-time passport applications, for which you may need to attend an interview at your nearest Identity and Passport Service (IPS) regional office. Allow three weeks for a renewal application or replacement of a lost, stolen or damaged passport.

Passport Validity

Most countries in the EU only require your passport to be valid for the duration of your stay. However, in case your return home is delayed it is a good idea make sure you have six month's validity remaining. Any time left on a passport (up to a maximum of nine months) will be added to the validity of your new passport on renewal.

Schengen Agreement

The Schengen Agreement allows people and vehicles to pass freely without border checks from country to country within the Schengen area (26 countries). Where there are no longer any border checks you should still not attempt to cross land borders without a full, valid passport. It is likely that random identity checks will be made for the foreseeable future in areas surrounding borders. The United Kingdom and Republic of Ireland do not fully participate in the Schengen Agreement.

Due to the current migrant crisis in Europe some countries have temporarily restored their borders. A current list of countries affected is available on the EU website: **ec.europa.eu/home-affairs/what-we-do/policies/borders-and-visas/schengen/reintroduction-border-control_en**.

Pets resident anywhere in the British Isles (excluding the Republic of Ireland) are able to travel freely within the British Isles and are not subject to PETS rules.

For details of how to obtain a Pet Passport visit www.defra.gov.uk or call 0370 241 1710.

Returning to the UK

On your return to the UK with your pet you will need to visit a vet between 24 and 120 hours prior to your return journey in order for your pet to be treated for tapeworm. The vet will need to sign your pet passport - ensure that they put the correct date against their signature or you may not fall within the correct time range for travel. Ask your campsite to recommend a local vet, or research vets near to the port you will be returning from before you travel.

Regulations for Pets

Some campsites do not accept dogs at all and some have restrictions on the number and breed of dogs allowed. Visit camc.com/overseasadvice for more information and country specific advice.

In popular tourist areas local regulations may ban dogs from beaches in the summer months.

Pet Travel Scheme (PETS)

The Pet Travel Scheme (PETS) allows owners of dogs, cats and ferrets from qualifying European countries, to bring their pets into the UK (up to a limit of five per person) without quarantine. The animal must have an EU pet passport, be microchipped and be vaccinated against rabies. Dogs must also have been treated for tapeworm. It also allows pets to travel from the UK to other EU qualifying countries.

There are country specific regulations regarding certain breeds of dogs. You can't import breeds classed as dangerous dogs to many countries, and other breeds will require additional documentation. For more information or to find out which breeds are banned or restricted visit camc.com/pets or call us on 01342 336766.

Travelling with Children

Some countries require evidence of parental responsibility for people travelling alone with children, especially those who have a different surname to them (including lone parents and grandparent). The authorities may want to see a birth certificate, a letter of consent from the child's parent (or other parent if you are travelling alone with your own child) and some evidence as to your responsibility for the child.

For further information on exactly what will be required at immigration contact the Embassy or Consulate of the countries you intend to visit.

Vehicle documents

Caravan Proof of Ownership (CRIS)

In Britain and Ireland, unlike most other European countries, caravans are not formally registered in the same way as cars. This may not be fully understood by police and other authorities on the Continent. You are strongly advised, therefore, to carry a copy of your Caravan Registration Identification Scheme (CRIS) document.

MOT Certificate

Carry your vehicle's MOT certificate (if applicable) as you may need to show it to the authorities if your vehicle is involved in an accident, or in the event of random vehicle checks. If your MOT certificate is due to expire while you are away you should have the vehicle tested before you leave home.

Tax

While driving abroad you still need to have current UK vehicle tax. If your vehicle's tax is due to expire while you are abroad you may apply to re-license the vehicle at a post office, by post, or in person at a DVLA local office, up to two months in advance.

Since October 2014 the DVLA have no longer issued paper tax discs - EU Authorities are aware of this change.

Vehicle Registration Certificate (V5C)

You must always carry your Vehicle Registration Certificate (V5C) and MOT Certificate (if applicable) when taking your vehicle abroad. If yours has been lost, stolen or destroyed you should apply to a DVLA local office on form V62. Call DVLA Customer Enquiries on 0300 790 6802 for more information.

Hired or Borrowed Vehicles

If using a borrowed vehicle you must obtain a letter of authority to use the vehicle from the registered owner. You should also carry the Vehicle Registration Certificate (V5C).

In the case of hired or leased vehicles, including company cars, when the user does not normally possess the V5C, ask the company which owns the vehicle to supply a Vehicle On Hire Certificate, form VE103, which is the only legal substitute for a V5C. The BVRLA, the trade body for the vehicle rental and leasing sector, provide advice on hired or leased vehicles - see www.bvrla.co.uk or call them on 01494 434747 for more information.

If you are caught driving a hired vehicle abroad without this certificate you may be fined and/or the vehicle impounded.

Visas

British citizens holding a full UK passport do not require a visa for entry into any EU countries, although you may require a permit for stays of more than three months. Contact the relevant country's UK embassy before you travel for information.

British subjects, British overseas citizens, British dependent territories citizens and citizens of other countries may need visas that are not required by British citizens. Again check with the authorities of the country you are due to visit at their UK embassy or consulate. Citizens of other countries should apply to their own embassy, consulate or High Commission.

Insurance

Car, Motorhome and Caravan Insurance

It is important to make sure your outfit is covered whilst you are travelling abroad. Your car or motorhome insurance should cover you for driving in the EU, but check what you are covered for before you travel. If you are travelling outside the EU or associated countries you'll need to inform your insurer and may have to pay an additional premium.

Make sure your caravan insurance includes travel outside of the UK, speak to your provider to check this. You may need to notify them of your dates of travel and may be charged an extra premium dependent on your level of cover.

The Caravan and Motorhome Club's Car, Caravan Cover and Motorhome Insurance schemes extend to provide policy cover for travel within the EU free of charge, provided the total period of foreign travel in any one year does not exceed 270 days for Car and Motorhome Insurance and 182 for Caravan Insurance. It may be possible to extend this period, although a charge may apply.

Should you be delayed beyond these limits notify your broker or insurer immediately in order to maintain your cover until you can return to the UK.

If your outfit is damaged during ferry travel (including while loading or unloading) it must be reported to the carrier at the time of the incident. Most insurance policies will cover short sea crossings (up to 65 hours) but check with your insurer before travelling.

Visit camc.com/insurance or call 01342 336610 for full details of our Caravan Cover or for Car or Motorhome Insurance call 0345 504 0334.

European Accident Statement

Your car or motorhome insurer may provide you with a European Accident Statement form (EAS), or you may be given one if you are involved in an accident abroad. The EAS is a standard form, available in different languages, which gives all parties involved in an accident the opportunity to agree on the facts. Signing the form doesn't mean that you are accepting liability, just that you agree with what has been stated on the form. Only sign an EAS if you are completely sure that you understand what has been written and always make sure that you take a copy of the completed EAS.

Vehicles Left Behind Abroad

If you are involved in an accident or breakdown abroad which prevents you taking your vehicle home, you must ensure that your normal insurance will cover your vehicle if left overseas while you return home. Also check if you're covered for the cost of recovering it to your home address.

In this event you should remove all items of baggage and personal belongings from your vehicles before leaving them unattended. If this isn't possible you should check with your insurer if extended cover can be provided. In all circumstances, you must remove any valuables and items liable for customs duty, including wine, beer, spirits and cigarettes.

Legal Costs Abroad

If an accident abroad leads to you being taken to court you may find yourself liable for legal costs – even if you are not found to be at fault. Most UK vehicle insurance policies include cover for legal costs or have the option to add cover for a small additional cost – check if you are covered before you travel.

Holiday Travel Insurance

A standard motor insurance policy won't cover you for all eventualities, for example vehicle breakdown, medical expenses or accommodation so it's important to also take out adequate travel insurance. Make sure that the travel insurance you take out is suitable for a caravan or motorhome holiday.

Remember to check exemptions and exclusions, especially those relating to pre-existing medical conditions or the use of alcohol. Be sure to declare any pre-existing medical conditions to your insurer.

The Club's Red Pennant Overseas Holiday Insurance is designed specifically for touring holidays and can cover both motoring and personal use. Depending on the level of cover chosen the policy will cover you for vehicle recovery and repair, holiday continuation, medical expenses and accommodation.

Visit camc.com/redpennant for full details or call us on 01342 336633.

Holiday Insurance for Pets

Taking your pet with you? Make sure they're covered too. Some holiday insurance policies, including The Club's Red Pennant, can be extended to cover pet expenses relating to an incident normally covered under the policy – such as pet repatriation in the event that your vehicle is written off.

However in order to provide cover for pet injury or illness you will need a separate pet insurance policy which covers your pet while out of the UK. For details of The Club's Pet Insurance scheme visit camc.com/petins or call 0345 504 0336.

Home Insurance

Your home insurer may require advance notification if you are leaving your home unoccupied for 30 days or more. There may be specific requirements, such as turning off mains services (except electricity), draining water down and having somebody check your home periodically. Read your policy documents or speak to your provider.

The Club's Home Insurance policy provides full cover for up to 90 days when you are away from home (for instance when touring) and requires only common sense precautions for longer periods of unoccupancy. See camc.com/homeins or call 0345 504 0335 for details.

Personal Belongings

The majority of travellers are able to cover their valuables such as jewellery, watches, cameras, laptops, and bikes under a home insurance policy. This includes the Club's Home Insurance scheme.

Specialist gadget insurance is now commonly available and can provide valuable benefits if you are taking smart phones, tablets, laptops or other gadgets on holiday with you. The Club offers a Gadget Insurance policy - visit camc.com/gadget or call 01342 779413 to find out more.

Customs

Caravans and Vehicles

You can temporarily import a caravan, trailer tent or vehicle from one EU country to another without any Customs formalities. Vehicles and caravans may be temporarily imported into non-EU countries generally for a maximum of six months in any twelve month period, provided they are not hired, sold or otherwise disposed of in that country.

If you intend to stay longer than six months, dispose of a vehicle in another country or leave your vehicle there in storage you should seek advice well before your departure from the UK.

Borrowed Vehicles

If you are borrowing a vehicle from a friend or relative, or loaning yours to someone, you should be aware of the following:

- The total time the vehicle spends abroad must not exceed the limit for temporary importation (generally six months).
- The owner of the caravan must provide the other person with a letter of authority.
- The owner cannot accept a hire fee or reward.

- The number plate on the caravan must match the number plate on the tow car.
- Both drivers' insurers must be informed if a caravan is being towed and any additional premium must be paid.

Currency

You must declare cash of €10,000 (or equivalent in other currencies) or more when travelling between the UK and a non-EU country. The term 'cash' includes cheques, travellers' cheques, bankers' drafts, notes and coins. You don't need to declare cash when travelling within the EU.

For further information contact HMRC Excise & Customs Helpline on 0300 200 3700.

Customs Allowances

Travelling within the European Union

If you are travelling to the UK from within the EU you can bring an unlimited amount of most goods without being liable for any duty or tax, but certain rules apply. The goods must be for your own personal use, which can include use as a gift (if the person you are gifting the goods to reimburses you this is not classed as a gift), and you must have paid duty and tax in the country where you purchased the goods. If a customs official suspects that any goods are not for your own personal use they can question you, make further checks and ultimately seize both the goods and the vehicle used to transport them. Although no limits are in place, customs officials are less likely to question you regarding your goods if they are under the following limits:

- 800 cigarettes
- 400 cigarillos
- 200 cigars
- 1kg tobacco
- 10 litres of spirits

- 20 litres of fortified wine (e.g. port or sherry)
- 90 litres of wine
- 110 litres of beer

The same rules and recommended limits apply for travel between other EU countries.

Travelling Outside the EU

There are set limits to the amount of goods you bring back into the UK from countries outside of the EU. All goods must be for your own personal use. Each person aged 17 and over is entitled to the following allowance:

- 200 cigarettes, or 100 cigarillos, or 50 cigars, or 250g tobacco
- 1 litre of spirits or strong liqueurs over 22% volume, or 2 litres of fortified wine, sparkling wine or any other alcoholic drink that's less than 22% volume
- 4 litres of still wine
- 16 litres of beer
- £390 worth of all other goods including perfume, gifts and souvenirs without having to pay tax and/or duty
- For further information contact HMRC National Advice Service on 0300 200 3700.

Medicines

There is no limit to the amount of medicines you can take abroad if they are obtained without prescription (i.e. over the counter medicines). Medicines prescribed by your doctor may contain controlled drugs (e.g. morphine), for which you will need a licence if you're leaving the UK for 3 months or more. Visit www.gov.uk/travelling-controlled-drugs or call 020 7035 0771 for a list of controlled drugs and to apply for a licence.

You don't need a licence if you carry less than 3 months' supply or your medication doesn't contain controlled drugs, but you should carry a letter from your doctor stating your name, a list of your prescribed drugs and dosages for each drug. You may have to show this letter when going through customs.

Personal Possessions

Visitors to countries within the EU are free to carry reasonable quantities of any personal possessions such as jewellery, cameras, and electrical equipment required for the duration of their stay. It is sensible to carry sales receipts for new items in case you need to prove that tax has already been paid.

Prohibited and Restricted Goods

Regardless of where you are travelling from the importation of some goods into the UK is restricted or banned, mainly to protect health and the environment. These include:

- Endangered animals or plants including live animals, birds and plants, ivory, skins, coral, hides, shells and goods made from them such as jewellery, shoes, bags and belts.

- Controlled, unlicensed or dangerous drugs.

- Counterfeit or pirated goods such as watches, CDs and clothes; goods bearing a false indication of their place of manufacture or in breach of UK copyright.

- Offensive weapons such as firearms, flick knives, knuckledusters, push daggers, self-defence sprays and stun guns.

- Pornographic material depicting extreme violence or featuring children

This list is not exhaustive; if in doubt contact HMRC on 0300 200 3700 (+44 2920 501 261 from outside the UK) or go through the red Customs channel and ask a Customs officer when returning to the UK.

Plants and Food

Travellers from within the EU may bring into the UK any fruit, vegetable or plant products without restriction as long as they are grown in the EU, are free from pests or disease and are for your own consumption. For food products Andorra, the Channel Islands, the Isle of Man, San Marino and Switzerland are treated as part of the EU. From most countries outside the EU you are not allowed to bring into the UK any meat or dairy products. Other animal products may be severely restricted or banned and it is important that you declare any such products on entering the UK. For up to date information contact the Department for Environment, Food and Rural Affairs (Defra) on 0345 33 55 77 or +44 20 7238 6951 from outside the UK. You can also visit www.defra.gov.uk to find out more.

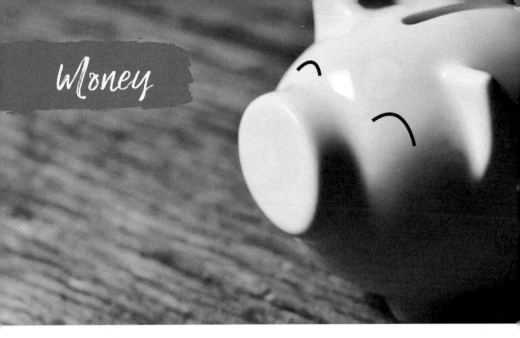

Money

Being able to safely access your money while you're away is a necessity for you to enjoy your break. It isn't a good idea to rely on one method of payment, so always have a backup plan. A mixture of a small amount of cash plus one or two electronic means of payment are a good idea.

Traveller's cheques have become less popular in recent years as fewer banks and hotels are willing or able to cash them. There are alternative options which offer the same level of security but are easier to use, such as prepaid credit cards.

Local Currency

It is a good idea to take enough foreign currency for your journey and immediate needs on arrival, don't forget you may need change for tolls or parking on your journey. Currency exchange facilities will be available at ports and on ferries but rates offered may not be as good as you would find elsewhere.

The Post Office, banks, exchange offices and travel agents offer foreign exchange. All should stock Euros but during peak holiday times or if you need a large amount it may be sensible to pre-order your currency. You should also pre-order less common currencies. Shop around and compare commission and exchange rates, together with minimum charges.

Banks and money exchanges in central and eastern Europe won't usually accept Scottish and Northern Irish bank notes and may be reluctant to change any sterling which has been written on or is creased or worn.

Foreign Currency Bank Accounts

Frequent travellers or those who spend long periods abroad may find a Euro bank account useful. Most such accounts impose no currency conversion charges for debit or credit card use and allow fee-free cash withdrawals at ATMs. Some banks may also allow you to spread your account across different currencies, depending on your circumstances. Speak to your bank about the services they offer.

Prepaid Travel Cards

Prepaid travel money cards are issued by various providers including the Post Office, Travelex, Lloyds Bank and American Express.

They are increasingly popular as the PIN protected travel money card offers the security of Traveller's Cheques, with the convenience of paying by card. You load the card with the amount you need before leaving home, and then use cash machines to make withdrawals or use the card to pay for goods and services as you would a credit or debit card. You can top the card up over the telephone or online while you are abroad. However there can be issues with using them with some automated payment systems, such as pay-at-pump petrol stations and toll booths, so you should always have an alternative payment method available.

These cards can be cheaper to use than credit or debit cards for both cash withdrawals and purchases as there are usually no loading or transaction fees to pay. In addition, because they are separate from your bank account, if the card is lost or stolen you bank account will still be secure.

Credit and Debit Cards

Credit and debit cards offer a convenient way of spending abroad. For the use of cards abroad most banks impose a foreign currency conversion charge of up to 3% per transaction. If you use your card to withdraw cash there will be a further commission charge of up to 3% and you will be charged interest (possibly at a higher rate than normal) as soon as you withdraw the money.

There are credit cards available which are specifically designed for spending overseas and will give you the best available rates. However they often have high interest rates so are only economical if you're able to pay them off in full each month.

If you have several cards, take at least two in case you encounter problems. Credit and debit 'Chip and PIN' cards issued by UK banks may not be universally accepted abroad so check that your card will be accepted if using it in restaurants or other situations where you pay after you have received goods or services

Contact your credit or debit card issuer before you leave home to let them know that you will be travelling abroad. In the battle against card fraud, card issuers frequently query transactions which they regard as unusual or suspicious, causing your card to be declined or temporarily stopped. You should always carry your card issuer's helpline number with you so that you can contact them if this happens. You will also need this number should you need to report the loss or theft of your card.

Dynamic Currency Conversion

When you pay with a credit or debit card, retailers may offer you the choice of currency for payment, e.g. a euro amount will be converted into sterling and then charged to your card account. This is known as a 'Dynamic Currency Conversion' but the exchange rate used is likely to be worse than the rate offered by your card issuer, so will work out more expensive than paying in the local currency.

Emergency Cash

If an emergency or theft means that you need cash in a hurry, then friends or relatives at home can send you emergency cash via money transfer services. The Post Office, MoneyGram and Western Union all offer services which, allows the transfer of money to over 233,000 money transfer agents around the world. Transfers take approximately ten minutes and charges are levied on a sliding scale.

Crossing the Channel

Booking Your Ferry

If travelling at peak times, such as Easter or school holidays, make reservations as early as possible. Each ferry will have limited room for caravans and large vehicles so spaces can fill up quickly, especially on cheaper crossings. If you need any special assistance request this at the time of booking.

When booking any ferry crossing, make sure you give the correct measurements for your outfit including bikes, roof boxes or anything which may add to the length or height of your vehicle - if you underestimate your vehicle's size you may be turned away or charged an additional fee.

The Caravan and Motorhome Club is an agent for most major ferry companies operating services. Call The Club's Travel Service on 01342 316 101 or see camc.com/ferries to book.

The table at the end of this section shows ferry routes from the UK to the Continent and Ireland. Some ferry routes may not be operational all year, and during peak periods there may be a limit to the number of caravans or motorhomes accepted. For the most up-to-date information visit camc.com/ferries or call the Club's Travel Services team.

On the Ferry

Arrive at the port with plenty of time before your boarding time. Motorhomes and car/caravan outfits will usually either be the first or last vehicles boarded onto the ferry. Almost all ferries are now 'drive on – drive off' so you won't be required to do any complicated manoeuvres. You may be required to show ferry staff that your gas is switched off before boarding the ferry.

Be careful using the ferry access ramps, as they are often very steep which can mean there is a risk of grounding the tow bar or caravan hitch. Drive slowly and, if your ground clearance is low, consider whether removing your jockey wheel and any stabilising devices would help.

Vehicles are often parked close together on ferries, meaning that if you have towing extension mirrors they could get knocked or damaged by people trying to get past your vehicle. If you leave them attached during the ferry crossing then make sure you check their position on returning to your vehicle.

Channel Tunnel

The Channel Tunnel operator, Eurotunnel, accepts cars, caravans and motorhomes (except those running on LPG) on their service between Folkestone and Calais. You can just turn up and see if there is availability on the day, however prices increase as it gets closer to the departure time so if you know your plans in advance it is best to book as early as possible.

On the Journey

You will be asked to open your roof vents prior to travel and you will also need to apply the caravan brake once you have parked your vehicle on the train. You will not be able to use your caravan until arrival.

Pets

It is possible to transport your pet on a number of ferry routes to the Continent and Ireland, as well as on Eurotunnel services from Folkestone to Calais. Advance booking is essential as restrictions apply to the number of animals allowed on any one crossing. Make sure you understand the carrier's terms and conditions for transporting pets. Brittany Ferries ask for all dogs to be muzzled when out of the vehicle but this varies for other operators so please check at the time of booking.

Once on board pets are normally required to remain in their owner's vehicle or in kennels on the car deck and you won't be able to access your vehicle to check on your pet while the ferry is at sea. On longer crossings you should make arrangements at the on-board information desk for permission to visit your pet in order to check its well-being. You should always make sure that ferry staff know your vehicle has a pet on board.

Information and advice on the welfare of animals before and during a journey is available on the website of the Department for Environment, Food and Rural Affairs (Defra), www.defra.gov.uk.

Gas

UK based ferry companies usually allow up to three gas cylinders per caravan, including the cylinder currently in use, however some may restrict this to a maximum of two cylinders. Some operators may ask you to hand over your gas cylinders to a member of the crew so that they can be safely stored during the crossing. Check that you know the rules of your ferry operator before you travel.

Cylinder valves should be fully closed and covered with a cap, if provided, and should remain closed during the crossing. Cylinders should be fixed securely in or on the caravan in the position specified by the manufacturer.

Gas cylinders must be declared at check-in and the crew may ask to inspect each cylinder for leakage before travel.

The carriage of spare petrol cans, whether full or empty, is not permitted on ferries or through the Channel Tunnel.

LPG Vehicles

Vehicles fully or partially powered by LPG can't be carried through the Channel Tunnel. Gas for domestic use (e.g. heating, lighting or cooking) can be carried, but the maximum limit is 47kg for a single bottle or 50kg in multiple bottles. Tanks must be switched off before boarding and must be less than 80% full; you will be asked to demonstrate this before you travel.

Most ferry companies will accept LPG-powered vehicles but you must let them know at the time of booking. During the crossing the tank must be no more than 75% full and it must be turned off. In the case of vehicles converted to use LPG, some ferry companies also require a certificate showing that the conversion has been carried out by a professional - before you book speak to the ferry company to see what their requirements are.

Club Sites Near Ports

If you've got a long drive to the ferry port, or want to catch an early ferry then an overnight stop near to the port gives you a relaxing start to your holiday. The following table lists Club sites which are close to ports.

Club Members can book online at camc.com or call 01342 327490. Non-members can book by calling the sites directly on the telephone numbers below when the sites are open.

Please note that Commons Wood, Fairlight Wood, Hunter's Moon and Old Hartley are open to Club members only. Non-members are welcome at all other sites listed below.

Port	Nearest Club Site	Tel No.
Cairnryan	New England Bay	01776 860275
Dover, Folkestone, Channel Tunnel	Bearsted	01622 730018
	Black Horse Farm*	01303 892665
	Daleacres	01303 267679
	Fairlight Wood	01424 812333
Fishguard, Pembroke	Freshwater East	01646 672341
Harwich	Cambridge Cherry Hinton*	01223 244088
	Commons Wood*	01707 260786
Holyhead	Penrhos	01248 852617
Hull	York Beechwood Grange*	01904 424637
	York Rowntree Park*	01904 658997
Newcastle upon Tyne	Old Hartley	0191 237 0256
Newhaven	Brighton*	01273 626546
Plymouth	Plymouth Sound	01752 862325
Poole	Hunter's Moon*	01929 556605
Portsmouth	Rookesbury Park	01329 834085
Rosslare	River Valley	00353 (0)404 41647
Weymouth	Crossways	01305 852032

* Site open all year

Ferry Routes and Operators

Route	Operator	Approximate Crossing Time	Maximum Frequency
Belgium			
Hull – Zeebrugge	P & O Ferries	12-14 hrs	1 daily
France			
Dover – Calais	P & O Ferries	1½ hrs	22 daily
Dover – Calais	DFDS Seaways	1½ hrs	10 daily
Dover – Dunkerque	DFDS Seaways	2 hrs	12 daily
Folkestone – Calais	Eurotunnel	35 mins	3 per hour
Newhaven – Dieppe	DFDS Seaways	4 hrs	2 daily
Plymouth – Roscoff	Brittany Ferries	6 hrs	2 daily
Poole – St Malo (via Channel Islands)*	Condor Ferries	5 hrs	1 daily (May to Sep)
Portsmouth – Caen	Brittany Ferries	6 / 7 hrs	3 daily (maximum)
Portsmouth – Cherbourg	Brittany Ferries	3 hrs	2 daily (maximum)
Portsmouth – Le Havre	Brittany Ferries	3¼ / 8 hrs	1 daily (minimum)
Portsmouth – St Malo	Brittany Ferries	9 hrs	1 daily
Ireland – Northern			
Cairnryan – Larne	P & O Irish Sea	1 / 2 hrs	7 daily
Liverpool (Birkenhead) – Belfast	Stena Line	8 hrs	2 daily
Cairnryan – Belfast	Stena Line	2 / 3 hrs	7 daily
Ireland – Republic			
Cork – Roscoff*	Brittany Ferries	14 hrs	1 per week
Dublin - Cherbourg	Irish Ferries	19 hrs	1 per week
Fishguard – Rosslare	Stena Line	3½ hrs	2 daily
Holyhead – Dublin	Irish Ferries	2-4 hrs	Max 4 daily
Holyhead – Dublin	Stena Line	2-4 hrs	Max 4 daily
Liverpool – Dublin	P & O Irish Sea	8 hrs	2 daily
Pembroke – Rosslare	Irish Ferries	4 hrs	2 daily
Rosslare – Cherbourg*	Irish Ferries	19½ hrs	3 per week
Rosslare – Cherbourg	Stena Line	19 hrs	3 per week
Rosslare – Roscoff*	Irish Ferries	19½ hrs	4 per week
Netherlands			
Harwich – Hook of Holland	Stena Line	7 hrs	2 daily
Hull – Rotterdam	P & O Ferries	11-12 hrs	1 daily
Newcastle – Ijmuiden (Amsterdam)	DFDS Seaways	15½ hrs	1 daily
Spain			
Portsmouth – Bilbao	Brittany Ferries	24 / 32 hrs	1 - 3 per week
Portsmouth or Plymouth – Santander	Brittany Ferries	20 / 32 hrs	4 per week

Not bookable through The Club's Travel Service.
Note: Services and routes correct at time of publication but subject to change.

Motoring advice

Preparing for Your Journey

The first priority in preparing your outfit for your journey should be to make sure it has a full service. Make sure that you have a fully equipped spares kit, and a spare wheel and tyre for your caravan – it is easier to get hold of them from your local dealer than to have to spend time searching for spares where you don't know the local area.

Club members should carry their UK Sites Directory & Handbook with them, as it contains a section of technical advice which may be useful when travelling.

The Club also has a free advice service covering a wide range of technical topics – download free information leaflets at camc.com/advice or contact the team by calling 01342 336611 or emailing technical@camc.com.

For advice on issues specific to countries other than the UK, Club members can contact the Travel Service Information Officer, email: travelserviceinfo@camc.com or call 01342 336766.

Weight Limits

From both a legal and a safety point of view, it is essential not to exceed vehicle weight limits. It is advisable to carry documentation confirming your vehicle's maximum permitted laden weight - if your Vehicle Registration Certificate (V5C) does not state this, you will need to produce alternative certification, e.g. from a weighbridge.

If you are pulled over by the police and don't have certification you will be taken to a weighbridge. If your vehicle(s) are then found to be overweight you will be liable to a fine and may have to discard items to lower the weight before you can continue on your journey.

Some Final Checks

Before you start any journey make sure you complete the following checks:

- All car and caravan or motorhome lights are working and sets of spare bulbs are packed.
- The coupling is correctly seated on the towball and the breakaway cable is attached.
- Windows, vents, hatches and doors are shut.
- On-board water systems are drained.
- Mirrors are adjusted for maximum visibility.
- Corner steadies are fully wound up and the brace is handy for your arrival on site.

- Any fires or flames are extinguished and the gas cylinder tap is turned off. Fire extinguishers are fully charged and close at hand.
- The over-run brake is working correctly.
- The jockey wheel is raised and secured, the handbrake is released.

Driving in Europe

Driving abroad for the first time can be a daunting prospect, especially when towing a caravan. Here are a few tips to make the transition easier:

- Remember that Sat Navs may take you on unsuitable roads, so have a map or atlas to hand to help you find an alternative route.
- It can be tempting to try and get to your destination as quickly as possible but we recommend travelling a maximum of 250 miles a day when towing.
- Share the driving if possible, and on long journeys plan an overnight stop.
- Remember that if you need to overtake or pull out around an obstruction you will not be able to see clearly from the driver's seat. If possible, always have a responsible adult in the passenger seat who can advise you when it is clear to pull out. If that is not possible then stay well back to get a better view and pull out slowly.
- If traffic builds up behind you, pull over safely and let it pass.
- Driving on the right should become second nature after a while, but pay particular attention when turning left, after leaving a rest area, petrol station or site or after a one-way system.
- Stop at least every two hours to stretch your legs and take a break.

Fuel

Grades of petrol sold on the Continent are comparable to those sold in the UK; 95 octane is frequently known as 'Essence' and 98 octane as 'Super'. Diesel may be called 'Gasoil' and is widely available across Europe. E10 petrol (containing 10% Ethanol) can be found in certain countries in Europe. Most modern cars are E10 compatible, but those which aren't could be damaged by filling up with E10. Check your vehicle handbook or visit www.acea.be and search for 'E10' to find the publication 'Vehicle compatibility with new fuel standards'.

Members of The Caravan and Motorhome Club can check current average fuel prices by country at camc.com/overseasadvice.

Away from major roads and towns it is a good idea not to let your fuel tank run too low as you may have difficulty finding a petrol station, especially at night or on Sundays. Petrol stations offering a 24-hour service may involve an automated process, in some cases only accepting credit cards issued in the country you are in.

Automotive Liquefied Petroleum Gas (LPG)

The increasing popularity of dual-fuelled vehicles means that the availability of LPG – also known as 'autogas' or GPL – has become an important issue for more drivers.

There are different tank-filling openings in use in different countries. Currently there is no common European filling system, and you might find a variety of systems. Most Continental motorway services will have adaptors but these should be used with care – see www.autogas.ltd.uk for more information.

Low Emission Zones

Many cities in countries around Europe have introduced 'Low Emission Zones' (LEZ's) in order to regulate vehicle pollution levels. Some schemes require you to buy a windscreen sticker, pay a fee or register your vehicle before entering the zone. You may also need to provide proof that your vehicle's emissions meet the required standard. Before you travel visit www.lowemissionzones.eu for maps and details of LEZ's across Europe. Also see the Country Introductions later in this guide for country specific information.

Motorhomes Towing Cars

If you are towing a car behind a motorhome, our advice would be to use a trailer with all four wheels of the car off the ground. Although most countries don't have specific laws banning A-frames, there may be laws in place which prohibit motor vehicle towing another motor vehicle.

Priority and Roundabouts

When driving on the Continent it can be difficult to work out which vehicles have priority in different situations. Watch out for road signs which indicate priority and read the Country Introductions later in this guide for country specific information.

Take care at intersections – you should never rely on being given right of way, even if you have priority; especially in small towns and villages where local traffic may take right of way. Always give way to public service and military vehicles and to buses and trams.

In some countries in Europe priority at roundabouts is given to vehicles entering the roundabout (i.e. on the right) unless the road signs say otherwise.

Public Transport

In general in built-up areas be prepared to stop to allow a bus to pull out from a bus stop when the driver is signalling his intention to do so.

Take particular care when school buses have stopped and passengers are getting on and off.

Overtaking trams in motion is normally only allowed on the right, unless on a one way street where you can overtake on the left if there is not enough space on the right. Do not overtake a tram near a tram stop. These may be in the centre of the road. When a tram or bus stops to allow passengers on and off, you should stop to allow them to cross to the pavement. Give way to trams which are turning across your carriageway. Don't park or stop across tram lines; trams cannot steer round obstructions!

Pedestrian Crossings

Stopping to allow pedestrians to cross at zebra crossings is not always common practice on the Continent as it is in the UK. Pedestrians expect to wait until the road is clear before crossing, while motorists behind may be taken by surprise by your stopping. The result may be a rear-end shunt or vehicles overtaking you at the crossing and putting pedestrians at risk.

Traffic Lights

Traffic lights may not be as easily visible as they are in the UK, for instance they may be smaller or suspended across the road with a smaller set on a post at the roadside. You may find that lights change directly from red to green, bypassing amber completely. Flashing amber lights generally indicate that you may proceed with caution if it is safe to do so but you must give way to pedestrians and other vehicles.

A green filter light should be treated with caution as you may still have to give way to pedestrians who have a green light to cross the road. If a light turns red as approached, continental drivers will often speed up to get through the light instead of stopping. Be aware that if you brake sharply because a traffic light has turned red as you approached, the driver behind might not be expecting it.

Motoring Equipment

Essential Equipment

The equipment that you legally have to carry differs by country. For a full list see the Essential Equipment table at the end of this chapter. Please note equipment requirements and regulations can change frequently. To keep up to date with the latest equipment information visit camc.com/overseasadvice.

Child Restraint Systems

Children under 10 years of age are not permitted to travel in front seats of vehicles, unless there are no rear seats in the vehicle, the rear seats are already occupied with other children, or there are no seat belts in the rear. In these situations a child must not be placed in the front seats in a rear-facing child seat, unless any airbag is deactivated. Children up to 10 must travel in an approved child seat or restraint system, adapted to their size. A baby up to 13kg in weight must be carried in a rear facing baby seat. A child between 9kg and 18kg in weight must be seated in a child seat. A child from 15kg in weight up to the age of 10 can use a booster seat with a seat belt.

Children must not travel in the front of a vehicle if there are rear seats available. If they travel in the front the airbag must be deactivated and again they must use an EU approved restraint system for their size.

Fire Extinguisher

As a safety precaution, an approved fire extinguisher should be carried in all vehicles. This is a legal requirement in several countries in Europe.

Lights

When driving in on the right headlights should be adjusted if they are likely to dazzle other road users. You can do this by applying beam deflectors, or some newer vehicles have a built-in adjustment system. Some high-density discharge (HID), xenon or halogen lights, may need to be taken to a dealer to make the necessary adjustment.

Remember also to adjust headlights according to the load being carried and to compensate for the weight of the caravan on the back of your car. Even if you do not intend to drive at night, it is important to ensure that your headlights are correctly adjusted as you may need to use them in heavy rain, fog or in tunnels. If using tape or a pre-cut adhesive mask remember to remove it on your return home.

All vehicle lights must be in working condition. If your lights are not in working order you may be liable for a fine of up to €450 and confiscation of your vehicle is a possibility in some European countries.

Headlight-Flashing

On the Continent headlight-flashing is used as a warning of approach or as an overtaking signal at night, and not, as is commonly the case in the UK, an indication that you are giving way. Be more cautious with both flashing your headlights and when another driver flashes you. If a driver flashes his headlights they are generally indicating that he has priority and you should give way, contrary to standard practice in the UK.

Hazard Warning Lights

Hazard warning lights should not be used in place of a warning triangle, but should be used in addition to it.

Nationality Plate

A nationality plate must be fixed to the rear of both your car or motorhome and caravan. Checks are made and a fine may be imposed for failure to display a nationality plate correctly. If your number plates have the Euro-Symbol on them there is no requirement to display an additional GB sticker within the EU and Switzerland. If your number plate doesn't have the EU symbol or you are planning to travel outside of the EU you will need a GB sticker.

GB is the only national identification code allowed for cars registered in the UK.

Reflective Jackets / Waistcoats

If you break down outside of a built-up area it is normally a legal requirement that anyone leaving the vehicle must be wearing a reflective jacket or waistcoat. Make sure that your jacket is accessible from inside the car as you will need to put it on before exiting the vehicle. Carry one for each passenger as well as the driver.

Route Planning

It is always a good idea to carry a road atlas or map of the countries you plan to visit, even if you have Satellite Navigation. You can find information on UK roads from Keep Moving – www.keepmoving.co.uk or call 09003 401100. Websites offering a European route mapping service include www.google.co.uk/maps, www.mappy.com or www.viamichelin.com.

Satellite Navigation/GPS

European postcodes don't cover just one street or part of a street in the same way as UK postcodes, they can cover a very large area. GPS co-ordinates and full addresses are given for site entries in this guide wherever possible, so that you can programme your device as accurately as possible.

It is important to remember that sat nav devices don't usually allow for towing or driving a large motorhome and may try to send you down unsuitable roads. Always use your common sense, and if a road looks unsuitable find an alternative route.

Use your sat nav in conjunction with the directions given in the site entries, which have been provided by members who have actually visited. Please note that directions given in site entries have not been checked by the Caravan and Motorhome Club.

In nearly all European countries it is illegal to use car navigation systems which actively search for mobile speed cameras or interfere with police equipment (laser or radar detection).

Car navigation systems which give a warning of fixed speed camera locations are legal in most countries with the exception of France, Germany, and Switzerland where this function must be de-activated.

Seat Belts

The wearing of seat belts is compulsory throughout Europe. On-the-spot fines will be incurred for failure to wear them and, in the event of an accident failure to wear a seat belt may reduce any claim for injury. See the country introductions for specific regulations on both seat belts and car seats.

Spares

Caravan Spares

It will generally be much harder to get hold of spare parts for caravans on the continent, especially for UK manufactured caravans.

It is therefore advisable to carry any commonly required spares (such as light bulbs) with you. Take contact details of your UK dealer or manufacturer with you, as they may be able to assist in getting spares delivered to you in an emergency.

Car Spares

Some car manufacturers produce spares kits; contact your dealer for details. The choice of spares will depend on the vehicle and how long you are away, but the following is a list of basic items which should cover the most common causes of breakdown:

- Radiator top hose
- Fan belt
- Fuses and bulbs
- Windscreen wiper blade
- Length of 12V electrical cable
- Tools, torch and WD40 or equivalent water repellent/ dispersant spray

Spare Wheel

Your local caravan dealer should be able to supply an appropriate spare wheel. If you have any difficulty in obtaining one, the Club's Technical Department can provide Club members with a list of suppliers on request.

Tyre legislation across Europe is more or less consistent and, while the Club has no specific knowledge of laws on the Continent regarding the use of space-saver spare wheels, there should be no problems in using such a wheel provided its use is in accordance with the manufacturer's instructions. Space-saver spare wheels are designed for short journeys to get to a place where it can be repaired and there will usually be restrictions on the distance and speed at which the vehicle should be driven.

Towbar

The vast majority of cars registered after 1 August 1998 are legally required to have a European Type approved towbar (complying with European Directive 94/20) carrying a plate giving its approval number and various technical details, including the maximum noseweight. Your car dealer or specialist towbar fitter will be able to give further advice.

All new motorhomes will need some form of type approval before they can be registered in the UK and as such can only be fitted with a type approved towbar. Older vehicles can continue to be fitted with non-approved towing brackets.

Tyres

Tyre condition has a major effect on the safe handling of your outfit. Caravan tyres must be suitable for the highest speed at which you can legally tow, even if you choose to drive slower.

Most countries require a minimum tread depth of 1.6mm but motoring organisations recommend at least 3mm. If you are planning a long journey, consider if they will still be above the legal minimum by the end of your journey.

Tyre Pressure

Tyre pressure should be checked and adjusted when the tyres are cold; checking warm tyres will result in a higher pressure reading. The correct pressures will be found in your car handbook, but unless it states otherwise to add an extra 4 - 6 pounds per square inch to the rear tyres of a car when towing to improve handling. Make sure you know what pressure your caravan tyres should be. Some require a pressure much higher than that normally used for cars. Check your caravan handbook for details.

Tyre Sizes

It is worth noting that some sizes of radial tyre to fit the 13" wheels commonly used on older UK caravans are virtually impossible to find in stock at retailers abroad, e.g. 175R13C.

After a Puncture

A lot of cars now have a liquid sealant puncture repair kit instead of a spare wheel. These should not be considered a permanent repair, and in some cases have been known to make repair of the tyre impossible. If you need to use a liquid sealant you should get the tyre repaired or replaced as soon as possible.

Following a caravan tyre puncture, especially on a single-axle caravan, it is advisable to have the non-punctured tyre removed from its wheel and checked inside and out for signs of damage resulting from overloading during the deflation of the punctured tyre.

Winter Driving

Snow chains must be fitted to vehicles using snow-covered roads in compliance with the relevant road signs. Fines may be imposed for non-compliance. Vehicles fitted with chains must not exceed 50 km/h (31mph).

They are not difficult to fit but it's a good idea to carry sturdy gloves to protect your hands when handling the chains in freezing conditions. Polar Automotive Ltd sells and hires out snow chains, contact them on 01892 519933, www.snowchains.com, or email: polar@snowchains.com.

In Andorra winter tyres are recommended. Snow chains must be used when road conditions necessitate their use and/or when road signs indicate.

Warning Triangles

In almost all European countries it is compulsory to carry a warning triangle which, in the event of vehicle breakdown or accident, must be placed (providing it is safe to do so) on the carriageway at least 30 metres from the vehicle. In some instances it is not compulsory to use the triangle but only when this action would endanger the driver.

A warning triangle should be placed on the road approximately 30 metres (100 metres on motorways) behind the broken down vehicle on the same side of the road. Always assemble the triangle before leaving your vehicle and walk with it so that the red, reflective surface is facing oncoming traffic. If a breakdown occurs round a blind corner, place the triangle in advance of the corner. Hazard warning lights may be used in conjunction with the triangle but they do not replace it.

Essential Equipment Table

The table below shows the essential equipment required for each country. Please note that this information was correct at the time of going to print but is subject to change.

For up to date information on equipment requirements for countries in Europe visit camc.com/overseasadvice.

Country	Warning Triangle	Spare Bulbs	First Aid Kit	Reflective Jacket	Additional Equipment to be Carried/Used
Andorra	Yes (2)	Yes	Rec	Yes	Dipped headlights in poor daytime visibility. Winter tyres recommended; snow chains when road conditions or signs dictate.
Austria	Yes	Rec	Yes	Yes	Winter tyres from 1 Nov to 15 April.*
Belgium	Yes	Rec	Rec	Yes	Dipped headlights in poor daytime visibility.
Croatia	Yes (2 for vehicle with trailer)	Yes	Yes	Yes	Dipped headlights at all times from last Sunday in Oct - last Sunday in Mar. Spare bulbs compulsory if lights are xenon, neon or LED. Snow chains compulsory in winter in certain regions.*
Czech Rep	Yes	Yes	Yes	Yes	Dipped headlights at all times. Replacement fuses. Winter tyres or snow chains from 1 Nov - 31st March.*
Denmark	Yes	Rec	Rec	Rec	Dipped headlights at all times. On motorways use hazard warning lights when queues or danger ahead.
Finland	Yes	Rec	Rec	Yes	Dipped headlights at all times. Winter tyres Dec - Feb.*
France	Yes	Rec	Rec	Yes	Dipped headlights recommended at all times. Legal requirement to carry a breathalyser, but no penalty for non-compliance.

Country	Warning Triangle	Spare Bulbs	First Aid Kit	Reflective Jacket	Additional Equipment to be Carried/Used
Germany	Rec	Rec	Rec	Rec	Dipped headlights recommended at all times. Winter tyres to be used in winter weather conditions.*
Greece	Yes	Rec	Yes	Rec	Fire extinguisher compulsory. Dipped headlights in towns at night and in poor daytime visibility.
Hungary	Yes	Rec	Yes	Yes	Dipped headlights at all times outside built-up areas and in built-up areas at night. Snow chains compulsory on some roads in winter conditions.*
Italy	Yes	Rec	Rec	Yes	Dipped headlights at all times outside built-up areas and in poor visibility. Snow chains from 15 Oct - 15 April.*
Luxembourg	Yes	Rec	Rec	Yes	Dipped headlights at night and daytime in bad weather.
Netherlands	Yes	Rec	Rec	Rec	Dipped headlights at night and in bad weather and recommended during the day.
Norway	Yes	Rec	Rec	Rec	Dipped headlights at all times. Winter tyres compulsory when snow or ice on the roads.*
Poland	Yes	Rec	Rec	Rec	Dipped headlights at all times. Fire extinguisher compulsory.
Portugal	Yes	Rec	Rec	Rec	Dipped headlights in poor daytime visibility, in tunnels and in lanes where traffic flow is reversible.
Slovakia	Yes	Rec	Yes	Yes	Dipped headlights at all times. Winter tyres compulsory when compact snow or ice on the road.*
Slovenia	Yes (2 for vehicle with trailer)	Yes	Rec	Yes	Dipped headlights at all times. Hazard warning lights when reversing. Use winter tyres or carry snow chains 15 Nov - 15 Mar.
Spain	Yes (2 Rec)	Rec	Rec	Yes	Dipped headlights at night, in tunnels and on 'special' roads (roadworks).
Sweden	Yes	Rec	Rec	Rec	Dipped headlights at all times. Winter tyres 1 Dec to 31 March.
Switzerland (inc Liechtenstein)	Yes	Rec	Rec	Rec	Dipped headlights recommended at all times, compulsory in tunnels. Snow chains where indicated by signs.

NOTES:
1) All countries: seat belts (if fitted) must be worn by all passengers.
2) Rec: not compulsory for foreign-registered vehicles, but strongly recommended
3) Headlamp converters, spare bulbs, fire extinguisher, first aid kit and reflective waistcoat are strongly recommended for all countries.
4) In some countries drivers who wear prescription glasses must carry a spare pair.
5) Please check information for any country before you travel. This information is to be used as a guide only and it is your responsibility to make sure you have the correct equipment.

* For more information and regulations on winter driving please see the Country Introduction.

Route Planning

ATLANTIC
OCEAN

N
W — E
S

| Motorways |
| Major roads |
| Main roads |
| Ferry routes |
| ⊕ Major airports |

UNITED KINGDOM

Cardiff
Bristol
LON
Poole
Plymouth
Weymouth
Portsmouth
Newhaven

English Channel

Diepp
Guernsey (British Crown Dependency)
Jersey (British Crown Dependency)
Cherbourg-Octeville
Le Havre
Roscoff
Caen
Brest
St Malo
Rennes

O

Nantes

Bay
of
Biscay

Poitiers
La Rochelle
Limoges

Bordeaux

Ferrol
Gijón/Xixón
Santiago de Compostela
Oviedo
Santander
Vigo
Bilbao
Ourense
León
Irun
Tou
Braga
Vitoria/Gasteiz
Pamplona/Iruña
Porto
Logroño
ANDORRA
Aveiro
Viseu
Valladolid
Zaragoza
Lleida
Manresa
Sabadell
Salamanca
SPAIN
Reus
PORTUGAL
Coimbra
Leiria
MADRID
Alcalá de Henares
LISBOA
Talavera de la Reina
Toledo
Setúbal
Badajoz
Sagunto
Évora
Torrent
Valencia
Palma de Mallor
Puertollano
Albacete
Eivissa
Eivissa (Ibiza)
Alcoy-Alcoi
Elda
Linares
Elche-Elx
Faro
Córdoba
Murcia
Sevilla
Lorca
El Puerto de Santa María
Jerez de la Frontera
Granada
Cartagena
Cádiz
Marbella
Malaga
Almería
Algeciras
GIBRALTAR (U.K.)
Tanger
Ceuta

© Collins Bartholomew Ltd 2020

Mountain roads

Mountain Passes

Mountain passes can create difficult driving conditions, especially when towing or driving a large vehicle. You should only use them if you have a good power to weight ratio and in good driving conditions. If in any doubt as to your outfit's suitability or the weather then stick to motorway routes across mountain ranges if possible.

The tables on the following pages show which passes are not suitable for caravans, and those where caravans are not permitted. Motorhomes aren't usually included in these restrictions, but relatively low powered or very large vehicles should find an alternative route. Road signs at the foot of a pass may restrict access or offer advice, especially for heavy vehicles. Warning notices are usually posted at the foot of a pass if it is closed, or if chains or winter tyres must be used.

Caravanners are particularly sensitive to gradients and traffic/road conditions on passes. The maximum gradient is usually on the inside of bends but exercise caution if it is necessary to pull out. Always engage a lower gear before taking a hairpin bend and give priority to vehicles ascending. On mountain roads it is not the gradient which puts strain on your car but the duration of the climb and the loss of power at high altitudes: approximately 10% at 915 metres (3,000 feet) and even more as you get higher. To minimise the risk of the engine overheating, take high passes in the cool part of the day, don't climb any faster than necessary and keep the engine pulling steadily. To prevent a radiator boiling, pull off the road safely, turn the heater and blower full on and switch off air conditioning. Keep an eye on water and oil levels. Never put cold water into a boiling radiator or it may crack. Check that the radiator is not obstructed by debris sucked up during the journey.

A long descent may result in overheating brakes; select the correct gear for the gradient and avoid excessive use of brakes. Even if you are using engine braking to control speed, caravan brakes may activate due to the overrun mechanism, which may cause them to overheat.

Travelling at altitude can cause a pressure build up in tanks and water pipes. You can prevent this by slightly opening the blade valve of your portable toilet and opening a tap a fraction.

Mountain Pass Information

The dates of opening and closing given in the following tables are approximate. Before attempting late afternoon or early morning journeys across borders, check their opening times as some borders close at night.

Gradients listed are the maximum which may be encountered on the pass and may be steeper at the inside of curves, particularly on older roads.

Gravel surfaces (such as dirt and stone chips) vary considerably; they can be dusty when dry and slippery when wet. Where known to exist, this type of surface has been noted.

In fine weather winter tyres or snow chains will only be required on very high passes, or for short periods in early or late summer. In winter conditions you will probably need to use them at altitudes exceeding 600 metres (approximately 2,000 feet).

Tunnels

Long tunnels are a much more commonly seen feature in Europe than in the UK, especially in mountainous regions. Tolls are usually charged for the use of major tunnels.

Dipped headlights are usually required by law even in well-lit tunnels, so switch them on before you enter. Snow chains, if used, must be removed before entering a tunnel in lay-bys provided for this purpose.

'No overtaking' signs must be strictly observed. Never cross central single or double lines. If overtaking is permitted in twin-tube tunnels, bear in mind that it is very easy to underestimate distances and speed once inside. In order to minimise the effects of exhaust fumes close all car windows and set the ventilator to circulate air, or operate the air conditioning system coupled with the recycled air option.

If you break down, try to reach the next lay-by and call for help from an emergency phone. If you cannot reach a lay-by, place your warning triangle at least 100 metres behind your vehicle. Modern tunnels have video surveillance systems to ensure prompt assistance in an emergency. Some tunnels can extend for miles and a high number of breakdowns are due to running out of fuel so make sure you have enough before entering the tunnel.

Tables and Maps

Much of the information contained in the following tables was originally supplied by The Automobile Association and other motoring and tourist organisations. The Caravan and Motorhome Club haven't checked this information and cannot accept responsibility for the accuracy or for errors or omissions to these tables.

The mountain passes, rail and road tunnels listed in the tables are shown on the following maps. Numbers and letters against each pass or tunnel in the tables correspond with the numbers and letters on the maps.

Converting Gradients

20% = 1 in 5	11% = 1 in 9
16% = 1 in 6	10% = 1 in 8
14% = 1 in 7	8% = 1 in 12
12% = 1 in 8	6% = 1 in 16

Abbreviations

MHV	Maximum height of vehicle
MLV	Maximum length of vehicle
MWV	Maximum width of vehicle
MWR	Minimum width of road
OC	Occasionally closed between dates
UC	Usually closed between dates
UO	Usually open between dates, although a fall of snow may obstruct the road for 24-48 hours.

Major Mountain Passes - Pyrenees and Northern Spain

Before using any of these passes, please read the advice at the beginning of this chapter.

Pass Height In Metres (Feet)	From To	Max Gradient	Conditions and Comments
❶ **Aubisque** (France) 1710 (5610)	Eaux Bonnes *Argelés-Gazost*	10%	UC mid Oct-Jun. MWR 3.5m (11'6") Very winding; continuous on D918 but easy ascent; descent including Col-d'Aubisque 1709m (5607 feet) and Col-du-Soulor 1450m (4757 feet); 8km (5 miles) of very narrow, rough, unguarded road with steep drop. **Not recommended for caravans.**
❷ **Bonaigua** (Spain) 2072 (6797)	Viella (Vielha) *Esterri-d'Aneu*	8.5%	UC Nov-Apr. MWR 4.3m (14'1") Twisting, narrow road (C28) with many hairpins and some precipitous drops. **Not recommended for caravans.** Alternative route to Lerida (Lleida) through Viella (Vielha) Tunnel is open all year.
③ **Cabrejas** (Spain) 1167 (3829)	Tarancon *Cuenca*	14%	UO. On N400/A40. Sometimes blocked by snow for 24 hours. MWR 5m (16')
④ **Col-d'Haltza and Col-de-Burdincurutcheta** (France) 782 (2565) and 1135 (3724)	St Jean-Pied-de-Port *Larrau*	11%	UO. A narrow road (D18/D19) leading to Iraty skiing area. Narrow with some tight hairpin bends; rarely has central white line and stretches are unguarded. Not for the faint-hearted. **Not recommended for caravans.**
⑤ **Envalira** (France – Andorra) 2407 (7897)	Pas-de-la-Casa *Andorra*	12.5%	OC Nov-Apr. MWR 6m (19'8") Good road (N22/CG2) with wide bends on ascent and descent; fine views. MHV 3.5m (11'6") on N approach near l'Hospitalet. Early start rec in summer to avoid border delays. Envalira Tunnel (toll) reduces congestion and avoids highest part of pass.
❻ **Escudo** (Spain) 1011 (3317)	Santander *Burgos*	17%	UO. MWR probably 5m (16'5") Asphalt surface but many bends and steep gradients. **Not recommended in winter.** On N632; A67/N611 easier route.
⑦ **Guadarrama** (Spain) 1511 (4957)	Guadarrama *San Rafael*	14%	UO. MWR 6m (19'8") On NVI to the NW of Madrid but may be avoided by using AP6 motorway from Villalba to San Rafael or Villacastin (toll).
⑧ **Ibañeta (Roncevalles)** (France – Spain) 1057 (3468)	St Jean-Pied-de-Port *Pamplona*	10%	UO. MWR 4m (13'1") Slow and winding, scenic route on N135.
⑨ **Manzanal** (Spain) 1221 (4005)	Madrid *La Coruña*	7%	UO. Sometimes blocked by snow for 24 hours. On A6.

Before using any of these passes, please read the advice at the beginning of this chapter.

Pass / Height in Metres (Feet)	From / To	Max Gradient	Conditions and Comments
10 Navacerrada (Spain) 1860 (6102)	Madrid / Segovia	17%	OC Nov-Mar. On M601/CL601. Sharp hairpins. Possible but **not recommended for caravans.**
11 Orduna (Spain) 900 (2953)	Bilbao / Burgos	15%	UO. On A625/BU556; sometimes blocked by snow for 24 hours. Avoid by using AP68 motorway.
12 Pajares (Spain) 1270 (4167)	Oviedo / Léon	16%	UO. On N630; sometimes blocked by snow for 24 hours. **Not recommended for caravans.** Avoid by using AP66 motorway.
13 Paramo-de-Masa (Spain) 1050 (3445)	Santander / Burgos	8%	UO. On N623; sometimes blocked by snow for 24 hours.
14 Peyresourde (France) 1563 (5128)	Arreau / Bagnères-de-Luchon	10%	UO. MWR 4m (13'1") D618 somewhat narrow with several hairpin bends, though not difficult. **Not recommended for caravans.**
15 Picos-de-Europa: Puerto-de-San-Roque, Puerto-de-Pontón, Puerto-de-Pandetrave (Spain), 1609 (5279)	Unquera / Riaño	12%	UO. MWR probably 4m (13'1") Desfiladero de la Hermida on N621 good condition. Puerto-de-San-Glorio steep with many hairpin bends. For confident drivers only.
	Riaño / Cangas-de-Onis		Puerto-de-Ponton on N625, height 1280 metres (4200 feet). Best approach fr S as from N is very long uphill pull with many tight turns.
	Portilla-de-la-Reina / Santa Marina-de-Valdeón		Puerto-de-Pandetrave, height 1562 metres (5124 feet) on LE245 not rec when towing as main street of Santa Marina steep & narrow.
16 Piqueras (Spain) 1710 (5610)	Logroño / Soria	7%	UO. On N111; sometimes blocked by snow for 24 hours.
17 Port (France) 1249 (4098)	Tarascon-sur-Ariège / Massat	10%	OC Nov-Mar. MWR 4m (13'1") A fairly easy, scenic road (D618), but narrow on some bends.
18 Portet-d'Aspet (France) 1069 (3507)	Audressein / Fronsac	14%	UO. MWR 3.5m (11'6") Approached from W by the easy Col-des-Ares and Col-de-Buret; well-engineered but narrow road (D618); care needed on hairpin bends. **Not recommended for caravans.**
19 Pourtalet (France – Spain) 1792 (5879)	Laruns / Biescas	10%	UC late Oct-early Jun. MWR 3.5m (11'6") A fairly easy, unguarded road, but narrow in places. Easier from Spain (A136), steeper in France (D934). **Not recommended for caravans.**

Before using any of these passes, please read the advice at the beginning of this chapter.

Pass Height In Metres (Feet)	From To	Max Gradient	Conditions and Comments
⑳ Puymorens (France) 1915 (6283)	Ax-les-Thermes *Bourg-Madame*	10%	OC Nov-Apr. MWR 5.5m (18') MHV 3.5m (11'6") A generally easy, modern tarmac road (N20). Parallel toll road tunnel available.
㉑ Quillane (France) 1714 (5623)	Axat *Mont-Louis*	8.5%	OC Nov-Mar. MWR 5m (16'5") An easy, straightforward ascent and descent on D118.
㉒ Somosierra (Spain) 1444 (4738)	Madrid *Burgos*	10%	OC Mar-Dec. MWR 7m (23') On A1/E5; may be blocked following snowfalls. Snow-plough swept during winter months but wheel chains compulsory after snowfalls. Well-surfaced dual carriageway; tunnel at summit.
㉓ Somport (France – Spain) 1632 (5354)	Accous *Jaca*	10%	UO. MWR 3.5m (11'6") A favoured, old-established route; not particularly easy and narrow in places with many unguarded bends on French side (N134); excellent road on Spanish side (N330). Use of road tunnel advised – see *Pyrenean Road Tunnels* in this section. NB Visitors advise re-fuelling no later than Sabiñánigo when travelling south to north.
㉔ Toses (Tosas) (Spain) 1800 (5906)	Puigcerda *Ribes-de-Freser*	10%	UO MWR 5m (16'5") A fairly straightforward, but continuously winding, two-lane road (N152) with with a good surface but many sharp bends; some unguarded edges. Difficult in winter.
㉕ Tourmalet (France) 2114 (6936)	Ste Marie-de-Campan *Luz-St Sauveur*	12.5%	UC Oct-mid Jun. MWR 4m (13'1") The highest French Pyrenean route (D918); approaches good, though winding, narrow in places and exacting over summit; sufficiently guarded. Rough surface & uneven edges on west side. **Not recommended for caravans.**
㉖ Urquiola (Spain) 713 (2340)	Durango (Bilbao) *Vitoria/Gasteiz*	16%	UO. Sometimes closed by snow for 24 hours. On BI623/A623. **Not recommended for caravans.**

Major Pyrenean Road Tunnels

Before using any of these tunnels, please read the advice at the beginning of this chapter.

	Tunnel	Route and Height Above Sea Level	General Information and Comments
AA	**Bielsa** (France – Spain) 3.2 km (2 miles)	**Aragnouet to Bielsa** 1830m (6000')	Open 24 hours but possibly closed October-Easter. On French side (D173) generally good road surface but narrow with steep hairpin bends and steep gradients near summit. Often no middle white line. Spanish side (A138) has good width and is less steep and winding. Used by heavy vehicles. No tolls.
BB	**Cadi** (Spain) 5 km (3 miles)	**Bellver de Cerdanya to Berga** 1220m (4000')	W of Toses (Tosas) pass on E9/C16; link from La Seo de Urgel to Andorra; excellent approach roads; heavy weekend traffic. Tolls charged.
CC	**Envalira** (France – Spain via Andorra) 2.8 km (1.75 miles)	**Pas de la Casa to El Grau Roig** 2000m (6562')	Tunnel width 8.25m. On N22/CG2 France to Andorra. Tolls charged.
DD	**Puymorens** (France –Spain) 4.8 km (2.9 miles)	**Ax-les-Thermes to Puigcerda** 1515m (4970')	MHV 3.5m (11'6"). Part of Puymorens pass on N20/E9. Tolls charged.
EE	**Somport** (France – Spain) 8.6 km (5.3 miles)	**Urdos to Canfranc** 1116m (3661')	Tunnel height 4.55m (14'9"), width 10.5m (34'). Max speed 90 km/h (56 mph); leave 100m between vehicles. On N134 (France), N330 (Spain). No tolls.
FF	**Vielha (Viella)** (Spain) 5.2 km (3.2 miles)	**Vielha (Viella) to Pont de Suert** 1635m (5390')	Tunnel height 5.3m, width 12m. Max speed 80km/h. 3 lane, well lit, modern tunnel on N230. Gentle gradients on both sides. Good road surface. Narrow on approach from Vielha. No tolls.

Keeping in Touch

Telephones

You might need to use a telephone at some point while you're away, whether to keep in touch with family and friends or call ahead to sites. Even if you don't plan to use one, it's best to make sure you have access to a phone in an emergency.

International Direct Dial Calls

Each country has a unique dialing code you must use if phoning from outside that country. You can find the international dialing code for any country by visiting www.thephonebook. bt.com. First dial the code then the local number. If the area code starts with a zero this should be omitted.

The international access code to dial the UK from anywhere in the world is 0044.

Ringing Tones

Ringing tones vary from country to country, so may sound very different to UK tones. Some ringing tones sound similar to error or engaged tones that you would hear on a UK line.

Using Mobile Phones

Mobile phones have an international calling option called 'roaming' which will automatically search for a local network when you switch your phone on. The EU abolished roaming charges in 2017, but you should contact your service provider to check if there are any charges for your tariff.

Storing telephone numbers in your phone's contact list in international format (i.e. use the prefix of +44 and omit the initial '0') will mean that your contacts will automatically work abroad as well as in the UK.

Global SIM Cards

If you're planning on travelling to more than one country consider buying a global SIM card. This will mean your mobile phone can operate on foreign mobile networks, which will be more cost effective than your service provider's roaming charges. For details of SIM cards available, speak to your service provider or visit www.0044.co.uk or www.globalsimcard.co.uk.

You may find it simpler to buy a SIM card or cheap 'pay-as-you-go' phone abroad if you plan to make a lot for local calls, e.g. to book campsites or restaurants. This may mean that you still have higher call charges for international calls (such as calling the UK).

Before buying a different SIM card, check with you provider whether your phone is locked against use on other networks.

Hands-Free

Legislation in Europe forbids the use of mobile or car phones while driving except when using hands-free equipment. In some European countries it is now also illegal to drive while wearing headphones or a headset - including hands-free kits.

If you are involved in an accident whilst driving and using a hand-held mobile phone, your insurance company may refuse to honour the claim.

Accessing the internet

If you have a phone plan that includes mobile data then you should be able to use this as normal within the European Union. Check with you network provider, and please note that this is likely to change if the UK leaves the EU.

Internet Access

Wi-Fi is available on lots of campsites in Europe, the cost may be an additional charge or included in your pitch fee. Most larger towns may have internet cafés or libraries where you can access the internet, however lots of fast food restaurants and coffee chains now offer free Wi-Fi for customers so you can get access for the price of a coffee or bite to eat.

Many people now use their smartphones for internet access. Another option is a dongle – a device which connects to your laptop to give internet access using a mobile phone network. While these methods are economical in the UK, overseas you will be charged data roaming charges which can run into hundreds or thousands of pounds depending on how much data you use. If you plan on using your smartphone or a dongle abroad speak to your service provider before you leave the UK to make sure you understand the costs or add an overseas data roaming package to your phone contract.

Making Calls from your laptop

If you download Skype to your laptop you can make free calls to other Skype users anywhere in the world using a Wi-Fi connection. Rates for calls to non-Skype users (landline or mobile phone) are also very competitively-priced. You will need a computer with a microphone and speakers, and a webcam is handy too. It is also possible to download Skype to an internet-enabled mobile phone to take advantage of the same low-cost calls – see www.skype.com.

Club Together

If you want to chat to other members either at home or while you're away, you can do so on The Club's online community Club Together. You can ask questions and gather opinions on the forums at camc.com/together.

Radio and Television

The BBC World Service broadcasts radio programmes 24 hours a day worldwide and you can listen on a number of platforms: online, via satellite or cable, DRM digital radio, internet radio or mobile phone. You can find detailed information and programme schedules at www.bbc.co.uk/worldservice.

Whereas analogue television signals were switched off in the UK during 2012, no date has yet been fixed for the switch off of analogue radio signals.

Digital Terrestrial Television

As in the UK, television transmissions in most of Europe have been converted to digital. The UK's high definition transmission technology may be more advanced than any currently implemented or planned in Europe. This means that digital televisions intended for use in the UK might not be able to receive HD terrestrial signals in some countries.

Satellite Television

For English-language TV programmes the only realistic option is satellite, and satellite dishes are a common sight on campsites all over Europe. A satellite dish mounted on the caravan roof or clamped to a pole fixed to the drawbar, or one mounted on a foldable free-standing tripod, will provide good reception and minimal interference. Remember however that obstructions to the south east (such as

tall trees or even mountains) or heavy rain, can interrupt the signals. A specialist dealer will be able to advise you on the best way of mounting your dish. You will also need a satellite receiver and ideally a satellite-finding meter.

The main entertainment channels such as BBC1, ITV1 and Channel 4 can be difficult to pick up in mainland Europe as they are now being transmitted by new narrow-beam satellites. A 60cm dish should pick up these channels in most of France, Belgium and the Netherlands but as you travel further afield, you'll need a progressively larger dish. See www.satelliteforcaravans.co.uk (created and operated by a Club member) for the latest changes and developments, and for information on how to set up your equipment.

Medical matters

Before You Travel

You can find country specific medical advice, including any vaccinations you may need, from www.nhs.uk/healthcareabroad, or speak to your GP surgery. For general enquiries about medical care abroad contact NHS England on 0300 311 22 33 or email england.contactus@nhs.uk.

If you have any pre-existing medical conditions you should check with your GP that you are fit to travel. Ask your doctor for a written summary of any medical problems and a list of medications , which is especially important for those who use controlled drugs or hypodermic syringes.

Always make sure that you have enough medication for the duration of your holiday and some extra in case your return is delayed. Take details of the generic name of any drugs you use, as brand names may be different abroad, your blood group and details of any allergies (translations may be useful for restaurants).

An emergency dental kit is available from High Street chemists which will allow you temporarily to restore a crown, bridge or filling or to dress a broken tooth until you can get to a dentist.

A good website to check before you travel is www.nathnac.org/travel which gives general health and safety advice, as well as highlighting potential health risks by country.

European Health Insurance Card

Before leaving home apply for a European Health Insurance Card (EHIC). British residents temporarily visiting another EU country are entitled to receive state-provided emergency treatment during their stay on the same terms as residents of those countries, but you must have a valid EHIC to claim these services.

To apply for your EHIC visit www.ehic.org.uk, call 0300 330 1350 or pick up an application form from a post office. An EHIC is required by each family member, with children under 16 included in a parent or guardian's application. The EHIC is free of charge, is valid for up to five years and can be renewed up to six months before its expiry date. Before you travel remember to check that your EHIC is still valid.

An EHIC is not a substitute for travel insurance and it is strongly recommended that you arrange full travel insurance before leaving home regardless of the cover provided by your EHIC. Some insurance companies require you to have an EHIC and some will waive the policy excess if an EHIC has been used.

If your EHIC is stolen or lost while you are abroad contact 0044 191 2127500 for help. If you experience difficulties in getting your EHIC accepted, telephone the Department for Work & Pensions for assistance on the overseas healthcare team line 0044 (0)191 218 1999 between 8am to 5pm Monday to Friday. Residents of the Republic of Ireland, the Isle of Man and Channel Islands, should check with their own health authorities about reciprocal arrangements with other countries.

Travel Insurance

Despite having an EHIC you may incur high medical costs if you fall ill or have an accident. The cost of bringing a person back to the UK in the event of illness or death is never covered by the EHIC.

Separate additional travel insurance adequate for your destination is essential, such as the Club's Red Pennant Overseas Holiday Insurance – see camc.com/redpennant.

First Aid

A first aid kit containing at least the basic requirements is an essential item, and in some countries it is compulsory to carry one in your vehicle (see the Essential Equipment Table in the chapter Motoring – Equipment). Kits should contain items such as sterile pads, assorted dressings, bandages and plasters, antiseptic wipes or cream, cotton wool, scissors, eye bath and tweezers. Also make sure you carry something for upset stomachs, painkillers and an antihistamine in case of hay fever or mild allergic reactions.

If you're travelling to remote areas then you may find it useful to carry a good first aid manual. The British Red Cross publishes a comprehensive First Aid Manual in conjunction with St John Ambulance and St Andrew's Ambulance Association.

Accidents and Emergencies

If you are involved in or witness a road accident the police may want to question you about it. If possible take photographs or make sketches of the scene, and write a few notes about what happened as it may be more difficult to remember the details at a later date.

For sports activities such as skiing and mountaineering, travel insurance must include provision for covering the cost of mountain and helicopter rescue. Visitors to the Savoie and Haute-Savoie areas should be aware that an accident or illness may result in a transfer to Switzerland for hospital treatment. There is a reciprocal healthcare agreement for British citizens visiting Switzerland but you will be required to pay the full costs of treatment and afterwards apply for a refund.

Sun Protection

Never under-estimate how ill exposure to the sun can make you. If you are not used to the heat it is very easy to fall victim to heat exhaustion or heat stroke. Avoid sitting in the sun between 11am and 3pm and cover your head if sitting or walking in the sun. Use a high sun protection factor (SPF) and re-apply frequently. Make sure you drink plenty of fluids.

Tick-Borne Encephalitis (TBE) and Lyme Disease

Hikers and outdoor sports enthusiasts planning trips to forested, rural areas should be aware of tick-borne encephalitis, which is transmitted by the bite of an infected tick. If you think you may be at risk, seek medical advice on prevention and immunisation before you leave the UK.

There is no vaccine against Lyme disease, an equally serious tick-borne infection, which, if left untreated, can attack the nervous system and joints. You can minimise the risk by using an insect repellent containing DEET, wearing long sleeves and long trousers, and checking for ticks after outdoor activity.

Avoid unpasteurised dairy products in risk areas. See www.tickalert.org or telephone 01943 468010 for more information.

Water and food

Water from mains supplies throughout Europe is generally safe, but may be treated with chemicals which make it taste different to tap water in the UK. If in any doubt, always drink bottled water or boil it before drinking.

Food poisoning is potential anywhere, and a complete change of diet may upset your stomach as well. In hot conditions avoid any food that hasn't been refrigerated or hot food that has been left to cool. Be sensible about the food that you eat – don't eat unpasteurised or undercooked food and if you aren't sure about the freshness of meat or seafood then it is best avoided.

Returning Home

If you become ill on your return home tell your doctor that you have been abroad and which countries you have visited. Even if you have received medical treatment in another country, always consult your doctor if you have been bitten or scratched by an animal while on holiday. If you were given any medicines in another country, it may be illegal to bring them back into the UK. If in doubt, declare them at Customs when you return.

Electricity and Gas

Electricity

General Advice

The voltage for mains electricity is 230V across the EU, but varying degrees of 'acceptable tolerance' mean you may find variations in the actual voltage. Most appliances sold in the UK are 220-240V so should work correctly. However, some high-powered equipment, such as microwave ovens, may not function well – check your instruction manual for any specific instructions. Appliances marked with 'CE' have been designed to meet the requirements of relevant European directives.

The table below gives an approximate idea of which appliances can be used based on the amperage which is being supplied (although not all appliances should be used at the same time). You can work it out more accurately by making a note of the wattage of each appliance in your caravan. The wattages given are based on appliances designed for use in caravans and motorhomes. Household kettles, for example, have at least a 2000W element. Each caravan circuit will also have a maximum amp rating which should not be exceeded.

Electrical Connections – EN60309-2 (CEE17)

EN60309-2 (formerly known as CEE17) is the European Standard for all newly fitted connectors. Most sites should now have these connectors, however there is no requirement to replace connectors which were installed before this was standardised so you may still find some sites where your UK 3 pin connector doesn't fit. For this reason it is a good idea

Amps	Wattage (Approx)	Fridge	Battery Charger	Air Conditioning	LCD TV	Water Heater	Kettle (750W)	Heater (1kW)
2	400	✓	✓					
4	900	✓	✓		✓	✓		
6	1300	✓	✓	*	✓	✓	✓	
8	1800	✓	✓	✓**	✓	✓	✓	✓**
10	2300	✓	✓	✓**	✓	✓	✓	✓**
16	3600	✓	✓	✓	✓	✓	✓	✓**

| * | Usage possible, depending on wattage of appliance in question |
| ** | Not to be used at the same time as other high-wattage equipment |

to carry a 2-pin adapter. If you are already on site and find your connector doesn't fit, ask campsite staff to borrow or hire an adaptor. You may still encounter a poor electrical supply on site even with an EN60309-2 connection.

If the campsite does not have a modern EN60309-2 (CEE17) supply, ask to see the electrical protection for the socket outlet. If there is a device marked with IDn = 30mA, then the risk is minimised.

Hooking Up to the Mains

Connection should always be made in the following order:

- Check your outfit isolating switch is at 'off'.
- Uncoil the connecting cable from the drum. A coiled cable with current flowing through it may overheat. Take your cable and insert the connector (female end) into your outfit inlet.
- Insert the plug (male end) into the site outlet socket.
- Switch outfit isolating switch to 'on'.
- Use a polarity tester in one of the 13A sockets in the outfit to check all connections are correctly wired. Never leave it in the socket. Some caravans have these devices built in as standard.

It is recommended that the supply is not used if the polarity is incorrect (see Reversed Polarity).

Warnings:

If you are in any doubt of the safety of the system, if you don't receive electricity once connected or if the supply stops then contact the site staff.

If the fault is found to be with your outfit then call a qualified electrician rather than trying to fix the problem yourself.

To ensure your safety you should never use an electrical system which you can't confirm to be safe. Use a mains tester such as the one shown on the right to test the electrical supply.

Always check that a proper earth connection exists before using the electrics. Please note that these testers may not pick up all earth faults so if there is any doubt as to the integrity of the earth system do not use the electrical supply.

Disconnection

- Switch your outfit isolating switch to 'off'.
- At the site supply socket withdraw the plug.
- Disconnect the cable from your outfit.

Motorhomes – if leaving your pitch during the day, don't leave your mains cable plugged into the site supply, as this creates a hazard if the exposed live connections in the plug are touched or if the cable is not seen during grass-cutting.

Reversed Polarity

Even if the site connector meets European Standard EN60309-2 (CEE17), British caravanners are still likely to encounter the problem known as reversed polarity. This is where the site supply 'live' line connects to the outfit's 'neutral' and vice versa. You should always check the polarity immediately on connection, using a polarity tester available from caravan accessory shops. If polarity is reversed the caravan mains electricity should not be used. Try using another nearby socket instead. Frequent travellers to the Continent can make up an adaptor themselves, or ask an electrician to make one for you, with the live

and neutral wires reversed. Using a reversed polarity socket will probably not affect how an electrical appliance works, however your protection is greatly reduced. For example, a lamp socket may still be live as you touch it while replacing a blown bulb, even if the light switch is turned off.

Shaver Sockets

Most campsites provide shaver sockets with a voltage of 220V or 110V. Using an incorrect voltage may cause the shaver to become hot or break. The 2-pin adaptor available in the UK may not fit Continental sockets so it is advisable to buy 2-pin adaptors on the Continent. Many modern shavers will work on a range of voltages which make them suitable for travelling abroad. Check you instruction manual to see if this is the case.

Gas

General Advice

Gas usage can be difficult to predict as so many factors, such as temperature and how often you eat out, can affect the amount you need. As a rough guide allow 0.45kg of gas a day for normal summer usage.

With the exception of Campingaz, LPG cylinders normally available in the UK cannot be exchanged abroad. If possible, take enough gas with you and bring back the empty

Site hooking up adaptor

Adaptateur de prise au site (secteur)
Campingplatz-anschluss (netz)

Extension lead to outfit

Câble de rallonge à la caravane
Verlâengerungskabel zum wohnwagen

Site outlet
Prise du site
Campingplatz-Steckdose

Mains adaptor
Adaptateur Secteur
Netzanschlußstacker

16A 230V AC

cylinders. Always check how many you can take with you as ferry and tunnel operators may restrict the number of cylinders you are permitted to carry for safety reasons.

The full range of Campingaz cylinders is widely available from large supermarkets and hypermarkets, although at the end of the holiday season stocks may be low. Other popular brands of gas are Primagaz, Butagaz, Totalgaz and Le Cube. A loan deposit is required and if you are buying a cylinder for the first time you may also need to buy the appropriate regulator or adaptor hose.

If you are touring in cold weather conditions use propane gas instead of butane. Many other brands of gas are available in different countries and, as long as you have the correct regulator, adaptor and hose and the cylinders fit in your gas locker these local brands can also be used.

Gas cylinders are now standardised with a pressure of 30mbar for both butane and propane within the EU. On UK-specification caravans and motorhomes (2004 models and later) a 30mbar regulator suited to both propane and butane use is fitted to the bulkhead of the gas locker. This is connected to the cylinder with a connecting hose (and

sometimes an adaptor) to suit different brands or types of gas. Older outfits and some foreign-built ones may use a cylinder-mounted regulator, which may need to be changed to suit different brands or types of gas.

Warnings:

- Refilling gas cylinders intended to be exchanged is against the law in most countries, however you may still find that some sites and dealers will offer to refill cylinders for you. Never take them up on this service as it can be dangerous; the cylinders haven't been designed for user-refilling and it is possible to overfill them with catastrophic consequences.

- Regular servicing of gas appliances is important as a faulty appliance can emit carbon monoxide, which could prove fatal. Check your vehicle or appliance handbook for service recommendations.

- Never use a hob or oven as a space heater.

The Caravan and Motorhome Club publishes a range of technical leaflets for its members including detailed advice on the use of electricity and gas – you can request copies or see camc.com/advice-and-training.

Safety and security

EU countries have good legislation in place to protect your safety wherever possible. However accidents and crime will still occur and taking sensible precautions can help to minimise your risk of being involved.

Beaches, Lakes and Rivers

Check for any warning signs or flags before you swim and ensure that you know what they mean. Check the depth of water before diving and avoid diving or jumping into murky water as submerged objects may not be visible. Familiarise yourself with the location of safety apparatus and/or lifeguards.

Use only the designated areas for swimming, watersports and boating and always use life jackets where appropriate. Watch out for tides, undertows, currents and wind strength and direction before swimming in the sea. This applies in particular when using inflatables, windsurfing equipment, body boards, kayaks or sailing boats. Sudden changes of wave and weather conditions combined with fast tides and currents are particularly dangerous.

Campsite Safety

Once you've settled in, take a walk around the site to familiarise yourself with its layout and locate the nearest safety equipment. Ensure that children know their way around and where your pitch is.

Natural disasters are rare, but always think about what could happen. A combination of heavy rain and a riverside pitch could lead to flash flooding, for example, so make yourself aware of site evacuation procedures.

Be aware of sources of electricity and cabling on and around your pitch – electrical safety might not be up to the same standards as in the UK.

Poison for rodent control is sometimes used on sites or surrounding farmland. Warning notices are not always posted and you are strongly advised to check if staying on a rural site with dogs or children.

Incidents of theft on campsites are rare but when leaving your caravan unattended make sure you lock all doors and shut windows. Conceal valuables from sight and lock up any bicycles.

Children

Watch out for children as you drive around the site and don't exceed walking pace.

Children's play areas are generally unsupervised, so check which are suitable for your children's ages and abilities. Read and respect the displayed rules. Remember it is your responsibility to supervise your children at all times.

Be aware of any campsite rules concerning ball games or use of play equipment, such as roller blades and skateboards. When your children attend organised activities, arrange when and where to meet afterwards. You should never leave children alone inside a caravan.

Fire

Fire prevention is important on sites, as fire can spread quickly between outfits. Certain areas of southern Europe experience severe water shortages in summer months leading to an increased fire risk. This may result in some local authorities imposing restrictions at short notice on the use of barbecues and open flames.

Fires can be a regular occurrence in forested areas, especially along the Mediterranean coast during summer months. They are generally extinguished quickly and efficiently but short term evacuations are sometimes necessary. If visiting forested areas familiarise yourself with local emergency procedures in the event of fire. Never use paraffin or gas heaters inside your caravan. Gas heaters should only be fitted when air is taken from outside the caravan. Don't change your gas cylinder inside the caravan. If you smell gas turn off the cylinder immediately, extinguish all naked flames and seek professional help.

Make sure you know where the fire points and telephones are on site and know the site fire drill. Make sure everyone in your party knows how to call the emergency services.

Where site rules permit the use of barbecues, take the following precautions to prevent fire:

- Never locate a barbecue near trees or hedges.
- Have a bucket of water to hand in case of sparks.
- Only use recommended fire-lighting materials.
- Don't leave a barbecue unattended when lit and dispose of hot ash safely.
- Never take a barbecue into an enclosed area or awning – even when cooling they continue to release carbon monoxide which can lead to fatal poisoning.

Swimming Pools

Familiarize yourself with the pool area before you venture in for a swim - check the pool layout and identify shallow and deep ends and the location of safety equipment. Check the gradient of the pool bottom as pools which shelve off sharply can catch weak or non-swimmers unawares.

Never dive or jump into a pool without knowing the depth – if there is a no diving rule it usually means the pool isn't deep enough for safe diving.

For pools with a supervisor or lifeguard, note any times or dates when the pool is not supervised. Read safety notices and rules posted around the pool.

On the Road

Don't leave valuables on view in cars or caravans, even if they are locked. Make sure items on roof racks or cycle carriers are locked securely.

Near to ports British owned cars have been targeted by thieves, both while parked and on the move, e.g. by flagging drivers down or indicating that a vehicle has a flat tyre. If you stop in such circumstances be wary of anyone offering help, ensure that car keys are not left in the ignition and that vehicle doors are locked while you investigate.

Always keep car doors locked and windows closed when driving in populated areas. Beware of a 'snatch' through open car windows at traffic lights, filling stations or in traffic jams. When driving through towns and cities keep your doors locked. Keep handbags, valuables and documents out of sight at all times.

If flagged down by another motorist for whatever reason, take care that your own car is locked and windows closed while you check outside, even if someone is left inside.

Be particularly careful on long, empty stretches of motorway and when you stop for fuel. Even if the people flagging you down appear to be officials (e.g. wearing yellow reflective jackets or dark, 'uniform-type' clothing) lock your vehicle doors. They may appear to be friendly and helpful, but could be opportunistic thieves. Have a mobile phone to hand and, if necessary, be seen to use it.

Road accidents are a increased risk in some countries where traffic laws may be inadequately enforced, roads may be poorly maintained, road signs and lighting inadequate, and driving standards poor. It's a good idea to keep a fully-charged mobile phone with you in your car with the number of your breakdown organisation saved into it. On your return to the UK there are increasing issues with migrants attempting to stowaway in vehicles, especially if you're travelling through Calais.

The UK government have issued the following instructions to prevent people entering the UK illegally:

- Where possible all vehicle doors and storage compartments should be fitted with locks.

- All locks must be engaged when the vehicle is stationary or unattended.
- Immediately before boarding your ferry or train check that the locks on your vehicle haven't been compromised.
- If you have any reason to suspect someone may have accessed your outfit speak to border control staff or call the police. Do not board the ferry or train or you may be liable for a fine of up to £2000.

Overnight Stops

Overnight stops should always be at campsites and not at motorway service areas, ferry terminal car parks, petrol station forecourts or isolated 'aires de services' on motorways where robberies are occasionally reported. If you decide to use these areas for a rest then take appropriate precautions, for example, shutting all windows, securing locks and making a thorough external check of your vehicle(s) before departing. Safeguard your property, e.g. handbags, while out of the caravan and beware of approaches by strangers.

For a safer place to take a break, there is a wide network of 'Aires de Services' in cities, towns and villages across Europe, many specifically for motorhomes with good security and overnight facilities. They are often less isolated and therefore safer than the motorway aires. It is rare that you will be the only vehicle staying on such areas, but take sensible precautions and trust your instincts.

Personal Security

Petty crime happens all over the world, including in the UK; however as a tourist you are more vulnerable to it. This shouldn't stop you from exploring new horizons, but there are a few sensible precautions you can take to minimise the risk.

- Leave valuables and jewellery at home. If you do take them, fit a small safe in your caravan or lock them in the boot of your car. Don't leave money or valuables in a car glovebox or on view. Don't leave bags in full view when sitting outside at cafés or restaurants, or leave valuables unattended on the beach.

- When walking be security-conscious. Avoid unlit streets at night, walk away from the kerb edge and carry handbags or shoulder bags on the side away from the kerb. The less of a tourist you appear, the less of a target you are.

- Keep a note of your holiday insurance details and emergency telephone numbers in more than one place, in case the bag or vehicle containing them is stolen.

- Beware of pickpockets in crowded areas, at tourist attractions and in cities. Be especially aware when using public transport in cities.

- Be cautious of bogus plain-clothes policemen who may ask to see your foreign currency or credit cards and passport. If approached, decline to show your money or to hand over your passport but ask for credentials and offer instead to go to the nearest police station.

- Laws and punishment vary from country to country so make yourself aware of anything which may affect you before you travel. Be especially careful on laws involving alcohol consumption (such as drinking in public areas), and never buy or use illegal drugs abroad.

- Respect customs regulations - smuggling is a serious offence and can carry heavy penalties. Do not carry parcels or luggage through customs for other people and never cross borders with people you do not know in your vehicle, such as hitchhikers.

The Foreign & Commonwealth Office produces a range of material to advise and inform British citizens travelling abroad about issues affecting their safety - www.gov.uk/foreign-travel-advice has country specific guides.

Money Security

We would rarely walk around at home carrying large amounts of cash, but as you may not have the usual access to bank accounts and credit cards you are more likely to do so on holiday. You are also less likely to have the same degree of security when online banking as you would in your own home. Take the following precautions to keep your money safe:

- Carry only the minimum amount of cash and don't rely on one person to carry everything. Never carry a wallet in your back pocket. Concealed money belts are the most secure way to carry cash and passports.

- Keep a separate note of bank account and credit/debit card numbers. Carry your credit card issuer/bank's 24-hour UK contact number with you.

- Be careful when using cash machines (ATMs) – try to use a machine in an area with high footfall and don't allow yourself to be distracted. Put your cash away before moving away from the cash machine.

- Always guard your PIN number, both at cash machines and when using your card to pay in shops and restaurants. Never let your card out of your sight while paying.

- If using internet banking do not leave the PC or mobile device unattended and make sure you log out fully at the end of the session.

Winter Sports

If you are planning a skiing or snowboarding holiday you should research the safety advice for your destination before you travel. A good starting point may be the relevant embassy for the country you're visiting. All safety instructions should be followed meticulously given the dangers of avalanches in some areas.

The Ski Club of Great Britain offer a lot of advice for anyone taking to the mountains, visit their website www.skiclub.co.uk to pick up some useful safety tips and advice on which resorts are suitable for different skill levels.

British Consular Services Abroad

British Embassy and Consular staff offer practical advice, assistance and support to British travellers abroad. They can, for example, issue replacement passports, help Britons who have been the victims of crime, contact relatives and friends in the event of an accident, illness or death, provide information about transferring funds and provide details of local lawyers, doctors and interpreters. But there are limits to their powers and a British Consul cannot, for example, give legal advice, intervene in court proceedings, put up bail, pay for legal or medical bills, or for funerals or the repatriation of bodies, or undertake work more properly done by banks, motoring organisations and travel insurers.

If you are charged with a serious offence, insist on the British Consul being informed. You will be contacted as soon as possible by a Consular Officer who can advise on local procedures, provide access to lawyers and insist that you are treated as well as nationals of the country which is holding you. However, they cannot get you released as a matter of course.

British and Irish embassy contact details can be found in the Country Introduction chapters.

Campsites

The quantity and variety of sites across Europe means you're sure to find one that suits your needs – from full facilities and entertainment to quiet rural retreats. If you haven't previously toured outside of the UK you may notice some differences, such as pitches being smaller or closer together. In hot climates hard ground may make putting up awnings difficult.

In the high season all campsite facilities are usually open, however bear in mind that toilet and shower facilities may be busy. Out of season some facilities such as shops and swimming pools may be closed and office opening hours may be reduced. If the site has very low occupancy the sanitary facilities may be reduced to a few unisex toilet and shower cubicles.

Booking a Campsite

To save the hassle of arriving to find a site full it is best to book in advance, especially in high season. If you don't book ahead arrive no later than 4pm (earlier at popular resorts) to secure a pitch, after this time sites fill up quickly. You also need to allow time to find another campsite if your first choice is fully booked.

You can often book directly via a campsite's website using a credit or debit card to pay a deposit if required. Please be aware that some sites regard the deposit as a booking or admin fee and will not deduct the amount from your final bill.

Overseas Travel Service

The Club's Overseas Travel Service offers members an site booking service on over 250 campsites in Europe. Full details of these sites plus information on ferry special offers and Red Pennant Overseas Holiday Insurance can be found in the Club's Venture Abroad brochure – call 01342 327410 to request a copy or visit camc.com/overseas.

Overseas Site Booking Service sites show heir booking code (e.g. G04) at the end of their listing. We can't make reservations for any other campsites in this guide.

Overseas Site Night Vouchers

The Club offers Overseas Site Night Vouchers which can be used at over 300 Club inspected sites in Europe. The vouchers cost £21.95 each (2019 cost) and you'll need one voucher per night to stay on a site in low season and two per night in high season. You'll also be eligible for the Club's special packaged ferry rates when you're buying vouchers. For more information and the view the voucher terms and conditions visit www.camc.com/overseasoffers or call 01342 327 410.

Caravan Storage

Storing your caravan on a site in Europe can be a great way to avoid a long tow and to save on ferry and fuel costs. Before you leave your caravan in storage always check whether your insurance covers this, as many policies don't.

If you aren't covered then look for a specialist policy - Towergate Insurance (tel: 01242 538431 or www.towergateinsurance.co.uk) or Look Insurance (tel: 0333 777 3035 or www.lookinsuranceservices.co.uk) both offer insurance policies for caravans stored abroad.

Facilities and Site Description

All of the site facilities shown in the site listings of this guide have been taken from member reports, as have the comments at the end of each site entry. Please remember that opinions and expectations can differ significantly from one person to the next.

The year of report is shown at the end of each site listing – sites which haven't been reported on for a few years may have had significant changes to their prices, facilities, and opening dates. It is always best to check any specific details you need to know before travelling by contacting the site or looking at their website.

Sanitary Facilities

Facilities normally include toilet and shower blocks with shower cubicles, wash basins and razor sockets. In site listings the abbreviation 'wc' indicates that the site has the kind of toilets we are used to in the UK (pedestal style). Some sites have footplate style toilets and, where this is known, you will see the abbreviation 'cont', i.e. continental. European sites do not always provide sink plugs, toilet paper or soap so take them with you.

Waste Disposal

Site entries show (when known) where a campsite has a chemical disposal and/or a motorhome service point, which is assumed to include a waste (grey) water dump station and toilet cassette-emptying point. You may find fewer waste water disposal facilities as on the continent more people use the site sanitary blocks rather than their own facilities.

Chemical disposal points may be fixed at a high level requiring you to lift cassettes in order to empty them. Disposal may simply be down a toilet. Wastemaster-style emptying points are not very common in Europe. Formaldehyde chemical cleaning products are banned in many countries. In Germany the 'Blue Angel' (Blaue Engel) Standard, and in the Netherlands the 'Milieukeur' Standard, indicates that the product has particularly good environmental credentials.

Finding a Campsite

Directions are given for all campsites listed in this guide and most listings also include GPS co-ordinates. Full street addresses are also given where available. The directions have been supplied by member reports and haven't been checked in detail by The Club.

For information about using satellite navigation to find a site see the Motoring Equipment section.

Overnight Stops

Many towns and villages across Europe provide dedicated overnight or short stay areas specifically for motorhomes, usually with security, electricity, water and waste facilities. These are known as 'Aires de Services', 'Stellplatz' or 'Aree di Sosta' and are usually well signposted with a motorhome icon. Facilities and charges for these overnight stopping areas will vary significantly.

Many campsites in popular tourist areas will also have separate overnight areas of hardstanding with facilities often just outside the main campsite area. There are guidebooks available which list just these overnight stops, Vicarious Books publish an English guide to

Aires including directions and GPS co-ordinates. Please contact 0131 208 3333 or visit their website www.vicarious-shop.com.

For security reasons you shouldn't spend the night on petrol station service areas, ferry terminal car parks or isolated 'Aires de Repos' or 'Aires de Services' along motorways.

Municipal Campsites

Municipal sites are found in towns and villages all over Europe, in particular in France. Once very basic, many have been improved in recent years and now offer a wider range of facilities. They can usually be booked in advance through the local town hall or tourism office. When approaching a town you may find that municipal sites are not always named and signposts may simply state 'Camping' or show a tent or caravan symbol. Most municipal sites are clean, well-run and very reasonably priced but security may be basic.

These sites may be used by seasonal workers, market traders and travellers in low season and as a result there may be restrictions or very high charges for some types of outfits (such as twin axles) in order to discourage this. If you may be affected check for any restrictions when you book.

Naturist Campsites

Some naturist sites are included in this guide and are shown with the word 'naturist' after their site name. Those marked 'part naturist' have separate areas for naturists. Visitors to naturist sites aged 16 and over usually require an INF card or Naturist Licence - covered by membership of British Naturism (tel 01604 620361, visit www.british-naturism.org.uk or email headoffice@british-naturism.org.uk) or you can apply for a licence on arrival at any recognised naturist site (a passport-size photograph is required).

Opening Dates and times

Opening dates should always be taken with a pinch of salt - including those given in this guide. Sites may close without notice due to refurbishment work, a lack of visitors or bad weather. Outside the high season it is always best to contact campsites in advance, even if the site advertises itself as open all year. Most sites will close their gates or barriers overnight – if you are planning to arrive late or are delayed on your journey you should call ahead to make sure you will be able to gain access to the site. There may be a late arrivals area outside of the barriers where you can pitch overnight. Motorhomers should also consider barrier closing times if leaving site in your vehicle for the evening.

Check out time is usually between 10am and 12 noon – speak to the site staff if you need to leave very early to make sure you can check out on departure. Sites may also close for an extended lunch break, so if you're planning to arrive or check out around lunchtime check that the office will be open.

Pets on Campsites

Dogs are welcome on many sites, although you may have to prove that all of their vaccinations are up to date before they are allowed onto the site. Certain breeds of dogs are banned in some countries and other breeds will need to be muzzled and kept on a lead at all times.
A list of breeds with restrictions by country can be found at camc.com/pets.

Sites usually charge for dogs and may limit the number allowed per pitch. On arrival make yourself aware of site rules regarding dogs, such as keeping them on a lead, muzzling them or not leaving them unattended in your outfit.

In popular tourist areas local regulations may ban dogs from beaches during the summer. Some dogs may find it difficult to cope with changes in climate. Also watch out for diseases transmitted by ticks, caterpillars, mosquitoes or sandflies - dogs from the UK will have no natural resistance. Consult your vet about preventative treatment before you travel.

Visitors to southern Spain and Portugal, parts of central France and northern Italy should be aware of the danger of Pine Processionary

Caterpillars from mid-winter to late spring. Dogs should be kept away from pine trees if possible or fitted with a muzzle that prevents the nose and mouth from touching the ground. This will also protect against poisoned bait sometimes used by farmers and hunters.

In the event that your pet is taken ill abroad a campsite should have information about local vets.

Most European countries require dogs to wear a collar identifying their owners at all times. If your dog goes missing, report the matter to the local police and the local branch of that country's animal welfare organisation.

See the Documents section of this book for more information about the Pet Travel Scheme.

Prices and Payment

Prices per night (for an outfit and two adults) are shown in the site entries. If you stay on site after midday you may be charged for an extra day. Many campsites have a minimum amount for credit card transactions, meaning they can't be used to pay for overnight or short stays. Check which payment methods are accepted when you check in.

Sites with automatic barriers may ask for a deposit for a swipe card or fob to operate it.

Extra charges may apply for the use of facilities such as swimming pools, showers or laundry rooms. You may also be charged extra for dogs, Wi-Fi, tents and extra cars.

A tourist tax, eco tax and/or rubbish tax may be imposed by local authorities in some European countries. VAT may also be added to your campsite fees.

Registering on Arrival

Local authority requirements mean you will usually have to produce an identity document on arrival, which will be held by the site until you check out. If you don't want to leave your passport with reception most sites accept a document such as the Camping Key Europe (CKE) or Camping Card International (CCI).

CKE are available for Club members to purchase by calling 01342 336633 or are free to members if you take out the 'motoring' level of cover from the Club's Red Pennant Overseas Holiday Insurance.

General Advice

If you've visiting a new site ask to take a look around the site and facilities before booking in. Riverside pitches can be very scenic but keep an eye on the water level; in periods of heavy rain this may rise rapidly.

Speed limits on campsites are usually restricted to 10 km/h (6 mph). You may be asked to park your car in a separate area away from your caravan, particularly in the high season.

The use of the term 'statics' in the campsite reports in this guide may to any long-term accommodation on site, such as seasonal pitches, chalets, cottages, fixed tents and cabins, as well as static caravans.

Complaints

If you want to make a complaint about a site issue, take it up with site staff or owners at the time in order to give them the opportunity to rectify the problem during your stay.

The Caravan and Motorhome Club has no control or influence over day to day campsite operations or administration of the sites listed in this guide. Therefore we aren't able to intervene in any dispute you should have with a campsite, unless the booking has been made through our Advanced Booking Service - see listings that have a booking code at the end of the entry (e.g. G04).

Campsite Groups

Across Europe there are many campsite groups or chains with sites in various locations.

You will generally find that group sites will be consistent in their format and the quality and variety of facilities they offer. If you liked one site you can be fairly confident that you will like other sites within the same group.

If you're looking for a full facility site, with swimming pools, play areas, bars and restaurants on site you're likely to find these on sites which are part of a group. You might even find organised excursions and activities such as archery on site.

Camilo Beach, Lagos

Highlights

With around 3000 hours of sunshine a year, 850 kilometres of spectacular beaches and a wonderfully vibrant and varied landscape, Portugal is a visitor's paradise.

The country has been heavily influenced by its nautical tradition and position on the Atlantic. Many local delicacies are fish-based dishes, such as grilled sardines and salt cod, while some of Portugal's most splendid architecture date from when it was a global maritime empire.

Ceramic tiles, or azelujos, are a common element of Portuguese designs. Often depicting aspects of Portuguese culture and history, these tiles are both beautiful and functional, and are a significant part of Portugal's heritage.

Portugal is the birthplace of port, and the Douro region is one of the oldest protected wine regions in the world. Taking its name from the city of Porto, this smooth, fortified wine is exclusively produced in the Duoro Valley of Northern Portugal.

Major towns and cities

- Lisbon – Portugal's capital is known for its museums and café culture.
- Porto – an extravagant city filled with beautiful and colourful sights.
- Braga – an ancient city with filled with churches and Roman ruins.
- Faro – the prefect base to explore the Algarve.

Attractions

- Jerónimos Monastery – this UNESCO heritage site houses two museums.
- Guimarães Castle – this medieval castle is known as the Cradle of Portugal.
- National Palace of Pena – a striking palace filled with wonderful works of art.
- Lisbon Oceanarium – enjoy stunning living ocean exhibits.

Find out more

www.visitportugal.com
E: info@visitportugal.com T: (0)1 21 11 40 200

Country Information

Population (approx): 10.8 million

Capital: Lisbon

Area: 92,100 sq km (inc Azores and Madeira)

Bordered by: Spain

Terrain: Rolling plains in south; mountainous and forested north of River Tagus

Climate: Temperate climate with no extremes of temperature; wet winters in the north influenced by the Gulf Stream; elsewhere Mediterranean with hot, dry summers and short, mild winters

Coastline: 1,794km

Highest Point (mainland Portugal): Monte Torre 1,993m

Language: Portuguese

Local Time: GMT or BST, i.e. the same as the UK all year

Currency: Euros divided into 100 cents; £1 = €1.16, €1 = £0.87 (October 2019)

Emergency numbers: Police 112; Fire brigade 112; Ambulance 112

Public Holidays 2020: Jan 1; Apr 10, 12, 25; May 1; Jun 10 (National Day), 11; Aug 15; Oct 5; Nov 1; Dec 1, 8, 25.

Other holidays and saints' days are celebrated according to region. School summer holidays run from the end of June to the end of August.

Entry Formalities

Holders of British and Irish passports may visit Portugal for up to three months without a visa. For stays of over three months you will need to apply for a Registration Certificate from the nearest office of Servico de Estrangeiros e Fronteiras (immigration authority) or go to www.sef.pt.

Medical Services

For treatment of minor conditions go to a pharmacy (farmacia). Staff are generally well trained and are qualified to dispense drugs, which may only be available on prescription in Britain. In large towns there is usually at least one pharmacy whose staff speak English, and all have information posted on the door indicating the nearest pharmacy open at night.

All municipalities have a health centre. State emergency health care and hospital treatment is free on production of a European Health Insurance Card (EHIC). You will have to pay for items such as X-rays, laboratory tests and prescribed medicines as well as dental treatment. Refunds can be claimed from local offices of the Administracão Regional de Saúde (regional health service).

For serious illness you can obtain the name of an English speaking doctor from the local police station or tourist office or from a British or American consulate.

Normal precautions should be taken to avoid mosquito bites, including the use of insect repellents, especially at night.

Opening Hours

Banks: Mon-Fri 8.30am-3pm; some banks in city centres are open until 6pm.

Museums: Tue-Sun 10am-5pm/6pm; closed Mon and may close 12.30pm-2pm.

Post Offices: Mon-Fri 9am-6pm; may close for an hour at lunch.

Shops: Mon-Fri 9am-1pm & 3pm-7pm, Sat 9am-1pm; large supermarkets open Mon-Sun 9am/9.30am-10pm/11pm.

Safety and Security

The crime rate is low but pickpocketing, bag snatching and thefts from cars can occur in major tourist areas. Be vigilant on public transport, at crowded tourist sites and in public parks where it is wise to go in pairs. Keep car windows closed and doors locked while driving in urban areas at night. There has been an increase in reported cases of items stolen from vehicles in car parks. Thieves distract drivers by asking for directions, for example, or other information. Be cautious if you are approached in this way in a car park.

Take care of your belongings at all times. Do not leave your bag on the chair beside you, under the table or hanging on your chair while you eat in a restaurant or café.

Death by drowning occurs every year on Portuguese beaches. Warning flags should be taken very seriously. A red flag indicates danger and you should not enter the water. If a yellow flag is flying you may paddle at the water's edge, but you may not swim. A green flag indicates that it is safe to swim, and a chequered flag means that the lifeguard is temporarily absent. Do not swim from beaches which are not manned by lifeguards. The police may fine bathers who disobey warning flags.

During long, hot, dry periods forest fires can occur, especially in northern and central parts of the country. Take care when visiting or driving through woodland areas: ensure that cigarettes are extinguished properly, do not light barbecues, and do not leave empty bottles behind.

Portugal shares with the rest of Europe an underlying threat from terrorism. Attacks could be indiscriminate and against civilian targets in public places including tourist sites.

British Embassy

RUA DE SÃO BERNARDO 33,
1249-082 LISBOA
Tel: 21 392 4000
www.ukinportugal.fco.gov.uk
There is also a British Consulate in Portimão.

Irish Embassy

VENIDA DA LIBERDADE No 200, 4th FLOOR
1250-147 LISBON
Tel: 213 308 200
www.embassyofireland.pt

Documents

Driving Licence

All valid UK driving licences should be accepted in Portugal but holders of an older all green style licence are advised to update it to a photocard before travelling. Alternatively carry an International Driving Permit, available from the AA, the RAC or selected Post Offices.

Passport

You must carry proof of identity which includes a photograph and signature, e.g. a passport or photocard licence, at all times.

Vehicle(s)

When driving you must carry your vehicle registration certificate (V5C), proof of insurance and MOT certificate (if applicable). There are heavy on the spot fines for those who fail to do so.

Money

The major credit cards are widely accepted and there are cash machines (Multibanco) throughout the country. A tax of €0.50 may be added to credit card transactions, especially at petrol stations. Carry your credit card issuers'/ banks' 24 hour UK contact numbers in case of loss or theft.

Driving

Many Portuguese drive erratically and vigilance is advised. By comparison with the UK, the accident rate is high. Particular blackspots are the N125 along the south coast, especially in the busy holiday season, and the coast road between Lisbon and Cascais. In rural areas you may encounter horse drawn carts and flocks of sheep or goats. Otherwise there are no special difficulties in driving except in Lisbon and Porto, which are unlimited 'free-for-alls'.

Accidents

The police must be called in the case of injury or significant material damage.

Alcohol

The maximum permitted level of alcohol is 50 milligrams in 100 millilitres of blood, i.e. lower than permitted in the UK (80 milligrams). For newly qualified drivers (those with under 3 year's experience), the legal limit is 20 milligrams per 100 millilitres of blood. It is advisable to adopt the 'no drink-driving' rule at all times.

Breakdown Service

The Automovel Club de Portugal (ACP) operates a 24 hour breakdown service covering all roads in mainland Portugal. Its vehicles are coloured red and white. Emergency telephones are located at 2km intervals on main roads and motorways. To contact the ACP breakdown service call +351 219 429113 from a mobile or 707 509510 from a landline.

The breakdown service comprises on the spot repairs taking up to a maximum of 45 minutes and, if necessary, the towing of vehicles. The charges for breakdown assistance and towing vary according to distance, time of day and day of the week, plus motorway tolls if applicable. Payment by credit card is accepted.

Alternatively, on motorways breakdown vehicles belonging to the motorway companies (their emergency numbers are displayed on boards along the motorways) and police patrols (GNR/Brigada de Trânsito) can assist motorists.

Child Restraint System

Children under 12 years of age and less than 1.35m in height are not allowed to travel in the front passenger seat. They must be seated in a child restraint system adapted to their size and weight in the rear of the vehicle, unless the vehicle only has two seats, or if the vehicle is not fitted with seat belts.

Children under the age of 3 years old can be seated in the front passenger seat as long as they are in a suitable rear facing child restraint system and the airbag has been deactivated.

Fuel

Credit cards are accepted at most filling stations but a small extra charge may be added and a tax of €0.50 is added to credit card transactions. There are no automatic petrol pumps. LPG (gáz liquido) is widely available.

Low Emission Zone

There is a Low Emission Zone in operation in Lisbon. There are 2 different zones within the city. In zone 1 vehicles must meet European Emission Standard 2 (EURO 3) and in zone 2 vehicles must meet EURO 2 standard. For more information visit www.lowemissionzones.eu.

Motorways

Portugal has more than 2,600km of motorways (auto-estradas), with tolls (portagem) payable on most sections. Take care not to use the 'Via Verde' green lanes reserved for motorists who subscribe to the automatic payment system – be sure to go through a ticket booth lane where applicable, or one equipped with the new electronic toll system.

Dual carriageways (auto vias) are toll free and look similar to motorways, but speed limits are lower.

It is permitted to spend the night on a motorway rest or service area with a caravan, although The Caravan and Motorhome Club does not recommend this practice for security reasons. Toll tickets are only valid for 12 hours and fines are incurred if this is exceeded.

Vehicle are classified for tolls as follows:

Class 1	Vehicle with or without trailer with height from front axle less than 1.10m.
Class 2	Vehicle with 2 axles, with or without trailer, with height from front axle over 1.10m.
Class 3	Vehicle or vehicle combination with 3 axles, with height from front axle over 1.10m.
Class 4*	Vehicle or vehicle combination with 4 or more axles with height from front axle over 1.10m.

* Drivers of high vehicles of the Range Rover/ Jeep variety, together with some MPVs, and towing a twin axle caravan pay Class 4 tolls.

Mountain Roads and Passes

There are no mountain passes or tunnels in Portugal. Roads through the Serra da Estrela near Guarda and Covilha may be temporarily obstructed for short periods after heavy snow.

Parking

In most cases vehicles must be parked facing in the same direction as moving traffic. Parking is very limited in the centre of main towns and cities and 'blue zone' parking schemes operate. Illegally parked vehicles may be towed away or clamped. Parking in Portuguese is 'estacionamento'.

Priority

In general at intersections and road junctions, road users must give way to vehicles approaching from the right, unless signs indicate otherwise. At roundabouts vehicles already on the roundabout, i.e. on the left, have right of way.

Do not pass stationary trams at a tram stop until you are certain that all passengers have finished entering or leaving the tram.

Roads

Roads are surfaced with asphalt, concrete or stone setts. Main roads generally are well surfaced and may be three lanes wide, the middle lane being used for overtaking in either direction.

Roads in the south of the country are generally in good condition, but some sections in the north are in a poor state. Roads in many towns and villages are often cobbled and rough.

Drivers entering Portugal from Zamora in Spain will notice an apparently shorter route on the CL527/N221 road via Mogadouro. Although this is actually the signposted route, the road surface is poor in places and this route is not recommended for trailer caravans. The recommended route is via the N122/IP4 to Bragança.

Road Signs and Markings

Road signs conform to international standards. Road markings are white or yellow. Signs on motorways (auto-estrada) are blue and on regional roads they are white with black lettering. Roads are classified as follows:

Code	Road Type
AE	Motorways
IP	Principal routes
IC	Complementary routes
EN	National roads
EM	Municipal roads
CM	Other municipal roads

Signs you might encounter are as follows:

Portuguese	English Translation
Atalho	Detour
Entrada	Entrance
Estacão de gasolina	Petrol station
Estacão de policia	Police station
Estacionamento	Parking
Estrada con portagem	Toll road
Saida	Exit

Speed Limits

	Open Road (km/h)	Motorway (km/h)
Car Solo	90-100	120
Car towing caravan/ trailer	70-80	100
Motorhome under 3500kg	90-100	120
Motorhome 3500-7500kg	70-90	100

Drivers must maintain a speed between 40 km/h (25 mph) and 60 km/h (37 mph) on the 25th April Bridge over the River Tagus in Lisbon. Speed limits are electronically controlled.

Visitors who have held a driving licence for less than one year must not exceed 90 km/h (56 mph) on any road subject to higher limits.

In built-up areas there is a speed limit of 50 km/h.

It is prohibited to use a radar detector or to have one installed in a vehicle.

Towing

Motorhomes are permitted to tow a car on a four wheel trailer, i.e. with all four wheels of the car off the ground. Towing a car on an A-frame (two back wheels on the ground) is not permitted.

Traffic Jams

Traffic jams are most likely to be encountered around Lisbon and Porto and on roads to the coast, such as the A1 Lisbon-Porto and the A2 Lisbon-Setúbal, which are very busy on Friday evenings and Saturday mornings. The peak times for holiday traffic are the last weekend in June and the first and last weekends in July and August.

Around Lisbon bottlenecks occur on the bridges across the River Tagus, the N6 to Cascais, the A1 to Vila Franca de Xira, the N8 to Loures and on the N10 from Setúbal via Almada.

Around Porto you may find traffic jams on the IC1 on the Arribada Bridge and at Vila Nova de Gaia, the A28/IC1 from Póvoa de Varzim and near Vila de Conde, and on the N13, N14 and the N15.

Major motorways are equipped with suspended signs which indicate the recommended route to take when there is traffic congestion.

Traffic Lights

There is no amber signal after the red. A flashing amber light indicates 'caution' and a flashing or constant red light indicates 'stop'. In Lisbon there are separate traffic lights in bus lanes.

Violation of Traffic Regulations

Speeding, illegal parking and other infringements of traffic regulations are heavily penalised.

You may incur a fine for crossing a continuous single or double white or yellow line in the centre of the road when overtaking or when executing a left turn into or off a main road, despite the lack of any other 'no left turn' signs. If necessary, drive on to a roundabout or junction to turn, or turn right as directed by arrows.

The police are authorised to impose on the spot fines and a receipt must be given. Most police vehicles are now equipped with portable credit card machines to facilitate immediate payment of fines.

Tolls

An electronic toll collecting system was introduced in Portugal during 2010. The following motorways have tolls but no toll booths: A27, A28, A24, A41, A42, A25, A29, A23, A13, A8, A19, A33, A22 and parts of the A17 and A4. Tolls for these motorways can be paid by one of the following options:

If you are crossing the border from Spain on the A24, A25 or A22 or the A28 (via the EN13) then you can use the EASYToll welcome points. You can input your credit card details and the machine reads and then matches your credit/debit card to your number-plate, tolls are deducted automatically from your credit card, and the EASYToll machine will issue you a 30 day receipt as proof that you have paid.

If you are entering Portugal on a road that does not have an EASYToll machine you can register on-line or at a CTT post office and purchase either €5, €10, €20 or €40 worth of tolls. You can purchase a virtual prepaid ticket up to 6

times a year. For more information visit www.ctt.pt – you can select 'ENG' at the top left of the screen to see the site in English.

Alternatively you can get a temporary device (DT) available from some motorway service stations, post offices and Via Verde offices.

A deposit of €27.50 is payable when you hire the DT and this is refundable when you return it to any of the outlets mentioned above. If you use a debit card, toll costs will automatically be debited from your card. If you pay cash you will be required to preload the DT. For further information see www.visitportugal.com and see the heading 'All about Portugal' then 'Useful Information'.

On motorways where this system applies you will see a sign: 'Lanço Com Portagem' or 'Electronic Toll Only', together with details of the tolls charged. Drivers caught using these roads without a DT will incur a minimum fine of €25.

The toll roads A1 to A15 and A21 continue to have manned toll booths. Most, but not all, accept credit cards or cash.

Toll Bridges

The 2km long 25th April Bridge in Lisbon crosses the River Tagus. Tolls are charged for vehicles travelling in a south-north direction only. Tolls also apply on the Vasco da Gama Bridge, north of Lisbon, but again only to vehicles travelling in a south-north direction. Overhead panels indicate the maximum permitted speed in each lane and, when in use, override other speed limit signs.

In case of breakdown, or if you need assistance, you should try to stop in the emergency hard shoulder areas, wait inside your vehicle and switch on your hazard warning lights until a patrol arrives. Emergency telephones are placed at frequent intervals. It is prohibited to carry out repairs, to push vehicles physically or to walk on the bridges.

Essential Equipment

Reflective Jackets/ Waistcoats

If your vehicle is immobilised on the carriageway you should wear a reflective jacket or waistcoat when getting out of your vehicle. This is a legal requirement for residents of Portugal and is recommended for visitors. Passengers who leave a vehicle, for example, to assist with a repair, should also wear one. Keep the jackets within easy reach inside your vehicle, not in the boot.

Warning Triangles

Use a warning triangle if, for any reason, a stationary vehicle is not visible for at least 100 metres. In addition, hazard warning lights must be used if a vehicle is causing an obstruction or danger to other road users.

Touring

Some English is spoken in large cities and tourist areas. Elsewhere a knowledge of French could be useful.

A Lisboa Card valid for 24, 48 or 72 hours, entitles the holder to free unrestricted access to public transport, including trains to Cascais and Sintra, free entry to a number of museums, monuments and other places of interest in Lisbon and surrounding areas, as well as discounts in shops and places offering services to tourists. These cards are obtainable from tourist information offices, travel agents, some hotels and Carris ticket booths, or by visiting www.welovecitycards.com.

Do ensure when eating out that you understand exactly what you are paying for; appetisers put on the table are not free. Service is included in the bill, but it is customary to tip 5 to 10% of the total if you have received good service. Rules on smoking in restaurants and bars vary according to the size of the premises. The areas where clients are allowed to smoke are indicated by signs and there must be adequate ventilation. Each town in Portugal devotes several days in the year to local celebrations which are invariably lively and colourful. Carnivals and festivals during the period before Lent, during Holy Week and during the grape harvest can be particularly spectacular.

Camping and Caravanning

There are numerous campsites in Portugal, and many of these are situated along the coast. Sites are rated from 1 to 4 stars.

There are 22 privately owned campsites in the Orbitur chain. Caravanners can join the Orbitur Camping Club for discounts of at lease 15% at these sites. The joining fee is €21, with a 50% discount for senior citizens. You can buy membership at Orbitur sites or www.orbitur.com. Casual/wild camping is not permitted.

Motorhomes

A number of local authorities now provide dedicated short stay areas for motorhomes called 'Áreas de Serviço'. It is rare that yours will be the only motorhome staying on such areas, but take sensible precautions and avoid any that are isolated.

Cycling

In Lisbon there are cycle lanes in Campo Grande gardens, also from Torre de Belém to Cais do Sodré (7km) along the River Tagus, and between Cascais and Guincho. Elsewhere in the country there are few cycle lanes.

Transportation of Bicycles

Legislation stipulates that the exterior dimensions of a vehicle should not be exceeded and, in practice, this means that only caravans or motorhomes are allowed to carry bicycles/motorbikes at the rear of the vehicle. Bicycles may not extend beyond the width of the vehicle or more than 45cms from the back. However, bicycles may be transported on the roof of cars provided that an overall height of 4 metres is not exceeded. Cars carrying bicycles/motorbikes on the back may be subject to a fine.

If you are planning to travel from Spain to Portugal please note that slightly different regulations apply and these are set out in the Spain Country Introduction.

Electricity and Gas

Usually current on campsites varies between 6 and 15 amps. Plugs have two round pins. CEE connections are commonplace.

The full range of Campingaz cylinders is available.

Public Transport

A passenger and vehicle ferry crosses the River Sado estuary from Setúbal to Tróia and there are frequent ferry and catamaran services for cars and passengers across the River Tagus from various points in Lisbon including Belém and Cais do Sodré.

Both Lisbon and Porto have metro systems operating from 6am to 1am. For routes and fares information see www.metrolisboa.pt and www.metrodoporto.pt (English versions).

Throughout the country buses are cheap, regular and mostly on time, with every town

connected. In Lisbon the extensive bus and tram network is operated by Carris, together with one lift and three funiculars which tackle the city's steepest hills. Buy single journey tickets on board from bus drivers or buy a rechargeable 'Sete Colinas' or Via Viagem card for use on buses and the metro.

In Porto buy a 'Euro' bus ticket, which can be charged with various amounts, from metro stations and transport offices. Validate tickets for each journey at machines on the buses. Also available is an 'Andante' ticket which is valid on the metro and on buses. Porto also has a passenger lift and a funicular so that you can avoid the steep walk to and from the riverside.

Taxis are usually cream in colour. In cities they charge a standard, metered fare; outside they may run on the meter or charge a flat rate and are entitled to charge for the return fare. Agree a price for your journey before setting off.

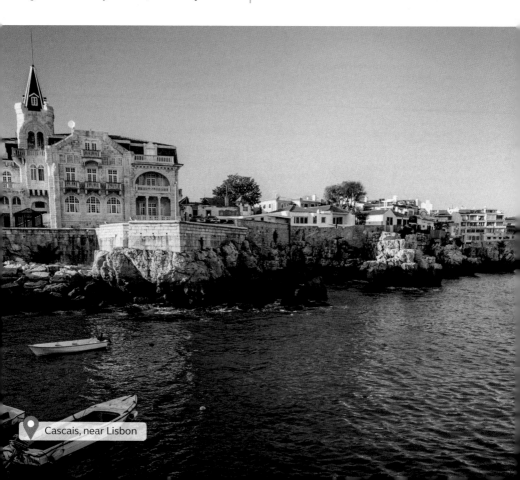

Cascais, near Lisbon

ALANDROAL *C3* (13km S Rural) *38.60645, -7.34674*
Camping Rosário, Monte das Mimosas, Rosário, 7250-999 Alandroal **268 459566; info@campingrosario.com; www.campingrosario.com**

🏕 €1 ♦♦ ⓦ 🛁 🗑 🖉 🦋 ⓨ 𝓨 ⑪ ⍤ 🏊 nr 🏔 ⚓

Fr E exit IP7/A6 at Elvas W junc 9; at 3rd rndabt take exit sp Espanha, immed 1st R dir Juromenha & Redondo. Onto N373 until exit Rosário. Fr W exit IP7/A6 junc 8 at Borba onto N255 to Alandroal, then N373 E sp Elvas. After 1.5km turn R to Rosário & foll sp to site. Sm, hdstg, pt shd, pt sl, EHU (6A) €2.35; sw nr; red long stay; TV; Eng spkn; adv bkg acc; boating; fishing; CKE. *"Remote site beside Alqueva Dam, excel touring base; dogs not acc Jul/Aug; ltd to 50 people max; excel site; idyllic; peaceful; clean & well maintained; v helpful owner."*
€22.50, 2 Jan-30 Sep.   **2019**

ALBUFEIRA *B4* (3km N Urban) *37.10617, -8.25395*
Camping Albufeira, Estrada de Ferreiras, 8200-555 Albufeira **289 587629 or 289 587630; geral@camping albufeira.net or info@campingalbufeira.net; www.campingalbufeira.net**

12 🐕 ♦♦ ⓦ 🛁 🛢 🗑 🖉 ⓜ 🦋 ⓨ 𝓨 ⑪ ⍤ 🏊 🏔 ⚓
🌲 sand 1.5km

Exit IP1/E1 sp Albufeira onto N125/N395 dir Albufeira; camp on L, sp. 4*, V lge, mkd, pt shd, pt sl, EHU (10-12A) €3; gas; red long stay; TV; 20% statics; phone; bus adj; Eng spkn; ccard acc; games area; games rm; bike hire; tennis; CKE. *"Friendly, secure site; excel pool area/bar; some pitches lge enough for US RVs; car wash; cash machine; security patrols; disco (soundproofed); sports park; pitches on lower pt of site prone to flooding in heavy rain; conv beach & town; poss lge rallies during Jan-Apr; camp bus to town high ssn."* **€27.60**   **2016**

ALCACER DO SAL *B3* (1km NW Rural) *38.38027, -8.51583* **Parque de Campismo Municipal de Alcácer do Sal,** Olival do Outeiro, 7580-125 Alcácer do Sal **265 612303; cmalcacer@mail.telepac.pt**

🏕 ♦♦ ⓦ 🛁 🛢 🗑 🖉 ⓜ 🦋 ⓨ 𝓨 ⍤ nr ⑪ 🏊 nr 🏔

Heading S on A2/IP1 turn L twd Alcácer do Sal on N5. Site on R 1km fr Alcácer do Sal. Sp at rndabt. Site behind supmkt. 2*, Sm, hdg, mkd, pt shd, pt sl, EHU (6-12A) €1.50 (rev pol); bbq; phone; bus 50m; Eng spkn; ccard acc; games area; clsd mid-Dec to mid-Jan; CKE. *"In rice growing area - major mosquito prob; historic town; spacious pitches; pool, paddling pool adj; poss full in winter - rec phone ahead; pleasant site behind supmkt; wifi at recep; san facs tired & not clean."* **€13.70, 15 Jan-15 Dec.**   **2017**

AMARANTE *C1* (3km NE Rural) *41.27805, -8.07027*
Camping Penedo da Rainha, Rua Pedro Alveollos, Gatão, 4600-099 Amarante **255 437630; ccporto@ sapo.pt**

🏕 🐕 ♦♦ ⓦ 🛁 🛢 ⅛ 🗑 🖉 ⓜ 🦋 𝓨 ⑪ ⍤ 🏊 🏔 🏊 ⚓

Fr IP4 Vila Real to Porto foll sp to Amarante & N15. On N15 cross bdge for Porto & immed take R slip rd. Foll sp thro junc & up rv to site. 2*, Lge, hdstg, shd, pt sl, terr, EHU (6A) €3.25; TV; phone; bus to Porto fr Amarante; Eng spkn; adv bkg acc; games rm; rv fishing adj; canoeing; cycling; CKE. *"Well-run site in steep woodland/parkland - take advice or survey rte bcf driving to pitch; excel facs but some pitches far fr facs; few touring pitches; friendly, helpful recep; plenty of shd; conv Amarante old town & Douro Valley; Sat mkt; not suitable for long o'fits, better for MH's."*
€14.00, 1 Jan-30 Nov.   **2017**

ARCO DE BAULHE *C1* (0.3km NE Rural) *41.48659, -7.95845* **Arco Unipessoal,** Lugar das Cruzes, 4860-067 Arco de Baúlhe (Costa Verde) **(351) 968176246; campismoarco@hotmail.com**

🏕 ♦♦ ⓦ 🛁 🗑 🖉 𝓨 ⑪ ⚓ (htd) 🛁

Dir A7 exit 12 Mondm/Cabeceiras, 2nd R at rndabt dir Arco de Baulhe. Call and they will lead you in. V narr rd access, no mv's over 7m. Med, pt shd, terr, EHU (6A); bbq; TV; Eng spkn; adv bkg rec; rv. *"New site run by couple with 20 yrs experience; quiet; centrally located for historic towns & nature parks; gd rest; lovely well maintained site with view; excel facs; 100m fr vill cent; beautiful mountain area."*
€23.00, 3 Apr-1 Oct.   **2019**

> ## "There aren't many sites open at this time of year"
>
> If you're travelling outside peak season remember to call ahead to check site opening dates – even if the entry says 'open all year'.

ARGANIL *C2* (3km N Rural) *40.2418, -8.06746* **Camp Municipal de Arganil,** 3300-432 Sarzedo **235 205706; camping@cm-arganil.pt; www.cm-arganil.pt**

🏕 ♦♦ ⓦ 🛁 🛢 🗑 🖉 ⓜ 🦋 ⓨ 𝓨 ⑪ ⍤ 🏊 nr 🏔 ⚓

Fr Coimbra on N17 twd Guarda; after 50km turn S sp Arganil on N342-4; site on L in 4km in o'skts of Sarzedo bef rv bdge; avoid Góis to Arganil rd fr SW. 2*, Med, pt shd, pt sl, terr, EHU (5-15A) €2.40; gas; bbq; red long stay; TV; phone; Eng spkn; ccard acc; canoeing adj; games area; fishing adj; CKE. *"Vg, well-run site; friendly owner; fine views; gd cent for touring; gd walks; ski in Serra da Estrela 50km Dec/Jan; interesting town; gd mkt (Thu)."*
€12.50, 1 Mar-31 Oct.   **2016**

AVEIRO *B2* (14km SW Coastal) *40.59960, -8.74981*
Camping Costa Nova, Estrada da Vagueira, Quinta
dos Patos, 3830-453 Ílhavo **234 393220; info@camping
costanova.com; www.campingcostanova.com**

🐕 €1.40 �100(htd) ⊞ ⚓ 🛗 🗑 ∥ MSP 🦋 ▼ ⑪ ♨ 🏊 /ሴ 🐾 ♐sand

**Site on Barra-Vagueira coast rd 1km on R after
Costa Nova.** 2*, V lge, mkd, unshd, EHU (2-6A) €2.40;
gas; bbq; red long stay; TV; 10% statics; phone; Eng
spkn; adv bkg acc; ccard acc; games rm; site clsd Jan;
fishing; bike hire; games area; CKE. *"Superb, peaceful
site adj nature reserve; helpful staff; gd, hot water to
shwrs only; sm pitches; sep car park high ssn; pool 4km;
vg; excel cycle track fr site."*
€22.50, 21 Mar-1 Oct.   **2019**

BRAGANCA *D1* (6km N Rural) *41.84361, -6.74722*
Inatel Parque Campismo Bragança, Estrada de Rabal,
5300-671 Meixedo **351 273 326 080 or 351 96 420
66 22; campismobraganca@gmail.com;
www.campismobraganca.com**

🐕 ♐♐♐ ⊞ ⚓ 🗑 ∥ 🦋 ▼ ⑪ ♨ 🏊 /ሴ

**Fr Bragança N for 6km on N103.7 twd Spanish
border. Site on R, sp Inatel.** 2*, Med, hdstg, pt shd,
pt sl, terr, EHU (6A) inc; gas; bus; Eng spkn; bike hire;
fishing. *"On S boundary of National Park; rv runs thro
site; friendly staff; gd rest; vg facs; lovely location by
rv."* **€12.50, 1 Jun-15 Sep.**   **2016**

CAMINHA *B1* (3km SW Coastal) *41.86611, -8.85888*
Camping ORBITUR-Caminha, Mata do Camarido,
N13, Km 90, 4910-180 Caminha **258 921295;
infocaminha@orbitur.pt; www.orbitur.pt**

12 🐕 €1.50 ♐♐♐ ⊞ ⚓ 🛗 🗑 ∥ MSP 🦋 ♀ ▼ ⑪ ♨ 🏊 /ሴ

🌴 sand 150m

**Foll seafront rd N13/E1 fr Caminha dir Viana/Porto,
at sp Foz do Minho turn R, site in approx 1km. Long
o'fits take care at ent.** 2*, Med, shd, terr, EHU (5-15A)
€3-4; gas; red long stay; TV; 5% statics; Eng spkn; adv
bkg acc; ccard acc; fishing; bike hire; CKE. *"Pleasant,
woodland site; pool 2.5km; care in shwrs - turn cold
water on 1st as hot poss scalding; Gerês National
Park & Viana do Castelo worth visit; poss to cycle to
Caminha; vg site, nr attractive beach and sh walk to
pleasant town."* **€38.60**   **2017**

CAMPO MAIOR *C3* (2km SE Rural) *39.00833, -7.04833*
Camping Rural Os Anjos, Estrada da Senhora da
Saúde, 7371-909 Campo Maior **268 688138 or
965 236625 (mob); info@campingosanjos.com;
www.campingosanjos.com**

🏕 ♿€1 ♚♚ wo ▲ ♨ ♿ ◐ ≋ 🦋 ♈ 🍴 ☎ nr ⚓

**Fr Elvas foll rd N373 to Campo Maior. Foll sm sp
thro vill. Site on L down country lane.** Sm, hdstg, pt
shd, terr, EHU (6A) €2.60; bbq; TV; phone; Eng spkn;
adv bkg rec; games rm; games area; CKE. *"Excel,
lovely, peaceful site; v helpful, friendly, Dutch owners;
gd touring base for unspoiled, diverse area; conv
Spanish border, Badajoz & Elvas; 15 Nov-15 Feb open
with adv bkg only; max 1 dog per pitch; Campo Maior
beautiful, white town; LS call or email bef arr; gd walks
& bike rides; v clean shwrs; lake sw 8km; fishing 8km;
watersports 8km; modern facs; fantastic views; excel."*
€17.00 2015

CASCAIS *A3* (7km NW Urban/Coastal) *38.72166,
-9.46666* **Camping ORBITUR-Guincho,** Lugar de
Areia, EN 247-6, Guincho 2750-053 Cascais **(214)
870450; infoguincho@orbitur.pt; www.orbitur.pt/
camping-orbitur-guincho**

🏕 🐕€3 ♚♚ wo ▲ ♨ ♿ ◐ ≋ / MSP 🦋 ♈ 🍴 ☎ 🅿 ⚓ /
⚓ ⛱ sand 800m

**Fr Lisbon take A5 W, at end m'way foll sp twd
Cascais. At 1st rndabt turn R sp Birre & Campismo.
Foll sp for 2.5km. Steep traff calming hump - care
needed.** 2*, V lge, mkd, hdg, shd, terr, EHU (6A)
inc; gas; bbq; red long stay; twin axles; TV (pitch);
50% statics; phone; Eng spkn; adv bkg acc; ccard acc;
games rm; horseriding 500m; tennis; watersports
1km; car wash; fishing 1km; golf 3km; bike hire; CKE.
*"Sandy, wooded site behind dunes; poss stretched &
v busy high ssn; poss diff lge o'fits due trees; steep rd
to beach; gd san facs, gd value rest; vg LS; buses to
Cascais for train to Lisbon; beautiful coastline within
20 min walk; rec lge o'fits prebook to ensure suitable
pitch."* **€37.00, E10.** 2017

See advertisement on previous page

CASTELO DE VIDE *C3* (7km SW Rural) *39.39805,
-7.48722* **Camping Quinta do Pomarinho,** N246,
Km 16.5, Castelo de Vide **(00351) 965 755 341;
info@pomarinho.com; www.pomarinho.com**

🏕 🐕 ♚♚ wo ▲ ♨ / 🦋 ♈ ☎ nr ⚓

**On N246 at km 16.5 by bus stop, turn into dirt
track. Site in 500m.** Sm, mkd, hdstg, unshd, EHU (6A)
€2.50-3.50; bus adj; Eng spkn; adv bkg acc; bike hire.
*"On edge of Serra de São Mamede National Park; gd
walking, fishing, birdwatching, cycling; vg; gd views twd
Serra de Sao Marmede; recep clsd 1-3pm; not many
ehu or flat lge pitches."* **€16.50** 2019

CASTRO VERDE *C4* (1km N Urban) *37.704976,
-8.087696* **Parque Campismo Castro Verde,** Rua
Timor Lorosae 7780, Castro Verde **286 320150;
parque.campismo@cm-castroverde.pt; https://cm-
castroverde.pt/pt/553/parque-de-campismo-
municipal.aspx**

🏕 🐕 ♚♚ wo ▲ ♨ / 🦋 ♈ ☎ nr 🏛

Sp fr Castro Verde town. Med, hdstg, pt shd, pt sl,
EHU; gas; twin axles; TV; Eng spkn; CCI. *"Vg site."*
2019

CELORICO DE BASTO *C1* (0.7km NW Rural)
41.39026, -8.00581 **Parque de Campismo de Celorico
de Basto,** Adaufe-Gemeos, 4890-361 Celorico de
Basto **(255) 323340 or 964-064436 (mob);
www.facebook.com/Celoricocamping/**

🏕 🐕€1.80 ♚♚ wo ▲ ♨ ◐ / MSP 🦋 ♈ 🍴 🅗 ☎ 🏛 /

**E fr Guimarães exit A7/IC5 S sp Vila Nune (bef x-ing
rv). Foll sp Fermil & Celorico de Basto, site sp. Rte
narr or winding or take the N210 fr Amarente
and foll sp to site.** 3*, Med, mkd, hdstg, shd, EHU
(6-16A) €2-3.20; gas; bbq; sw nr; red long stay; TV;
10% statics; phone; ccard acc; games area; fishing adj;
CKE. *"Peaceful, well-run site; gd facs; pool 500m; gd
cycling & walking; vg."* **€16.00** 2019

CHAVES *C1* (6km S Rural) *41.70166, -7.50055* **Camp
Municipal Quinta do Rebentão,** Vila Nova de Veiga,
5400-764 Chaves **276 322733; parquedecampismo@
chaves.pt; www.ccchaves.com**

🐕 ♚♚ wo ▲ ♿ ◐ / 🦋 ♈ 🍴 ☎ nr 🏛

**Fr o'skts Chaves take N2 S. After about 3km in vill
of Vila Nova de Veiga turn E at sp thro new estate,
site in about 500m.** 1*, Med, hdstg, pt shd, terr, EHU
(6A) inc; bbq; sw nr; phone; bus 800m; Eng spkn; adv
bkg acc; bike hire; fishing 4km; games rm; CKE. *"Gd
site in lovely valley but remote; excel helpful, friendly
staff; facs block quite a hike fr some terr pitches; old
but clean facs; Chaves interesting, historical Roman
town; baker visits every morn; vg rest (clsd Mon in LS)
& bar; site clsd Dec; pool adj; easy access; wifi at recep."*
€15.00, 1 Feb-30 Nov. 2019

COIMBRA *B2* (6km SE Urban) *40.18888, -8.39944*
Coimbra Camping, Rua de Escola, Alto do Areeiro,
Santo António dos Olivais, 3030-011 Coimbra **239
086692; coimbra@cacampings.com; www.coimbra
camping.com**

🏕 🐕€2.60 ♚♚(htd) wo ▲ ♨ ♿ ◐ / MSP 🦋 ♈ 🍴 🅗 ☎ 🏛

**Fr S on AP1/IP1 at junc 11 turn twd Lousa & in 1km
turn twd Coimbra on IC2. In 9.5km turn R at rndabt
onto Ponte Rainha, strt on at 3 rndabts along Avda
Mendes Silva. Then turn R along Estrada des Beiras
& cross rndabt to Rua de Escola. Or fr N17 dir Beira
foll sp sports stadium/campismo. Fr N ent Coimbra
on IC2, turn L onto ring rd & foll Campismo sps.**
4*, V lge, hdstg, pt shd, pt sl, terr, EHU (6A) €3.90 (rev
pol); gas; bbq; sw nr; red long stay; TV; 10% statics;
bus 100m; Eng spkn; adv bkg acc; ccard acc; bike hire;
games area; tennis; games rm; sauna; CKE. *"Vg site &
facs; health club; pool adj; v interesting, lively university
town."* **€23.70** 2017

COIMBRAO *B2 (0.5km NW Urban) 39.90027, -8.88805* **Camping Coimbrão,** 185 Travessa do Gomes, 2425-452 Coimbrão **244 606007; camping coimbrao@web.de**

12 ♦♦♦ ᵂᴰ ♨ ᴥ 🛒 🗑 ⫽ ᴹˢᴾ 💥 ♈ 🐾nr ⋔ ⚓

Site down lane in vill cent. Care needed lge o'fits, but site worth the effort. Sm, unshd, EHU (6-10A) €2.20-3.30; bbq; sw nr; red long stay; TV; bus 200m; Eng spkn; fishing 4km. *"Excel site; helpful & friendly staff; gd touring base; gd loc for exploring; office open 0800-1200 & 1500-2200; canoeing 4km; German owners."* **€16.70**   **2017**

COVILHA *C2 (48km NW Rural) 40.40406, -7.58770* **Vale do Rossim,** Penhas Douradas, 6270 Gouveia **275 981 029; vrecoresort@gmail.com; valedo rossimecoresort.com**

12 🐕 ♦♦♦(htd) ᵂᴰ ♨ ♈ ᴥ 🛒 ⫽ ᴹˢᴾ 💥 ♈ 🍸 ⑪ 🗑 ⚓

20km W on N232 fr Manteigas. Turn L at sp. Site 1km at end of rd. Sm, pt shd, pt sl, EHU (6A) €3.50; gas; bbq; sw nr; twin axles; phone; Eng spkn; adv bkg acc; ccard acc. *"High in mountains by lake wth beaches; sw, kayaking, biking, climbing, walking; rest & bar by lake; peaceful, rural site in beautiful surroundings; friendly, helpful staff; vg."* **€11.00**   **2016**

ELVAS *C3 (2km SW Urban) 38.87305, -7.1800* **Parque de Campismo da Piedade,** 7350-901 Elvas **268 628997 or 268 622877**

🐕 ♦♦♦ ᵂᴰ ♨ ᴥ 🗑 ⫽ 🍸 ⑪ 🗑 🐾nr ⋔

Exit IP7/E90 junc 9 or 12 & foll site sp dir Estremoz. 1*, Med, mkd, hdstg, pt shd, sl, EHU (16A) inc; gas; bbq; phone; bus 500m; CKE. *"Attractive aqueduct & walls; Piedade church & relics adj; traditional shops; pleasant walk to town; v quiet site, even high ssn; adequate san facs; conv NH en rte Algarve; c'vans parked to cls; noisy; facs need updating."* **€20.00, 1 Apr-15 Sep.**   **2018**

ERMIDAS SADO *B4 (11km W Rural) 38.01805, -8.48500* **Camping Monte Naturista O Barão (Naturist),** Foros do Barão, 7566-909 Ermidas-Sado **936710623 (mob); info@montenaturista.com; www.montenaturista.com**

12 🐕 €1 ♦♦♦ ᵂᴰ ♨ ♈ ᴥ 🛒 ⫽ ᴹˢᴾ 💥 ♈ 🍸 ⚓

Fr A2 turn W onto N121 thro Ermidas-Sado twd Santiago do Cacém. At x-rds nr Areláos turn R at bus stop (km 17.5) dir Barão. Site in 1km along unmade rd. Sm, mkd, pt shd, pt sl, EHU (6A) €3.20; bbq; red long stay; TV; 10% statics; Eng spkn; adv bkg acc; ccard acc; games area; CKE. *"Gd, peaceful 'retreat-type' site in beautiful wooded area; meals Tue, Thurs, Sat & Sun; friendly atmosphere; spacious pitches - sun or shd; rec."* **€22.50**   **2016**

EVORA *C3 (3km SW Urban) 38.55722, -7.92583* **Camping Orbitur Evora,** Estrada das Alcaçovas, Herdade Esparragosa, 7005-206 Évora **(266) 705190; evora@orbitur.pt; www.orbitur.pt**

12 🐕 €3 ♦♦♦ ᵂᴰ ♨ ᴥ 🛒 ⫽ ᴹˢᴾ 💥 ♈ 🍸 🗑 🐾 ⋔ ⚓ 🏊

Fr N foll N18 & by-pass, then foll sps for Lisbon rd at each rndabt or traff lts. Fr town cent take N380 SW sp Alcaçovas, foll site sp, site in 2km. NB Narr gate to site. 3*, Med, mkd, hdstg, pt shd, pt sl, EHU (6A) €3.50-4.60 (long lead poss req, rev pol); gas; red long stay; TV; phone; bus; Eng spkn; adv bkg acc; ccard acc; games area; car wash; tennis; CKE. *"Conv town cent, Évora World Heritage site with wealth of monuments & prehistoric sites nrby; cycle path to town; free car parks just outside town walls; poss flooding some pitches after heavy rain; beautiful site."* **€29.00**   **2019**

> ## "I like to fill in the reports as I travel from site to site"
>
> You'll find report forms at the back of this guide, or you can fill them in online at camc.com/europereport.

EVORAMONTE *C3 (6km NE Rural) 38.79276, -7.68701* **Camping Alentejo,** Novo Horizonte, 7100-300 Evoramonte **268 959283 or 936 799249 (mob); info@campingalentejo.com; www.camping alentejo.com**

12 🐕 €1 ♦♦♦ ᵂᴰ ♨ ᴥ 🛒 ⫽ ᴹˢᴾ 💥 ♈ ⚓

Fr E exit A6/E90 junc 7 Estremoz onto N18 dir Evora. Site in 8km at km 236. Sm, hdstg, pt shd, terr, EHU (16A) inc; bbq; bus adj; Eng spkn; adv bkg acc; horseriding; CKE. *"Excel site; gd birdwatching, v friendly and helpful owner; conv NH on the way to S; easy parking; excel modern clean facs; gd library in off; bus stop outside gate to Evora; care req ent site; MH stay at lower price if no hookups; improved site; gd; secure."* **€15.00**   **2018**

FIGUEIRA DA FOZ *B2 (7km S Urban/Coastal) 40.11861, -8.85666* **Camping ORBITUR-Gala,** N109, Km 4, Gala, 3090-458 Figueira da Foz **233 431231; infogala@orbitur.pt; www.orbitur.pt**

12 🐕 €1.50 ♦♦♦ ᵂᴰ ♨ ᴥ 🛒 ⫽ ᴹˢᴾ 🍸 ⑪ 🗑 🐾 ⋔ ⚓ (htd) 🏊 🌴 sand 400m

Fr Figueira da Foz on N109 dir Leiria for 3.5km. After Gala site on R in approx 400m. Ignore sp on R 'Campismo' after long bdge. 3*, Lge, hdstg, shd, terr, EHU (6-10A) €3-4; gas; bbq; red long stay; TV; 80% statics; phone; Eng spkn; adv bkg acc; ccard acc; fishing 1km; car wash; tennis; games rm; CKE. *"Gd, renovated site adj busy rd; luxury san facs (furthest fr recep); excel pool; busy site; in pine woods."* **€29.00**   **2016**

GERES *C1 (14km NW Rural) 41.76305, -8.19111*
Parque de Campismo de Cerdeira, Rue de Cerdeira
400, Campo do Gerês, 4840-030 Terras do Bouro
(253) 351005; info@parquecerdeira.com;
www.parquecerdeira.com

12 🐕 €3 ♦♦♦ �🆆🅳 ♨ ♿ 🔲 ⩊ 🦋 🍴 ⑭ 🎿 ⅍ ♠

Fr N103 Braga-Chaves rd, 28km E of Braga turn N
onto N304 at sp to Poussada. Cont N for 18km to
Campo de Gerês. Site in 1km; well sp. 3*, V lge, shd,
EHU (5-10A) €4; gas; sw; TV; 10% statics; bus 500m;
Eng spkn; ccard acc; canoeing; bike hire; fishing 2km;
CKE. *"Beautiful scenery; unspoilt area; fascinating old
vills nrby & gd walking; ltd facs LS; Nat pk campsite;
wooded site; san facs modern & clean."* **€30.00**   **2018**

"We must tell the Club about that great site we found"

Get your site reports in by mid-August and we'll
do our best to get your updates into the next
edition.

GUIMARAES *B1 (32km E Rural) 41.46150, -8.01120*
Quinta Valbom, Quintã 4890-505 Ribas **351 253 653
048; info@quintavalbom.nl; www.quintavalbom.nl**

🐕 ♦♦♦ ♨ ♿ 🔲 ⩊ 🦋 ⑭ 🍴 🎿

Fr Guimaraes take A7 SE. Exit 11 onto N206 Fafe/
Gandarela. Turn R bef tunnel twds Ribas. Foll blue
& red signs of campsite. Med, mkd, pt shd, terr, EHU
(10A); bbq; twin axles; Eng spkn; adv bkg acc; CCI.
*"Very nice site; friendly, extremely helpful Dutch
owners; quiet surroundings; lots of space in beautiful
setting; if driving c'van, park at white chapel and call
campsite for their 4WD assistance up last bit of steep
hill; owner won't acc c'vans over 6mtrs."*
€26.70, 1 Apr-1 Oct.   **2017**

GUIMARAES *B1 (6km SE Rural) 41.42833, -8.26861*
Camping Parque da Penha, Penha-Costa, 4800-026
Guimarães **253 515912 or 253 515085; geral@
turipenha.pt; www.turipenha.pt**

🐕 ♦♦♦ ♨ ♿ ⑭ 🍴 ⑭ nr ⅍ ⚶ 🎿

Take N101 SE fr Guimarães sp Felgueiras. Turn R
at sp for Nascente/Penha. Site sp. 1*, Lge, hdstg,
shd, pt sl, terr, EHU (6A); gas; phone; bus; Eng
spkn; adv bkg acc; fishing; car wash; CKE. *"Excel
staff; gd san facs; lower terrs not suitable lge o'fits;
densely wooded hilltop site; conv Guimarães World
Heritage site European City of Culture 2012; cable
car down to Guimaraes costs €5 return; excel rest."*
€19.00, 1 May-15 Sep.   **2017**

LAGOS *B4 (7km W Rural/Coastal) 37.10095,
-8.73220* **Camping Turiscampo,** N125 Espiche,
8600-109 Luz-Lagos **282 789265; info@turiscam-
po.com; www.turiscampo.com**

12 🐕 €1.50 ♦♦♦ (htd) �🆆🅳 ♨ ♿ 🔲 ⩊ 🅼🆂🅿 🦋 ⑭ 🍴 ⑭ 🎿 🎿
⅍ ♠ ♒ 🎿 ⚶ 🏖 sand 2km

Exit A22/IC4 junc 1 to Lagos then N125 fr Lagos
dir Sagres, site 3km on R. 4*, Lge, hdstg, mkd, hdg,
shd, pt sl, terr, EHU (6A) inc - extra for 10A; gas; bbq;
red long stay; TV; 25% statics; phone; bus to Lagos
100m; Eng spkn; adv bkg acc; ccard acc; games area;
tennis 2km; bike hire; games rm; fishing 2.5km; CKE.
*"Superb, well-run, busy site; fitness cent; v popular
for winter stays & rallies; all facs (inc excel pool) open
all yr; gd san facs; helpful staff; lovely vill, beach &
views; varied & interesting area, Luz worth visit; vg."*
€44.00, E07.   **2019**

See advertisement opposite

LAMAS DE MOURO *C1 (2km S Rural) 42.03587,
-8.19644* **Camping Lamas de Mouro,** 4960-170
Lamas de Mouro **(251) 466041; geral@camping-
lamas.com; www.camping-lamas.com**

12 🐕 €2 ♦♦♦ �🆆🅳 ♨ 🔲 ⩊ 🦋 🍴 ⑭ 🎿 🎿 ⅍ ♠ 🎿

Fr N202 at Melgaco foll sp Peneda- Gerês National
Park, cont R to rd sp Porta de Lamas de Mouro. Cont
1km past park info office, site on L in pine woods.
2*, Med, pt shd, EHU (10A) €3; cooking facs; phone;
bus 1km; CKE. *"Ideal for walking in National Park;
natural pool."* **€15.00**   **2017**

"I need an on-site restaurant"

We do our best to make sure site information
is correct, but it is always best to check any
must-have facilities are still available or will
be open during your visit.

LAMEGO *C1 (0.5km NW Urban) 41.09017, -7.82212*
Camping Lamego, EN2 Lugar da Raposeira, 5101-
909 Lamego **351 969 021 408; campinglamego@
gmail.com; campinglamego.wix.com**

12 ♦♦♦ (htd) �🆆🅳 ♨ ♿ 🔲 ⩊ 🅼🆂🅿 🦋 ⑭ 🍴 ⑭

Foll N225. Turn L onto N2. Sm, hdstg, pt shd, EHU
(6A) €4; Eng spkn. *"Easy walk to Bom Jesus do Monte;
site only suitable for MH's; san facs new & excel (2016);
v friendly owners; excel."* **€15.00**   **2016**

OPEN ALL YEAR // HEATED INDOOR POOL // OUTDOOR POOL // SPA & GYM

Algarve ~ Portugal

TURISCAMPO
CAMPING CLUB ALGARVE

 (+351) 282 789 265

 info@turiscampo.com

 www.turiscampo.com

 LeadingCampings

 yelloh! VILLAGE

E.N.125, Km17 Espiche, 8600-109 Luz - Lagos - Algarve

PORTUGAL

LISBOA *B3* (1/km SW Coastal) *38.653909, -9.238510*
Camping ORBITUR-Costa de Caparica, Ave Afonso de Albuquerque, Quinta de S. António, 2825-450 Costa de Caparica **212 901366 or 903894; caparica@orbitur.pt; www.orbitur.pt**

🔢 🚲 ⛳3 👬 wo ♨ 🔥 📺 ∥ msp ♒ 🍽 ⊕ 🛒 ♿ ✂ 🎣 sand 1km

Take A2/IP7 S fr Lisbon; after Rv Tagus bdge turn W to Costa de Caparica. At end of rd turn N twd Trafaria, & site on L. Well sp fr a'strada. 3*, Lge, mkd, hdg, shd, terr, EHU (6A) €3; gas; bbq; red long stay; TV; 75% statics; phone; bus to Lisbon; Eng spkn; adv bkg acc; ccard acc; car wash; games rm; tennis; fishing; CKE. *"Gd, clean, well run site; heavy traff into city; rec use free parking at Monument to the Discoveries & tram to city cent; ferry to Belém; ltd facs LS; pleasant, helpful staff; pool 800m; aircraft noise early am & late pm."* **€44.00** **2019**

See advertisement

LOURICAL *B2* (5km SW Rural) *39.99149, -8.78880*
Campismo O Tamanco, Rua do Louriçal 11, Casas Brancas, 3105-158 Louriçal **236 952551; tamanco@me.com; www.campismo-o-tamanco.com**

🔢 🚲 👬 wo ♨ 🔥 🛒 ∥ msp 🦋 ♒ 🍽 ⊕ 🛒 🎣 (htd) 🏊
🏖 sand 5km

S on N109 fr Figuera da Foz S twds Leiria foll sp at rndabt Matos do Corrico onto N342 to Louriçal. Site 800m on L. 3*, Med, hdstg, hdg, mkd, pt shd, EHU inc (6A) €2.25-3.50; gas; bbq; sw nr; red long stay; twin axles; 5% statics; bus 500m; Eng spkn; adv bkg acc; CKE. *"Excel; friendly Dutch owners; chickens & ducks roaming site; superb mkt on Sun at Louriçal; a bit of real Portugal; gd touring base; mkd walks thro pine woods; v clean; relaxed; sm farm animal area."* **€25.00** **2016**

MEDA *C2* (0.5km N Urban) *40.96972, -7.25916*
Parque de Campismo Municipal, Av. Professor Adriano Vasco Rodrigues, 6430 Mêda **(351) 925 480 500 or (351) 279 883 270; campismo@cm-meda.pt; www.cm-meda.pt/turismo/Paginas/Parque_Camsimo.aspx**

🔢 👬 wo ♨ 🔥 🛒 msp ♒ 🍽 ⊕ 🛒 🎣

Head N fr cent of town, take 1st R, take 1st L & site on L within the Meda Sports Complex. Sm, hdstg, pt shd, pt sl,. *"Pt of the Municipal Sports Complex with facs avail; conv for town cent & historic ctr; lovely sm site; lge pitches; some pull thro; blocks essential; clean modern san facs."* **€16.00** **2017**

MONTARGIL *B3* (4km N Rural) *39.10083, -8.14472*
Camping ORBITUR, Baragem de Montargil, N2, 7425-017 Montargil **242 901207; infomontargil@orbitur.pt; www.orbitur.pt**

🔢 🚲 ⛳1.50 👬 wo ♨ 🔥 🛒 ∥ msp ♒ 🍽 ⊕ 🛒 ♿ ✂ 🚣 🎣

Fr N251 Coruche to Vimiero rd, turn N on N2, over dam at Barragem de Montargil. Fr Ponte de Sor S on N2 until 3km fr Montargil. Site clearly sp bet rd & lake. 3*, Med, hdstg, mkd, pt shd, terr, EHU (6-10A) €3-4; gas; bbq; red long stay; TV (pitch); 60% statics; phone; Eng spkn; adv bkg acc; ccard acc; fishing; car wash; tennis; games rm; boating; watersports; CKE. *"Friendly site in beautiful area."* **€26.70** **2016**

NAZARE *B2* (2km N Rural) *39.62036, -9.05630*
Camping Vale Paraíso, N242, 2450-138 Nazaré **262 561800; info@valeparaiso-naturpark.com; www.valeparaiso-naturpark.com**

🔢 🚲 ⛳2.10 👬 wo ♨ 🔥 🛒 ∥ msp 🦋 ♒ 🍽 ⊕ 🛒 ♿ 🚣
🏊 🏖 sand 2km

Site thro pine reserve on N242 fr Nazaré to Leiria. 3*, V lge, hdstg, mkd, shd, terr, EHU (4-10A) €3; gas; red long stay; TV; 20% statics; bus; Eng spkn; adv bkg acc; ccard acc; games area; games rm; bike hire; site clsd 19-26 Dec; fishing; CKE. *"Gd, clean site; well run; gd security; pitches vary in size & price, & divided by concrete walls, poss not suitable lge o'fits, bus outside gates to Nazare, exit down steep hill."* **€23.60** **2017**

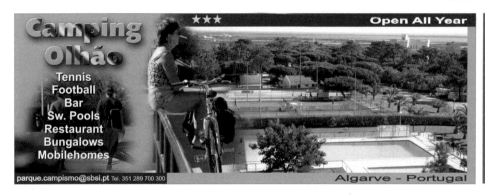
PORTUGAL

OLHAO *C4* (2km NE Rural) *37.03527, -7.82250*
Camping Olhão, Pinheiros do Marim, 8700-912
Olhão 289 700300; parque.campismo@sbsi.pt;
www.sbsi.pt

12 🏕 €1.60 ♦♦♦ wc ♨ ⚕ ⚙ ⁄ MsP ⁇ ⛱ ① 🍴 📶 🏔 ⛲ 🎣
🏊 1.5km

Turn S twd coast fr N125 1.5km E of Olhão by
filling stn. Clearly sp on S side of N125, adj Ria
Formosa National Park. 3*, V lge, mkd, hdg,
shd, pt sl, EHU (6A) €2.40; gas; red long stay;
TV; 75% statics; phone; bus adj, train 1.5km;
Eng spkn; adv bkg acc; ccard acc; tennis; games
area; horseriding 1km; bike hire; games rm; CKE.
*"Pleasant, helpful staff; sep car park for some pitches;
car wash; security guard; excl pool; gd san facs; very
popular long stay LS; many sm sandy pitches, some
diff access for lge o'fits; gd for cycling, birdwatching;
ferry to islands."* **€22.30** 2019

See advertisement above

OLIVEIRA DO HOSPITAL *C2* (9km NE Rural)
40.40338, -7.82684 **Camping Toca da Raposa,**
3405-351 Meruge 238 601547 or 926 704218 (mob);
campingtocadaraposa@gmail.com; toca-da-
raposa.com

🏕 ♦♦♦ wc ♨ ⚕ ⁄ MsP 🦋 ⁇ ⛱ ① 📶 🏔 ⛲

Fr N: N170 Oliveira Do Hospital head SW. Drive
thro EM540-2, EM503-1, R. Principal, Estr. Principal
and EM504-3 to Coimbra. Foll sp to site. Sm, hdg,
pt shd, pt sl, terr, EHU (6A) €2.50; gas; bus; Eng spkn.
*"Charming; lovely pool; bar & eve meals; friendly Dutch
owner; vg."* **€18.50, 15 Mar-1 Nov.** 2017

ORTIGA *C3* (6km SE Rural) *39.48277, -8.00305*
Parque Campismo de Ortiga, Estrada da Barragem,
6120-525 Ortiga 241 573464; campismo@cm-macao.pt

12 🏕 ♦♦♦ wc ♨ ⚕ ⚙ ⁄ 🦋 ⛱ ① nr 📶 nr 🏔

Exit A23/IP6 junc 12 S to Ortiga. Thro Ortiga &
foll site sp for 1.5km. Site beside dam. Sm, mkd,
hdstg, pt shd, terr, EHU (10A) €1.50; bbq; sw nr; TV;
50% statics; Eng spkn; watersports; CKE. *"Lovely site
in gd position; useful NH; dogs free; lge o'fits should
avoid acc thro town."* **€21.00** 2016

PENACOVA *B2* (3km N Rural) *40.27916, -8.26805*
Camp Municipal de Camp de Penacova (Vila Nova),
Rua dos Barqueiros, Vila Nova, 3360-204 Penacova
919 121967; penaparque2@iol.pt

♦♦♦ ♨ ⁄ ⁇ ⛱ ① nr ⚙ 📶 nr 🏔

IP3 fr Coimbra, exit junc 11, cross Rv Mondego N
of Penacova & foll to sp to Vila Nova & site. Med, pt
shd, EHU (6A) €1; bbq; sw nr; TV; phone; bus 150m;
Eng spkn; bike hire; fishing; CKE. *"Open, attractive
site."* **€20.00, 31 May-30 Sep.** 2017

PONTE DA BARCA *B1* (11km E Rural) *41.82376,
-8.31723* **Camping Lima Escape (formerly Entre-
Ambos-os-Rios),** Lugar da Igreja, Entre-Ambos-os-
Rios, 4980-613 Ponte da Barca 258 588361 or 964
969309; info@lima-escape.pt; www.lima-escape.pt

🏕 €0.60 ♦♦♦ ♨ ⚙ ⁄ ⁇ ⛱ ① nr ⚙ 📶 nr 🏔 🎣

N203 E fr Ponte da Barca, pass ent sp for vill. Site
sp N twd Rv Lima, after 1st bdge. 2*, Lge, shd, pt sl,
EHU (6A) €1.20; gas; TV; phone; bus 100m; adv bkg
acc; fishing; canoeing; CKE. *"Beautiful, clean, well run
& maintained site in pine trees; well situated for
National Park; vg rest."*
€29.00, 2 Jan-10 Nov, 1 Dec-30 Dec. 2019

PORTO *B1* (17km N Coastal) *41.2675, -8.71972*
Camping Orbitur-Angeiras, Rua de Angeiras,
Matosinhos, 4455-039 Lavra 229 270571;
infoangeiras@orbitur.pt; www.orbitur.pt

12 🏕 €1.50 ♦♦♦ wc ♨ ⚕ ⚙ ⁄ MsP ⁇ ⛱ ① ⚙ 📶 🏔 🎣 ⛲
🎣 🏊 sand 400m

Fr ICI/A28 take turn-off sp Lavra, site sp at end
of slip rd. Site in approx 3km - app rd potholed &
cobbled. 3*, Lge, shd, pt sl, EHU (6A) €3-4 (check
earth); gas; bbq; red long stay; TV (pitch); 70% statics;
phone; bus to Porto at site ent; Eng spkn; adv bkg
acc; ccard acc; car wash; games area; tennis; games
rm; fishing; CKE. *"Friendly & helpful staff; gd rest; gd
pitches in trees at end of site but ltd space lge o'fits;
ssnl statics all yr; fish & veg mkt in Matosinhos; excel
new san facs (2015); vg pool; poss noisy on Sat nights
(beach parties)."* **€40.70** 2017

PORTO *B1* (32km SE Rural) *41.03972, -8.42666*
Campidouro Parque de Medas, Lugar do Gavinho, 4515-397 Medas-Gondomar **224 760162; geral@ campidouro.pt; www.campidouro.pt**

🔢 🐕 👪 wc ♨ ♿ 🖥 ⚓ 🗑 MSP 🦋 🍴 Y ⓓ ⚡ ⚠ 🏊 ⛵ 🛶

Take N12 dir Gondomar off A1. Almost immed take R exit sp Entre-os-Rios. At rndabt pick up N108 & in approx 14km. Sp for Medas on R, thro hamlet & forest for 3km & foll sp for site on R. Long, steep app. New concrete access/site rds. 3*, Lge, mkd, hdstg, pt shd, terr, serviced pitches; EHU (6A) inc (poss rev pol); gas; bbq; sw; TV; 90% statics; phone; bus to Porto; Eng spkn; adv bkg acc; ccard acc; games rm; tennis; boating; fishing; CKE. *"Beautiful site on Rv Douro; helpful owners; gd rest; clean facs; sm level area (poss cr by rv & pool) for tourers - poss noisy at night & waterlogged after heavy rain; bus to Porto (just outside site) rec as parking diff (ltd buses at w/end)."*
€26.00 2016

PORTO *B1* (9km SW Urban/Coastal) *41.10777, -8.65611* **Camping ORBITUR-Madalena,** Rua do Cerro 608, Praia da Madalena, 4405-736 Vila Nova de Gaia **(227) 122520; infomadalena@orbitur.pt; www.orbitur.pt/camping-orbitur-madalena**

🔢 🐕 €2.20 👪 ♨ ♨ ♿ 🖥 ⚓ MSP 🍴 Y ⓓ 🗑 ⚠ 🏊 ⛵
🛶 🌴 sand 250m

Fr Porto ring rd IC1/A44 take A29 exit dir Espinho. In 1km take exit slip rd sp Madalena opp Volvo agent. Watch for either 'Campismo' or 'Orbitur' sp to site along winding, cobbled rd (beware campismo sp may take you to another site nrby). 4*, Lge, pt shd, pt sl, terr, EHU (6A)inc; gas; bbq; red long stay; TV; 40% statics; phone; bus to Porto; Eng spkn; adv bkg acc; ccard acc; car wash; games area; tennis; games rm; CKE. *"Site in forest; restricted area for tourers; slight aircraft noise; some uneven pitches; poss ltd facs LS; excel bus to Porto cent fr site ent - do not take c'van into Porto; facs in need of refurb (2013)."*
€22.00 2017

"Satellite navigation makes touring much easier"

Remember most sat navs don't know if you're towing or in a larger vehicle – always use yours alongside maps and site directions.

SANTIAGO DO CACEM *B4* (17km NW Coastal) *38.10777, -8.78690* **Camping Lagoa de Santo Andre,** Lagoa de Santo Andre, 7500-024 Vila Nova de Santo Andre **269 708550**

👪 ♨ ⚓ Y ⓓ ⚡

Take N261 sp Melides out of town & foll sps to Lagoa de Santo Andre to site on L of rd. On shore but fenced off fr unsafe banks of lagoon. 1*, Med, pt shd, pt sl, EHU inc (4-6A); sw; boating; fishing. *"Ltd facs LS."*
€19.50, 1 Jan-23 Dec, 26 Dec-31 Dec. 2019

SANTO ANTONIO DAS AREIAS *C3* (5km N Rural) *39.41370, -7.37575* **Quinta Do Maral (Naturist),** PO Box 57, Cubecudos, 7330-205 Santo Antonio das Areias **(963) 462169; info@quintadomaral.com; www.quintadomaral.com**

🔢 🐕 👪 wc ♨ ♿ 🖥 ⚓ MSP 🦋 🍴 Y ⚓ 🏊

Take N359 twds Santo Antonio Das Areias/Beira. Pass turn off to Santo Antonio in dir to Beira. At Ranginha turn L to Cubecudos. Turn R past vill sp by a school bldg, keep on this rd for 1.7km. Campsite on L, white hse with blue stripe. Do not use sat nav as they lead to unsuitable rds. Sm, hdg, pt shd, EHU (6-16A); bbq; twin axles; red long stay; TV; 5% statics; Eng spkn; adv bkg rec. *"In S Mamede nature park; vill & castle of Marvao an hr's walk; young, friendly owners; excel."* **€18.50** 2016

SANTO ANTONIO DAS AREIAS *C3* (0km S Rural) *39.40992, -7.34075* **Camping Asseiceira,** Asseiceira, 7330-204 Santo António das Areias **(245) 992940 or (960) 150352 (mob); gary-campingasseiceira@ hotmail.com; www.campingasseiceira.com**

🐕 👪 wc ♨ ♿ 🖥 ⚓ 🦋 🍴 Y ⓓ 🗑 nr ⚓ nr 🏊

Fr N246-1 turn off sp Marvão/Santo António das Areias. Turn L to Santo António das Areias then 1st R on ent town then immed R again, up sm hill to rndabt. At rndabt turn R then at next rndabt cont strt on. There is a petrol stn on R, cont down hill for 400m. Site on L. Sm, pt shd, pt sl, EHU (10A) €4; bus 1km; CKE. *"Attractive area; peaceful, well-equipped, remote site among olive trees; clean, tidy; gd for walking, birdwatching; helpful, friendly, British owners; excel san facs, maintained to a high standard; nr Spanish border; excel; ideal cent for walking, cycling, visit hilltop castle Marvao; access & pitches poss tight for lge o'fits."* **€19.00, 1 Jan-31 Oct.** 2019

SAO MARCOS DA SERRA *B4* (5km SE Rural) *37.3350, -8.3467* **Campismo Rural Quinta Odelouca,** Vale Grande de Baixo, CxP 644-S, 8375-215 São Marcos da Serra **282 361718 or 915 656685; info@ quintaodelouca.com; www.quintaodelouca.com**

🐕 €1 👪 wc ♨ 🖥 ⚓ 🦋 🍴 ⚓

Fr N (Ourique) on IC1 pass São Marcos da Serra & in approx 2.5km turn R & cross blue rlwy bdge. At bottom turn L & at cont until turn R for Vale Grande (paved rd changes to unmade). Foll sp to site. Fr S exit A22 junc 9 onto IC1 dir Ourique. Pass São Bartolomeu de Messines & at km 710.5 turn L & cross blue rlwy bdge, then as above. 2*, Sm, pt shd, terr, EHU (6-10A) €3.50; bbq (elec, gas, sep area); sw; twin axles; Eng spkn; adv bkg rec; CKE. *"Helpful, friendly Dutch owners; beautiful views; gd walks; vg; v little shd; access via bad rd; excel; internet free but unreliable and weak signal."*
€23.00, 1 Feb-30 Sep. 2019

PORTUGAL

SAO PEDRO DE MOEL *B2* (1km E Urban/Coastal)
39.75861, -9.02583 **Camping ORBITUR-São Pedro de Moel,** Rua Volta do Sete, São Pedro de Moel, 2430 Marinha Grande 244 599168; **infospedro@orbitur.pt; www.orbitur.pt**

🔢 🚐 €1.50 ♦♦♦ wc 🚿 ♿ 🍽 ⚡ MsP 🦋 ⏰ 🍴 ⓦ 🛒 🛎 ⚠ 🏄
🏊 (htd) 🅿 🏖 sand 500m

Site at end of rd fr Marinha Grande to beach; turn R at 1st rndabt on ent vill. Site S of lighthouse. 3*, V lge, hdstg, mkd, hdg, shd, terr, EHU (6A) €3-4 (poss rev pol); gas; bbq; red long stay; TV (pitch); 10% statics; phone; Eng spkn; adv bkg acc; ccard acc; waterslide; fishing; car wash; tennis; games rm; bike hire; CKE. *"Friendly, well-run, clean site in pine woods; easy walk to shops, rests; heavy surf; gd cycling to beaches; São Pedro smart resort; ltd facs LS site in attractive area and well run."* **€28.60, W18.** **2016**

"I like to fill in the reports as I travel from site to site"

You'll find report forms at the back of this guide, or you can fill them in online at camc.com/europereport.

SAO TEOTONIO *B4* (7km W Coastal) *37.52560, -8.77560* **Parque de Campismo da Zambujeira,** Praia da Zambujeira, 7630-740 Zambujeira do Mar **(283)** 958 407; **info@campingzambujeira; www.camping zambujeira.com**

🚐 €4 ♦♦♦ wc 🚿 ⚡ MsP 🍴 ⓦ 🛒 🛎 ⚠ 🏖 sand 1km

S on N120 twd Lagos, turn W when level with São Teotónio on unclassified rd to Zambujeira. Site on L in 7km, bef vill. 2*, V lge, pt shd, pt sl, EHU (6-10A) €3.50; gas; red long stay; TV; phone; bus adj; Eng spkn; tennis. *"Welcoming, friendly owners; in pleasant rural setting; hot water to shwrs only; sh walk to unspoilt vill with some shops & rest; cliff walks; nice site; facs & pool gd; rest food basic."* **€18.00, 1 Apr-31 Oct.** **2016**

SERPA *C4* (1km SW Urban) *37.94090, -7.60404* **Parque Municipal de Campismo Serpa,** Rua da Eira São Pedro, 7830-303 Serpa 284 540193; **parque campismoserpa@cm-serpa.pt; http://www.cm-serpa.pt/artigos.asp?id=885**

🔢 🚐 ♦♦♦ wc 🚿 ♿ 🍽 ⚡ 🍴 nr ⓦ nr 🛒 nr

Fr IP8 take 1st sp for town; site well sp fr most dirs - opp sw pool. Do not ent walled town. Med, pt shd, pt sl, EHU (6A) €1.25; gas; bbq; sw nr; 20% statics; phone; adv bkg acc; CKE. *"Popular gd site; daily mkt 500m; pool adj; simple, high quality facs; interesting, historic town."* **€10.00** **2019**

TAVIRA *C4* (5km E Rural/Coastal) *37.14506, -7.60223* **Camping Ria Formosa,** Quinta da Gomeira, 8800-591 Cabanas-Tavira 281 328887; **info@campingria formosa.com; www.campingriaformosa.com**

🔢 🚐 €2 ♦♦♦ (htd) wc 🚿 ♿ 🍽 ⚡ MsP 🦋 ⏰ 🍴 ⓦ 🛒 🛎 ⚠
🏊 🅿 🏖 sand 1.2km

Fr spain onto A22 take exit junc 17 (bef tolls) Fr N125 turn S at Conceição dir 'Cabanas Tavira' & 'Campismo'. Cross rlwy line & turn L to site, sp. 3*, V lge, hdstg, mkd, pt shd, terr, EHU (16A) €3; gas; bbq; red long stay; TV; bus 100m, train 100m; Eng spkn; adv bkg acc; ccard acc; games area; car wash; bike hire; CKE. *"Excel, comfortable site; friendly, welcoming owner & staff; vg, modern san facs; various pitch sizes; cycle path to Tavira, excel facs."* **€24.00** **2019**

TOMAR *B2* (9km NE Rural) *39.63833, -8.33694* **Camping Pelinos,** Casal das Aboboreiras, 2300-093 Tomar 249 301814; **info@campingpelinos.com; www.campingpelinos.com**

🚐 ♦♦♦ wc 🚿 ♿ 🍽 ⚡ 🦋 ⏰ 🍴 ⓦ 🛒 ⚠ 🏊

N fr Tomar on N110, turn R to Calçadas at traff lts opp g'ge, foll site sp. Steep descent to site. 1*, Sm, pt shd, sl, terr, EHU (6A); bbq (elec, gas); TV; phone; bus 100m; Eng spkn; adv bkg acc; table tennis; CKE. *"Lake sw, watersports & fishing 7km; vg; lovely site; no shops nrby; v helpful Dutch couple; dogs 2 max; walks fr site; ltd wifi on pitch."* **€20.50, 15 Mar-1 Oct.** **2019**

TOMAR *B2* (1km NW Urban) *39.60694, -8.41027* **Campismo Parque Municipal,** 2300-000 Tomar 249 329824; **camping@cm-tomar.pt; www.cm-tomar.pt**

🔢 🚐 ♦♦♦ (htd) wc 🚿 ♿ 🍽 ⚡ MsP 🦋 ⏰ 🍴 nr ⓦ 🛒 🛎 ⚠

Fr S on N110 foll sp to town cent at far end of stadium. Fr N (Coimbra) on N110 turn R immed bef bdge. Med, mkd, pt shd, FHU (10A) inc; bbq; TV; Eng spkn; adv bkg acc; ccard acc; CKE. *"Useful base for touring Alcobaca, Batalha & historic monuments in Tomar; conv Fatima; Convento de Cristo worth visit; vg, popular, improved site; lovely walk to charming rvside town; easy access for lge vehicle, sh walk thro gdns to Knights Templar castle; free wifi nr recep; camp entry ticket gives free access to adj pool; pool adj; v helpful, friendly staff; great site."* **€19.00** **2016**

TORRES NOVAS *B2* (13.5km SE Urban) *39.400100, -8.485829* **Parque De Campismo Municipal Da Golega,** Largo do Parque de Campismo 7, 2150-269 Golega 249 979003; **cm-golega.pt**

🔢 🚐 €1.77 wc 🚿 ⚡ ⓦ nr 🛒 nr

Sp fr main rd. Med, pt shd, EHU (10A); twin axles; Eng spkn. *"Vg; ideal for visiting lovely nature reserve; easy walk to town."* **€10.00** **2019**

VILA NOVA DE CERVEIRA *B1* (5km E Rural)
41.94362, -8.69365 **Parque de Campismo Convívio,** Rua de Badão, 1 Bacelo, 4920-020 Candemil **251 794401; info@campingconvivio.net; www.camping convivio.net**

Fr Vila Nova de Cerveira dir Candemil on N13/N302, turn L at Bacelo, site sp. Sm, pt shd, terr, EHU (6A); bbq; red long stay; Eng spkn; adv bkg acc; games rm; CKE. *"V helpful Dutch owners; gd area to visit; vg."* **€21.00, 1 Mar-15 Oct.** 2017

VILA NOVA DE MILFONTES *B4* (1km N Coastal)
37.73194, -8.78277 **Camping Milfontes,** Apartado 81, 7645-300 Vila Nova de Milfontes **(283) 996140; reservas@camping-milfontes.com; www.camping-milfontes.com**

S fr Sines on N120/IC4 for 22km; turn R at Cercal on N390 SW for Milfontes on banks of Rio Mira; clear sp. 2*, V lge, hdg, mkd, pt shd, EHU (6A) €3 (long lead poss req); gas; TV; 80% statics; phone; bus 600m; ccard acc; CKE. *"Pitching poss diff for lge o'fits due trees & statics; supmkt & mkt 5 mins walk; nr fishing vill at mouth Rv Mira with beaches & sailing on rv; pleasant site."* **€27.00** 2019

See advertisement

VILA REAL *C1* (1km NE Urban) *41.30361, -7.73694* **Camping Vila Real,** Rua Dr Manuel Cardona, 5000-558 Vila Real **259 324724**

On IP4/E82 take Vila Real N exit & head S into town. Foll 'Centro' sp to Galp g'ge; at Galp g'ge rndabt, turn L & in 30m turn L again. Site at end of rd in 400m. Site sp fr all dirs. 2*, Med, pt shd, pt sl, terr, EHU (6A); gas; bbq; 10% statics; phone; bus 150m; tennis; CKE. *"Conv upper Douro; pool complex adj; gd facs ltd when site full; gd mkt in town (15 min walk); Lamego well worth a visit; excel rest adj."* **€18.70, 1 Feb-31 Dec.** 2017

VILA REAL DE SANTO ANTONIO *C4* (14km W Rural) *37.18649, -7.55003* **Camping Caliço Park,** Sitio do Caliço, 8900-907 Vila Nova de Cacela **281 951195; geral@calico-park.com; www.calico-park.com**

On N side of N125 Vila Real to Faro rd. Sp on main rd & in Vila Nova de Cacela vill, visible fr rd. 1*, Lge, hdstg, shd, pt sl, terr, EHU (6A) €2.80; gas; red long stay; 80% statics; phone; Eng spkn; adv bkg acc; ccard acc; bike hire; CKE. *"Friendly staff; noisy in ssn & rd noise; not suitable for m'vans or tourers in wet conditions - ltd touring pitches & poss diff access; gd NH."* **€17.00** 2016

VILA REAL DE SANTO ANTONIO *C4* (3km W Coastal) *37.17972, -7.44361* **Parque Municipal de Campismo,** 8900 Monte Gordo **281 510970; geral@cm-vrsa.pt; http://www.cm-vrsa.pt/pt/menu/459/parque-de-campismo.aspx**

Fr Faro on N125 turn R sp Monte Gordo. Site on sea front in 500m. Or fr Spain over bdge at border, exit junc 9 to Vila Real over rlwy line. Strt over rndabt & turn R at T-junc, site sp just bef ent town. 1*, shd, Pt sl, EHU (10A) €1.90 (long cable poss req); gas; bbq; red long stay; TV; 10% statics; phone; bus, train to Faro 3km; Eng spkn; ccard acc; canoeing; CKE. *"Former campsite now MH stop; sp through town; san facs avail but shwrs cold water; MH svr pnt."* **€13.50** 2019

VILAMOURA *B4* (4.8km N Rural) *37.112371, -8.106409* **Vilamoura Rustic Motorhome Aire,** N125 436A, 8100 Consiguinte, Loule **289 149315 or 918 721948 (mob) or 917 428356 (mob); info@vilamoura-rustic-motorhome-aire.com; www.vilamoura-rustic-motorhome-aire.com**

Fr A22 (tollrd) take exit for Quarteria and drive for 3km for exit Quarteria/Portimao. Turn R at exit to join N125 and drive for approx 6km W direct to site. Sm, hdstg, pt shd, EHU (6A) €0.50 per KW; bbq; twin axles; TV; bus 200m; Eng spkn; adv bkg acc; games area; bike hire. *"Boutique, adults only (18+), MH & c'van Aire; outdoor cinema; Sky Sports; events throughout the year; vg; run by past CAMC memb."* **€10.00** 2019

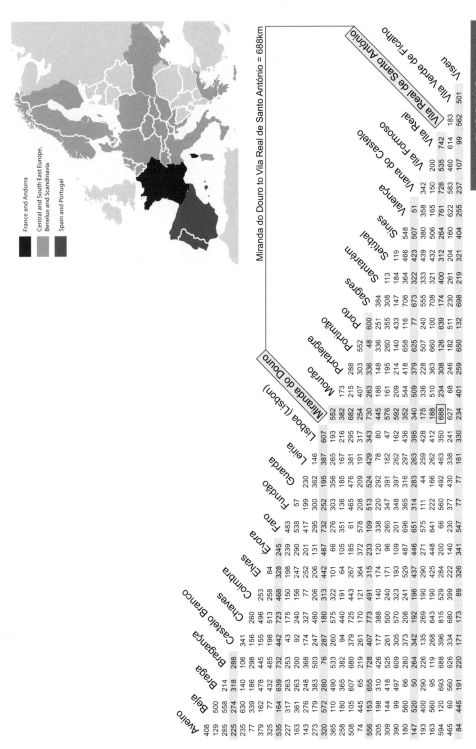

Miranda do Douro to Vila Real de Santo António = 688km

France and Andorra

Central and South East Europe, Benelux and Scandinavia

Spain and Portugal

91

PORTUGAL

Spain

Barcelona

Highlights

Boasting lively cities, beautiful beaches and an energetic and diverse culture, it's easy to see why Spain is one of the most popular destinations in the world.

From Gaudi's Sagrada Familia in the bustling centre of Barcelona to the ancient monuments of Andalusia, Spain rich history explore. After a long day of sightseeing, what better way to relax that on one of Spain's many beaches, with a glass of Sangria in hand.

Music and dance are deeply ingrained in Spanish culture, and the flamenco is one of the best loved examples of the Spanish arts. Known for its distinctive flair and passion, this dance is now popular worldwide, but there is nowhere better to soak in a performance than in its homeland.

Tapas and sangria and some of Spain's most popular fare, but there is plenty of choice for those looking to try something different. Orxata is a refreshing drink made of tigernuts, water and sugar, and is served ice-cold.

Major towns and cities

- Madrid – this vibrant capital is filled with culture.
- Barcelona – a city on the coast, filled with breathtaking architecture.
- Alicante – home to the Castle of Santa Barbara, a huge medieval fortress.
- Valencia – set on the Mediterranean sea, this city has numerous attractions on offer.

Attractions

- Mosque-Cathedral of Córdoba – this site has been a place of worship since the 8th century
- Sagrada Familia – designed by Catalan architect, Antoni Gaudí, this basilica is one of Barcelona's most famous sights.
- Guggenheim Museum, Bilbao – a museum for modern and contemporary art, housed in a ground-breaking 20th century building.

Find out more

www.spain.info
E: infosmile@tourspain.es T: (0)9 13 43 35 00

Country Information

Population (approx): 46.5 million

Capital: Madrid

Area: 506,000 sq km (inc Balearic & Canary Islands)

Bordered by: Andorra, France, Portugal

Terrain: High, rugged central plateau, mountains to north and south

Climate: Temperate climate; hot summers, cold winters in the interior; more moderate summers and cool winters along the northern and eastern coasts; very hot summers and mild/warm winters along the southern coast

Coastline: 4,964km

Highest Point (mainland Spain): Mulhacén (Granada) 3,478m

Languages: Castilian Spanish, Catalan, Galician, Basque

Local Time: GMT or BST + 1, i.e. 1 hour ahead of the UK all year

Currency: Euros divided into 100 cents; £1 = €1.16, €1 = £0.87 (October 2019)

Emergency numbers: Police 092; Fire brigade 080; Ambulance (SAMUR) 061. Operators speak English. Civil Guard 062. All services can be reached on 112.

Public Holidays 2020: Jan 1, 6; Apr 9, 10, 13; May 1; Aug 15; Oct 12; Nov 1; Dec 6 (Constitution Day), 8, 25.

Several other dates are celebrated for fiestas according to region. School summer holidays stretch from mid June to mid September.

Entry Formalities

Holders of valid British and Irish passports are permitted to stay up to three months without a visa. EU residents planning to stay longer are required to register in person at the Oficina de Extranjeros (Foreigners Office) in their province of residence or at a designated police station. You will be issued with a certificate confirming that the registration obligation has been fulfilled.

Medical Services

Basic emergency health care is available free from practitioners in the Spanish National Health Service on production of a European Health Insurance Card (EHIC). Some health centres offer both private and state provided health care and you should ensure that staff are aware which service you require. In some parts of the country you may have to travel some distance to attend a surgery or health clinic operating within the state health service. It is probably quicker and more convenient to use a private clinic, but the Spanish health service will not refund any private health care charges.

In an emergency go to the casualty department (urgencias) of any major public hospital. Urgent treatment is free in a public ward on production of an EHIC; for other treatment you will have to pay a proportion of the cost.

Medicines prescribed by health service practitioners can be obtained from a pharmacy (farmacia) and there will be a charge unless you are an EU pensioner. In all major towns there is a 24 hour pharmacy.

Dental treatment is not generally provided under the state system and you will have to pay for treatment.

The Department of Health has two offices in Spain to deal with health care enquiries from British nationals visiting or residing in Spain. These are at the British Consultate offices in Alicante and Madrid, Tel: 965-21 60 22 or 917-14 63 00.

Opening Hours

Banks : Mon-Fri 8.30am/9am-2pm/2.30pm, Sat 9am-1pm (many banks are close Sat during summer).

Museums: Tue-Sat 9am/10am-1pm/2pm & 3pm/4pm-6pm/8pm. Sun 9am/10am-2pm; most close Mon.

Post Offices: Mon-Fri 8.30am-2.30pm & 5pm-8pm/8.30pm, Sat 9am/9.30am-1pm/1.30pm.

Shops: Mon-Sat 9am/10am-1.30pm/2pm & 4pm/4.30pm-8pm/8.30pm; department stores and shopping centres don't close for lunch.

Regulations for pets

Dogs must be kept on a lead in public places and in a car they should be isolated from the driver by means of bars, netting or kept in a transport carrier.

Safety and Security

Street crime exists in many Spanish towns and holiday resorts. Keep all valuable personal items such as cameras or jewellery out of sight. The authorities have stepped up the police presence in tourist areas but nevertheless, you should remain alert at all times (including at airports, train and bus stations, and even in supermarkets and their car parks).

In Madrid particular care should be taken in the Puerto de Sol and surrounding streets, including the Plaza Mayor, Retiro Park and Lavapies, and on the metro. In Barcelona this advice also applies to the Ramblas, Monjuic, Plaza Catalunya, Port Vell and Olympic Port areas. Be wary of approaches by strangers either asking directions or offering help, especially around cash machines or at tills, as they may be trying to distract attention.

A few incidents have been reported of visitors being approached by a bogus police officer asking to inspect wallets for fake euro notes, or to check their identity by keying their credit card PIN into an official looking piece of equipment carried by the officer. If in doubt ask to see a police officer's official identification, refuse to comply with the request and offer instead to go to the nearest police station.

Spanish police have set up an emergency number for holidaymakers with English speaking staff and offering round the clock assistance - call 902 10 2 112. An English speaking operator will take a statement about the incident, translate it into Spanish and fax or email it to the nearest police station. You still have to report in person to a police station if you have an accident, or have been robbed or swindled, and the helpline operator will advise you where to find the nearest one.

Motorists travelling on motorways – particularly those north and south of Barcelona, in the Alicante region, on the M30, M40 and M50 Madrid ring roads and on the A4 and A5 – should be wary of approaches by bogus policemen in plain clothes travelling in unmarked cars. In all traffic related matters police officers will be in uniform. Unmarked vehicles will have a flashing electronic sign in the rear window reading 'Policía' or 'Guardia Civil' and will normally have blue flashing lights incorporated into their headlights, which are activated when the police stop you.

In non-traffic related matters police officers may be in plain clothes but you have the right to ask to see identification. Genuine officers may ask you to show them your documents but would not request that you hand over your bag or wallet. If in any doubt, converse through the car window and telephone the police on 112 or the Guardia Civil on 062 and ask them for confirmation that the registration number of the vehicle corresponds to an official police vehicle.

On the A7 motorway between the La Junquera and Tarragona toll stations be alert for 'highway pirates' who flag down foreign registered and hire cars (the latter have a distinctive number plate), especially those towing caravans. Motorists are sometimes targeted in service areas, followed and subsequently tricked into stopping on the hard shoulder of the motorway. The usual ploy is for the driver or passenger in a passing vehicle, which may be 'official-looking', to suggest by gesture that there is something seriously wrong with a rear wheel or exhaust pipe. If flagged down by other motorists or a motorcyclist in this way, be extremely wary. Within the Barcelona urban area thieves may also employ the 'punctured tyre' tactic at traffic lights.

In instances such as this, the Spanish Tourist Office advises you not to pull over but to wait until you reach a service area or toll station. If you do get out of your car when flagged down take care it is locked while you check outside, even if someone is left inside. Car keys should never be left in the ignition.

Spain shares with the rest of Europe an underlying threat from terrorism. Attacks could be indiscriminate and against civilian targets in public places including tourist areas.

The Basque terrorist organisation, ETA, has been less active in recent years and on 20 October 2011 announced a "definitive cessation of armed activity." However you should always be vigilant and follow the instructions of local police and other authorities.

Coast guards operate a beach flag system to indicate the general safety of beaches for swimming: red – danger / do not enter the water; yellow – take precautions; green – all clear. Coast guards operate on most of the popular beaches, so if in doubt, always ask. During the summer months stinging jellyfish frequent Mediterranean coastal waters.

There is a risk of forest fires during the hottest months and you should avoid camping in areas with limited escape routes. Take care to avoid actions that could cause a fire, e.g. disposal of cigarette ends.

Respect Spanish laws and customs. Parents should be aware that Spanish law defines anyone under the age of 18 as a minor, subject to parental control or adult supervision. Any unaccompanied minor coming to the attention of the local authorities for whatever reason is deemed to be vulnerable under the law and faces being taken into a minors centre for protection until a parent or suitable guardian can be found.

British Embassy & Consulate-General

TORRE ESPACIO, PASEO DE LA CASTELLANA 259D
28046 MADRID
Tel: 917 14 63 00
www.ukinspain.fco.gov.uk/en/

British Consulate-General

AVDA DIAGONAL 477-13, 08036 BARCELONA
Tel: 933 66 02 00

There are also British Consulates in Alicante and Málaga.

Irish Embassy

IRELAND HOUSE, PASEO DE LA CASTELLANA 46-4
28046 MADRID
Tel: 914 36 40 93
www.embassyofireland.es

There are also Irish Honorary Consulates in Alicante, Barcelona, Bilbao, El Ferrol, Málaga and Seville.

Customs Regulations

Under Spanish law the number of cigarettes which may be exported is set at eight hundred. Anything above this amount is regarded as a trade transaction which must be accompanied by the required documentation. Travellers caught with more than 800 cigarettes face seizure of the cigarettes and a large fine.

Documents

Driving Licence

The British EU format pink driving licence is recognised in Spain. Holders of the old style all green driving licence are advised to replace it with a photocard version. Alternatively, the old style licence may be accompanied by an International Driving Permit available from the AA, the RAC or selected Post Offices.

Passport

Visitors must be able to show some form of identity document if requested to do so by the police and you should carry your passport or photocard licence at all times.

Vehicle(s)

When driving in Spain it is compulsory at all times to carry your driving licence, vehicle registration certificate (V5C), insurance certificate and MOT certificate (if applicable). Vehicles imported by a person other than the owner must have a letter of authority from the owner.

Money

All bank branches offer foreign currency exchange, as do many hotels and travel agents.

The major credit cards are widely accepted as a means of payment in shops, restaurants and petrol stations. Smaller retail outlets in non commercial areas may not accept payments by credit card – check before buying. When shopping carry your passport or photocard driving licence if paying with a credit card as you will almost certainly be asked for photographic proof of identity.

Keep a supply of loose change as you could be asked for it frequently in shops and at kiosks.

Driving

Drivers should take particular care as driving standards can be erratic, e.g. excessive speed and dangerous overtaking, and the accident rate is higher than in the UK. Pedestrians should take particular care when crossing roads (even at zebra crossings) or walking along unlit roads at night.

Accidents

The Central Traffic Department runs an assistance service for victims of traffic accidents linked to an emergency telephone network along motorways and some roads. Motorists in need of help should ask for 'auxilio en carretera' (road assistance). The special ambulances used are connected by radio to hospitals participating in the scheme.

It is not necessary to call the emergency services in case of light injuries. A European Accident Statement should be completed and signed by both parties and, if conditions allow, photos of the vehicles and the location should be taken. If one of the drivers involved does not want to give his/her details, the other should call the police or Guardia Civil.

Alcohol

The maximum permitted level of alcohol is 50 milligrams in 100 millilitres of blood, i.e. less than in the UK (80 milligrams) and it reduces to 30 milligrams for drivers with less than two years experience, drivers of vehicles with more than 8 passenger seats and for drivers of vehicles over 3,500kg. After a traffic accident all road users involved have to undergo a breath test. Penalties for refusing a test or exceeding the legal limit are severe and may include immobilisation of vehicles, a large fine and suspension of your driving licence. This limit applies to cyclists as well as drivers of private vehicles.

Breakdown Service

The motoring organisation, Real Automóvil Club de España (RACE), operates a breakdown service and assistance may be obtained 24 hours a day by telephoning the national centre in Madrid on 915 93 33 33. After hearing a message in Spanish press the number 1 to access the control room where English is spoken.

RACE's breakdown vehicles are blue and yellow and display the words 'RACE Asistencia' on the sides. This service provides on the spot minor repairs and towing to the nearest garage. Charges vary according to type of vehicle and time of day, but payment for road assistance must be made in cash.

Child Restraint System

Children under the age of 12 years old and under the height of 1.35m must use a suitable child restraint system adapted for their size and weight (this does not apply in taxis in urban areas). Children measuring more than 1.35m in height may use an adult seatbelt.

Fuel

Credit cards are accepted at most petrol stations, but you should be prepared to pay cash if necessary in remote areas.

LPG (Autogas) can be purchased from some Repsol filling stations. Details of approximately 33 sales outlets throughout mainland Spain can be found on www.mylpg.eu.

Lights

Dipped headlights is now compulsory for all vehicles on all roads at night and in tunnels. Bulbs are more likely to fail with constant use and you are recommended to carry spares.

Dipped headlights must be used at all times on 'special' roads, e.g. temporary routes created at the time of road works such as the hard shoulder, or in a contra-flow lane.

Headlight flashing is only allowed to warn other road users about an accident or a road hazard, or to let the vehicle in front know that you intend to overtake.

Motorways

The Spanish motorway system has been subject to considerable expansion in recent years with more motorways under construction or planned. The main sections are along the Mediterranean coast, across the north of the country and around Madrid. Tolls are charged on most autopistas but many sections are toll-free, as are autovias. Exits on autopistas are numbered consecutively from Madrid. Exits on autovias are numbered according to the kilometre point from Madrid.

Many different companies operate within the motorway network, each setting their own tolls which may vary according to the time of day and classification of vehicles.

Avoid signposted 'Via T' lanes showing a circular sign with a white capital T on a blue background where toll collection is by electronic device only. Square 'Via T' signs are displayed above mixed lanes where other forms of payment are also accepted.

Rest areas with parking facilities, petrol stations and restaurants or cafés are strategically placed and are well signposted. Emergency telephones are located at 2km intervals.

Motorway signs near Barcelona are confusing. To avoid the city traffic when heading south, follow signs for Barcelona, but once signs for Tarragona appear follow these and ignore Barcelona signs.

Mountain Passes and Tunnels

Some passes are occasionally blocked in winter following heavy falls of snow. Check locally for information on road conditions.

Parking

Parking regulations vary depending on the area of a city or town, the time of day, the day of the week, and whether the date is odd or even. In many towns parking is permitted on one side of the street for the first half of the month and on the other side for the second half of the month. Signs marked '1-15' or '16-31' indicate these restrictions.

Yellow road markings indicate parking restrictions. Parking should be in the same direction as the traffic flow in one way streets or on the right hand side when there is two way traffic. Illegally parked vehicles may be towed away or clamped but, despite this, you will frequently encounter double and triple parking.

In large cities parking meters have been largely replaced by ticket machines and these are

often located in areas known as 'zona azul', i.e. blue zones. The maximum period of parking is usually one and a half hours between 8am and 9pm. In the centre of some towns there is a 'zona O.R.A.' where parking is permitted for up to 90 minutes against tickets bought in tobacconists and other retail outlets.

In many small towns and villages it is advisable to park on the edge of town and walk to the centre, as many towns can be difficult to navigate due to narrow, congested streets.

Madrid

In Madrid, there is a regulated parking zone where parking spaces are shown by blue or green lines (called SER). Parking is limited to 1 or 2 hours in these areas for visitors and can be paid by means of ticket machines of by mobile phone.

Pedestrians

Jaywalking is not permitted. Pedestrians may not cross a road unless a traffic light is at red against the traffic, or a policeman gives permission. Offenders may be fined.

Priority and Overtaking

As a general rule traffic coming from the right has priority at intersections. When entering a main road from a secondary road drivers must give way to traffic from both directions. Traffic already on a roundabout (i.e. from the left) has priority over traffic joining it. Trams and emergency vehicles have priority at all times over other road users and you must not pass trams that are stationary while letting passengers on or off.

Motorists must give way to cyclists on a cycle lane, cycle crossing or other specially designated cycle track. They must also give way to cyclists when turning left or right.

You must use your indicators when overtaking. If a vehicle comes up behind you signalling that it wants to overtake and if the road ahead is clear, you must use your right indicator to acknowledge the situation.

Roads

There are approximately 16,200km of highways and dual carriageways. Roads marked AP (autopista) are generally toll roads and roads marked A (autovía) or N (nacional) are dual carriageways with motorway characteristics – but not necessarily with a central reservation – and are toll-free. In recent years some major national roads have been upgraded to Autovías and have two identifying codes or have changed codes, e.g. the N-I from Madrid to Irún near the French border is now known as the A1 or Autovía del Norte. Autovías are often as fast as autopistas and are generally more scenic.

Roads managed by regional or local authorities are prefixed with the various identification letters such as C, CV, GR, L or T.

All national roads and roads of interest to tourists are generally in good condition, are well signposted, and driving is normally straightforward. Hills often tend to be longer and steeper than in parts of the UK and some of the coastal roads are very winding, so traffic flows at the speed of the slowest lorry.

As far as accidents are concerned the N340 coast road, especially between Málaga and Fuengirola, is notorious, as are the Madrid ring roads, and special vigilance is necessary.

Road humps are making an appearance on Spanish roads and recent visitors report that they may be high, putting low stabilisers at risk.

Andorra

The main road to Barcelona from Andorra is the C14/C1412/N141b via Ponts and Calaf. It has a good surface and avoids any high passes. The N260 along the south side of Andorra via Puigcerda and La Seo de Urgel also has a good surface.

Road Signs and Markings

Road signs conform to international standards. Lines and markings are white. Place names may appear both in standard (Castilian) Spanish and in a local form, e.g. Gerona/Girona, San Sebastián/Donostia, Jávea/Xàbio, and road atlases and maps usually show both.

You may encounter the following signs:

Spanish	English Translation
Carretera de peaje	Toll road
Ceda el paso	Give way
Cuidado	Caution

Spanish	
Curva peligrosa	
Despacio	
Desviación	
Dirección única	
Embotellamiento	
Estacionamiento prohibido	N
Estrechamiento	Narrow lane
Gravillas	Loose chippings/gravel
Inicio	Start
Obras	Roadworks
Paso prohibido	No entry
Peligro	Danger
Prioridad	Right of way
Salida	Exit
Todas direcciones	All directions

Many non motorway roads have a continuous white line on the near (verge) side of the carriageway. Any narrow lane between this line and the side of the carriageway is intended primarily for pedestrians and cyclists and not for use as a hard shoulder.

A continuous line also indicates 'no stopping' even if it is possible to park entirely off the road and it should be treated as a double white line and not crossed except in a serious emergency. If your vehicle breaks down on a road where there is a continuous white line along the verge, it should not be left unattended as this is illegal and an on the spot fine may be levied.

Many road junctions have a continuous white centre line along the main road. This line must not be crossed to execute a left turn, despite the lack of any other 'no left turn' signs. If necessary, drive on to a 'cambio de sentido' (change of direction) sign to turn.

Traffic police are keen to enforce both the above regulations.

Watch out for traffic lights which may be mounted high above the road and hard to spot. The international three colour traffic light system is used in Spain. Green, amber and red arrows are used on traffic lights at some intersections.

	Open Road (km/h)	Motorway (km/h)
Car Solo	90-100	120
Car towing caravan/trailer	70-80	80
Motorhome under 3500kg	80-90	100
Motorhome 3500-7500kg	80	90

In built-up areas speed is limited to 50km/h (31mph) except where signs indicate a lower limit. Reduce your speed to 20km/h (13mph) in residential areas. On motorways and dual carriageways in built-up areas, speed is limited to 80km/h (50mph) except where indicated by signs.

Outside built-up areas motorhomes under 3500kg are limited to 100km/h (62mph) and those over 3500kg are limited to 90km/h (56 mph) on motorways and dual carriageways. On other main roads motorhomes under 3500kg are limited to 80-90km/h (50-56mph) and those over 3500kg are limited to 80km/h (50mph)

It is prohibited to own, transport or use radar detectors.

Foreign Registered Vehicles

When a radar camera detects a foreign registered vehicle exceeding the speed limit, a picture of the vehicle and its number plate will be sent not only to the relevant traffic department, but also to the nearest Guardia Civil mobile patrol. The patrol will then stop the speeding vehicle and impose an on the spot fine which non-residents must pay immediately, otherwise the vehicle will be confiscated until the fine is paid.

This is to prevent offenders flouting the law and avoiding paying their fines, as pursuing them is proving costly and complicated for the Spanish authorities.

Towing

Motorhomes are prohibited from towing a car unless the car is on a special towing trailer with all four wheels of the car off the ground.

Any towing combination in excess of 10 metres in length must keep at least 50 metres from the vehicle in front except in built-up areas, on roads where overtaking is prohibited, or where there are several lanes in the same direction.

Traffic Jams

Roads around the large cities such as Madrid, Barcelona, Zaragoza, Valencia and Seville are extremely busy on Friday afternoons when residents leave for the mountains or coast, and again on Sunday evenings when they return. The coastal roads along the Costa Brava and the Costa Dorada may also be congested. The coast road south of Torrevieja is frequently heavily congested as a result of extensive holiday home construction.

Summer holidays extend from mid June to mid September and the busiest periods are the last weekend in July, the first weekend in August and the period around the Assumption holiday in mid August.

Traffic jams occur on the busy AP7 from the French border to Barcelona during the peak summer holiday period. An alternative route now exists from Malgrat de Mar along the coast to Barcelona using the C32 where tolls are lower than on the AP7.

The Autovía de la Cataluña Central (C25) provides a rapid east-west link between Gerona and Lleida via Vic, Manresa and Tàrrega. There is fast access from Madrid to La Coruña in the far north-west via the A6/AP6.

Information on road conditions, traffic delays, etc can be found on http://infocar.dgt.es/etraffic.

Violation of Traffic Regulations

The police are empowered to impose on the spot fines. Visiting motorists must pay immediately otherwise a vehicle will be confiscated until the fine is paid. An official receipt should be obtained. An appeal may be made within 15 days and there are instructions on the back of the receipt in English. RACE can provide legal advice - tel: 900 100 901.

Essential Equipment

Reflective Jacket/ Waistcoat

If your vehicle is immobilised on the carriageway outside a built-up area you must wear a reflective jacket or waistcoat when getting out of your vehicle. This also applies to passengers who may leave the vehicle

Reflectors/Marker Boards for Caravans

Any vehicle or vehicle combination, i.e. car plus caravan over 12 metres in length, must display reflector marker boards at the rear of the towed vehicle. These aluminium boards must have a yellow centre with a red outline, be reflective and comply with ECE70 standards. They must be positioned between 50cm and 150cm off the ground and must be 500mm x 250mm or 565mm x 200mm in size. Alternatively a single horizontal reflector may be used measuring 1300mm x 250mm or 1130mm x 200mm.

To buy these aluminium marker boards contact www.hgvdirect.co.uk, tel: 0845 6860008. Contact your local dealer or caravan manufacturer for advice on fitting them to your caravan.

Warning Triangles

All vehicles must carry warning triangles. They should be placed 50 metres behind and in front of broken down vehicles.

Touring

A fixed price menu or 'menú del dia' offers good value. Service is generally included in restaurant bills but a tip of approximately €1 per person up to 10% of the bill is appropriate if you have received good service. Smoking is not allowed in indoor public places, including bars, restaurants and cafés.

Spain is one of the world's top wine producers, enjoying a great variety of high quality wines of which cava, rioja and sherry are probably the best known. Local beer is generally drunk as an aperitif to accompany tapas.

Spaniards tend to get up later and stay out later at night than their European neighbours. Out of the main tourist season and in non-tourist areas it may be difficult to find a restaurant open in the evening before 9pm.

Taking a siesta is still common practice, although it is now usual for businesses to stay open during the traditional siesta hours.

Spain's many different cultural and regional influences are responsible for the variety and originality of fiestas held each year. Over 200 have been classified as 'of interest to tourists' while others have gained international fame, such as La Tomatina mass tomato throwing battle held each year in August in Buñol near Valencia. Find a full list of fiestas at www.spain.info/uk or from tourist offices. Each town will also celebrate its local Saint's Day which is always a very happy and colourful occasion.

The Madrid Card, valid for one, two or three days, gives free use of public transport, free entry to various attractions and museums, as well as free tours and discounts at restaurants and shows. You can buy the card from www.madridcard.com or by visiting the City Tourist Office in Plaza Mayor, or on Madrid Visión tour buses. Similar generous discounts can be obtained with the Barcelona Card, valid from two to five days, which can be purchased from tourist offices or online at www.barcelonacard.org. Other tourist cards are available in Burgos, Córdoba, Seville and Zaragoza.

The region of Valencia and the Balearic Islands are prone to severe storms and torrential rainfall between September and November and are probably best avoided at that time. Monitor national and regional weather on www.wmo.int.

Gibraltar

For information on Gibraltar contact:

GIBRALTAR GOVERNMENT TOURIST OFFICE
150 STRAND, LONDON WC2R 1JA
Tel: 020 7836 0777
www.gibraltar.gov.gi

info@gibraltar.gov.uk

There are no campsites on the Rock, the nearest being at San Roque and La Línea de la Concepción in Spain. The only direct access to Gibraltar from Spain is via the border at La Línea which is open 24 hours a day. You may cross on foot and it is also possible to take cars or motorhomes to Gibraltar.

A valid British passport is required for all British nationals visiting Gibraltar. Nationals of other countries should check entry requirements with the Gibraltar Government Tourist Office.

There is currently no charge for visitors to enter Gibraltar but Spanish border checks can cause delays and you should be prepared for long queues. As roads in the town are extremely narrow and bridges low, it is advisable to park on the outskirts. Visitors advise against leaving vehicles on the Spanish side of the border owing to the high risk of break-ins.

An attraction to taking the car into Gibraltar includes English style supermarkets and a wide variety of competitively priced goods free of VAT. The currency is sterling and British notes and coins circulate alongside Gibraltar pounds and pence, but note that Gibraltar notes and coins are not accepted in the UK. Scottish and Northern Irish notes are not generally accepted in Gibraltar. Euros are accepted but the exchange rate may not be favourable.

Disabled visitors to Gibraltar may obtain a temporary parking permit from the police station on production of evidence confirming their disability. This permit allows parking for up to two hours (between 8am and 10pm) in parking places reserved for disabled people.

Violence or street crime is rare but there have been reports of people walking from La Línea to Gibraltar at night being attacked and robbed.

If you need emergency medical attention while on a visit to Gibraltar, treatment at primary healthcare centres is free to UK passport holders under the local medical scheme. Non UK nationals need a European Health Insurance Card (EHIC). You are not eligible for free treatment if you go to Gibraltar specifically to be treated for a condition which arose elsewhere, e.g in Spain.

Camping and Caravanning

There are more than 1,200 campsites in Spain with something to suit all tastes – from some of the best and biggest holiday parks in Europe, to a wealth of attractive small sites offering a personal, friendly welcome. Most campsites are located near the Mediterranean, especially on the Costa Brava and Costa del Sol, as well as in the Pyrenees and other areas of tourist interest. Campsites are indicated by blue road signs. In general pitch sizes are small at about 80 square metres.

Many popular coastal sites favoured for long winter stays may contain tightly packed pitches with long-term residents putting up large awnings, umbrellas and other structures. Many sites allow pitches to be reserved from year to year, which can result in a tight knit community of visitors who return every year.

If you're planning to stay on sites in the popular coastal areas between late spring and October, or in January and February, it is advisable to arrive early in the afternoon or to book in advance.

Although many sites claim to be open all year, if you're planning a visit out of season, always check first. It is common for many 'all year' sites to open only at weekends during the winter and facilities may be very limited.

Motorhomes

A number of local authorities now provide dedicated or short stay areas for motorhomes called 'Áreas de Servicio'.

For details see the websites www.lapaca.org or www.viajarenautocaravana.com for a list of regions and towns in Spain and Andorra which have at least one of these areas.

It is rare that yours will be the only motorhome staying on such areas, but take sensible precautions and avoid any that are isolated.

Some motorhome service points are situated in motorway service areas. Use these only as a last resort and do not be tempted to park overnight. The risk of a break-in is high.

Recent visitors to tourist areas on Spain's Mediterranean coast report that the parking of motorhomes on public roads and, in some instances, in public parking areas, may be prohibited in an effort to discourage 'wild camping'. Specific areas where visitors have encountered this problem include Alicante, Dénia, Palamós and the Murcian coast. Police are frequently in evidence moving parked motorhomes on and it is understood that a number of owners of motorhomes have been fined for parking on sections of the beach belonging to the local authority.

Cycling

There are around 2,200km of dedicated cycle paths in Spain, many of which follow disused railway tracks. Known as 'Vias Verdes' (Green Ways), they can be found mainly in northern Spain, in Andalucia, around Madrid and inland from the Costa Blanca. For more information see the website www.viasverdes.com or contact the Spanish Tourist Office.

There are cycle lanes in major cities and towns such as Barcelona, Bilbao, Córdoba, Madrid, Seville and Valencia. Madrid alone has over 100km of cycle lanes.

It is compulsory for all cyclists, regardless of age, to wear a safety helmet on all roads outside built-up areas. At night, in tunnels or in bad weather, bicycles must have front and rear lights and reflectors. Cyclists must also wear a reflective waistcoat or jacket while riding at night on roads outside built-up areas (to be visible from a distance of 150 metres) or when visibility is bad.

Strictly speaking, cyclists have right of way when motor vehicles wish to cross their path to turn left or right, but great care should always be taken. Do not proceed unless you are sure that a motorist is giving way.

Spanish regulations stipulate that motor cycles or bicycles may be carried on the rear of a vehicle providing the rack to which the motorcycle or bicycle is fastened has been designed for the purpose. Lights, indicators, number plate and any signals made by the driver must not be obscured and the rack should not compromise the carrying vehicle's stability.

An overhanging load, such as bicycles, should not extend beyond the width of the vehicle but may exceed the length of the vehicle by up to 10% (up to 15% in the case of indivisible items). The load must be indicated by a 50cm x 50cm square panel with reflective red and white diagonal stripes. These panels may

be purchased in the UK from motorhome or caravan dealers/accessory shops. There is currently no requirement for bicycle racks to be certified or pass a technical inspection.

If you are planning to travel from Spain to Portugal please note that slightly different official regulations apply. These are set out in the Portugal Country Introduction.

Electricity and Gas

The current on campsites should be a minimum of 4 amps but is usually more. Plugs have two round pins. Some campsites do not yet have CEE connections.

Campingaz is widely available in 901 and 907 cylinders. The Cepsa Company sells butane gas cylinders and regulators, which are available in large stores and petrol stations, and the Repsol Company sells butane cylinders at their petrol stations throughout the country.

French and Spanish butane and propane gas cylinders are understood to be widely available in Andorra.

Public Transport

Madrid boasts an extensive and efficient public transport network including a metro system, suburban railways and bus routes. You can purchase a pack of ten tickets which offer better value than single tickets. In addition, tourist travel passes for use on all public transport are available from metro stations, tourist offices and travel agencies and are valid for one to seven days – you will need to present your passport when buying them. Single tickets must be validated before travel. For more information see www.ctm-madrid.es.

Metro systems also operate in Barcelona, Bilbao, Seville and Valencia and a few cities operate tram services including La Coruña, Valencia, Barcelona and Bilbao.
The Valencia service links Alicante, Benidorm and Dénia.

Various operators run year round ferry services from Spain to North Africa, the Balearic Islands and the Canary Islands. All enquiries should be made through their UK agent:

SOUTHERN FERRIES
22 SUSSEX STREET, LONDON SW1V 4RW
www.southernferries.co.uk
mail@southernferries.co.uk

AGUILAR DE CAMPOO *1B4* (3km W Rural) *42.78694, -4.30222* **Monte Royal Camping,** Carretera Virgen del Llano 34800 Aguilar de Campóo (Palencia) **979-18 10 07; info@campingmonteroyal.com; www.camping monteroyal.com**

12 🛉 ♦♦♦ wᴅ ♨ ∥ 🐾 ℗ ⵂ ⍴ 🐾 nr 🛝

App site fr S on N611 fr Palencia. At Aguilar de Campóo turn W at S end of rv bdge at S end of town. Site on L in 3km; sp at edge of reservoir. Fr N take 3rd exit fr rndabt on N611. Do not tow thro town. 2*, Med, mkd, shd, pt sl, EHU (6A) inc; sw; twin axles; 50% statics; ccard acc; horseriding; watersports; fishing; lake 400yds; CKE. *"Useful, peaceful NH 2 hrs fr Santander; ltd/basic facs LS & poss stretched high ssn; barking dogs poss problem; friendly staff; gd walking, cycling & birdwatching in National Park; unrel opening dates LS; facs and site run down (2019); poor."* €22.00   2019

AGUILAS *4G1* (2km SW Coastal) *37.3925, -1.61111* **Camping Bellavista,** Ctra de Vera, Km 3, 30880 Águilas (Murcia) **968-44 91 51; info@campingbellavista.com; www.campingbellavista.com**

12 🛉 €2.50 ♦♦♦ wᴅ ♨ ∥ ᴍsᴘ 🐾 ⍴ ℗ nr 🛝 🐾 🛝

🏖 sand 300m

Site on N332 Águilas to Vera rd on R at top of sh, steep hill, 100m after R turn to El Cocon. Well mkd by flags. Fr S by N332 on L 400m after fuel stn, after v sharp corner. Sm, hdg, hdstg, pt shd, pt sl, EHU (10A) €5.20 or metered; gas; bbq; red long stay; 10% statics; Eng spkn; adv bkg acc; ccard acc; bike hire; CKE. *"Gd autumn/winter stay; clean, tidy site with excel facs; ltd pitches for lge o'fits; helpful owner; fine views; rd noise at 1 end; excel town & vg beaches; v secure site."* €34.20   2019

AGUILAS *4G1* (11km NW Rural) *37.45387, -1.64488* **Camping La Quinta Bella,** Finca El Charcon 31, 30889 Aguilas **968 43 85 35; info@quintabella.com; www.quintabella.com**

12 🛉 ♦♦♦ (htd) wᴅ ♨ 🐾 ∥ ᴍsᴘ 🐾 ⍴ ⵂ ℗ nr 🛝

Fr AP7 exit at junc 878 onto RM11. Foll sp to Los Arejos. In 2km turn R foll sp to site. Med, mkd, hdstg, EHU; gas; bbq; twin axles; 30% statics; Eng spkn; adv bkg acc; ccard acc; CKE. *"V lge pitches; ideal for carnival & Easter parades; v friendly English owners; boules; m'homes should have other transport; excel."* €20.00   2016

AINSA *3B2* (6km NW Rural) *42.43004, 0.07881* **Camping Boltaña,** Ctra N260, Km 442, Ctra Margudgued, 22340 Boltaña (Huesca) **974-50 23 47; info@campingboltana.com; www.campingboltana. com**

12 🛉 €4.25 ♦♦♦ (htd) wᴅ ♨ 🐾 🐾 🛝 ∥ ᴍsᴘ 🐾 ⍴ ⵂ 🐾 ℗ ☰ 🐾 🛝 🐾 🛝 (htd) 🛝

Follow N260 NW for 5km. After petrol stn turn L sp Barcabo. Cross bdge and keep L. Site ent on R in 1km. 1*, Lge, hdstg, mkd, hdg, shd, pt sl, terr, EHU (4-10A) €6.50; gas; twin axles; red long stay; 30% statics; phone; Eng spkn; adv bkg acc; ccard acc; horseriding 500m; fishing 600m; clsd 15 Dec-15 Jan; bike hire; games area; tennis 1km; games rm. *"Conv Ordesa National Park; adventure sports; san facs stretched high ssn; friendly, helpful staff; Ainsa old town worth visit; excel."* €35.00   2019

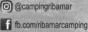
ALBARRACIN *3D1* (2km E Rural) *40.41228, -1.42788*
Camp Municipal Ciudad de Albarracín, Camino de
Gea s/n, 44100 Albarracín (Teruel) **978-71 01 97 or
657-49 84 33 (mob); campingalbarracin5@hotmail.
com; www.campingalbarracin.com**

Fr Teruel take A1512 to Albarracín. Go thro vill, foll
camping sps. 2*, Lge, pt shd, pt sl, EHU (16A) €3.85;
gas; bbq; 10% statics; phone; adv bkg acc; ccard acc;
CKE. *"Gd site; immac san facs; pool adj in ssn; sports
cent adj; gd touring base & gd walking fr site; rec;
friendly staff; gd rest & shop; views striking, gd Sierras;
site extended to nearly dbl; Albaraccin beautiful
ancient town."* **€20.00, 4 Mar-27 Nov.**   2019

ALBERCA, LA *1D3* (6km N Rural) *40.52181, -6.13762*
Camping Sierra de Francia, Ctra Salamanca-La
Alberca, Km 73, 37623 El Caserito (Salamanca) **923-
45 40 81; info@campingsierradefrancia.com;
www.campingsierradefrancia.com**

Fr Cuidad Rodrigo take C515. Turn R at El Cabaco,
site on L in approx 2km. Med, hdg, mkd, shd, EHU
(3-6A) €3.75; gas; bbq; 10% statics; ccard acc;
horseriding; bike hire. *"Conv 'living history' vill of La
Alberca & Monasterio San Juan de la Peña; dogs free;
excel views."* **€23.50, 1 Apr-15 Sep.**   2017

ALCARAZ *4F1* (6km E Rural) *38.67301, -2.40462*
Camping Sierra de Peñascosa, Ctra Peñascosa-
Bogarra, Km 1, 02313 Peñascosa (Albacete) **967-38
25 21; informacion@campingpenascosa.com;
www.campingsierrapenascosa.com**

Fr N322 turn E bet km posts 279 & 280 sp
Peñascosa. In vill foll site sp for 1km beyond vill.
Gravel access track & narr ent. 2*, Sm, mkd, hdstg,
shd, terr, EHU (6A) €4; gas; ccard acc; bike hire;
CKE. *"Not suitable lge o'fits or faint-hearted; pitches
sm, uneven & amongst trees - care needed when
manoeuvring; open w/end in winter; historical sites nr."*
€21.00   2016

ALCOSSEBRE *3D2* (2.5km NE Rural/Coastal)
40.27016, 0.30646 **Camping Ribamar**, Partida
Ribamar s/n, 12579 Alcossebre (Castellón) **964 76
1601; info@campingribamar.com; www.camping-
ribamar.com**

Exit AP7 at junc 44 into N340 & foll sp to Alcossebre,
then dir Sierra de Irta & Las Fuentes. Turn in dir of
sea & foll sp to site in 2km - pt rough rd. Med, hdstg,
mkd, hdg, pt shd, pt sl, terr, EHU (6/10A) €4.50-6.50
(metered for long stay); gas; red long stay; TV;
25% statics; Eng spkn; adv bkg acc; tennis; games area;
games rm; CKE. *"Excel, refurbished tidy site in 'natural
park'; warm welcome; realistic pitch sizes; variable
prices; excel san facs; beware caterpillars in spring - poss
dangerous for dogs."* **€47.00, W04.**   2017

See advertisement

ALGAMITAS *2G3* (3km SW Rural) *37.01934, -5.17440*
Camping El Peñon, Ctra Algámitas-Pruna, Km 3,
41661 Algámitas (Sevilla) **955-85 53 00; info@
algamitasaventura.es; www.algamitasaventura.es**

Fr A92 turn S at junc 41 (Arahal) to Morón de la
Frontera on A8125. Fr Morón take A406 & A363
dir Pruna. At 1st rndabt at ent Pruna turn L onto
SE9225 to Algámitas. Site on L in approx 10km -
steep app rd. Sm, hdg, mkd, hdstg, pt shd, EHU (16A)
€3.32; gas; bbq; 50% statics; adv bkg acc; ccard acc;
site clsd 13-24 Nov; games area; CKE. *"Conv Seville,
Ronda & white vills; walking, hiking & horseriding fr site;
excel rest; excel, clean san facs; vg site - worth effort to
find."* **€15.00**   2016

SPAIN

ALHAURIN DE LA TORRE *2H4* (4km W Rural) *36.65174, -4.61064* **Camping Malaga Monte Parc,** 29130 Alhaurín de la Torre (Málaga) **951-29 60 28;** info@malagamonteparc.com; www.malagamonteparc.com

12 ♿ €1.70 👥 (htd) 🆆 ♨ ⚓ 🔥 🚐 ♪ 🐾 ℘ 🍴 ⓘ 🏧 🚻nr ⚓

W fr Málaga on AP7 or N340 take exit for Churriana/ Alhaurín de la Torre. Thro Alhuarín de la Torre take A404 W sp Alhaurín el Grande, site on R, sp. Sm, hdg, mkd, hdstg, shd, pt sl, EHU (6A) inc; bbq; TV; 10% statics; bus 200m; Eng spkn; adv bkg acc; ccard acc; golf nr; CKE. *"Vg site; well-appointed, clean san facs; friendly Welsh owner; all facs open all year; sm pitches; gd position to tour Costa Del Sol."* **€25.00** **2019**

ALICANTE *4F2* (12.5km NE Coastal) *38.41333, -0.40556* **Camping Bon Sol,** Camino Real de Villajoyosa 35, Playa Muchavista, 03560 El Campello (Alicante) **965-94 13 83;** info@campingbonsol.es; www.campingbonsol.es

12 👥 🆆 ♨ ⚓ 🔥 ♪ ℘ 🍴 ⓘ 🚻 🐾sand

Exit AP7 N of Alicante at junc 67 onto N332 sp Playa San Juan; on reaching coast rd turn N twds El Campello; site sp. 2*, Sm, hdstg, mkd, pt shd, serviced pitches; EHU (10A); red long stay; adv bkg acc; ccard acc; CKE. *"Diff ent for long o'fits; helpful friendly staff; poss cold shwrs; vg."* **€20.00** **2016**

ALLARIZ *1B2* (1.5km W Rural) *42.18443, -7.81811* **Camping Os Invernadeiros,** Ctra Allariz-Celanova, Km 3, 32660 Allariz (Ourense) **988-44 20 06;** reatur@allariz.com

12 🐕 €2 👥 ♨ ♪ 🦋 ℘ 🍴 🏧 🚻 ⛺

Well sp off N525 Orense-Xinzo rd & fr A52. Steep descent to site off rd OU300. Height limit 2.85m adj recep - use gate to R. 3*, Sm, pt shd, EHU (6A) €4.50; gas; red long stay; 10% statics; Eng spkn; ccard acc; horseriding; bike hire; CKE. *"Vg; steep slope into site, level exit is avail; pool 1.5km; site combined with horseriding stable; rv walk adj; facs v clean; hot water; short rv side walk to interesting town; site sp in town as Camping Hippe."* **€24.00** **2019**

ALMERIA *4G1* (18km W Coastal) *36.79738, -2.59128* **Camping Roquetas,** Ctra Los Parrales s/n, 04740 Roquetas de Mar (Almería) **950-34 90 85 or 950-34 38 09;** info@campingroquetas.com; www.campingroquetas.com

12 🐕 €2.25 👥 🆆 ♨ ⚓ 🔥 🚐 ♪ MSP 🦋 ℘ 🍴 🏧 🚻 ⚓ 🛁 🐾shgl 400m

Fr A7 take exit 429; ahead at rndabt A391 sp Roquetas. Turn L at rndabt sp camping & foll sp to site. V lge, pt shd, EHU (10-16A) €6.35-7.45; gas; red long stay; TV; 10% statics; phone; bus 1km; Eng spkn; adv bkg rec; ccard acc; tennis; CKE. *"Double-size pitches in winter; helpful staff; gd clean facs; tidy site but poss dusty; artificial shd; many long term visitors in winter; gd dedicated cycle path along sea front."* **€24.00** **2017**

ALQUEZAR *3B2* (1.5km SW Rural) *42.16454, 0.01527* **Camping Alquézar,** Ctra. Barbastro s/n. 22145 Alquézar, Huesca **34 974 318 300; camping@alquezar.com; campingalquezar.com**

12 🐕 👥 🆆 ♨ ♨ 🔥 🚐 ♪ MSP 🦋 ℘ 🍴 ⓘ 🏧 🚻 ⛺

A22 Huesca - Barbastro. Take N240 W of Barbastro, dir Barbastro. Then A1232 & A1233 to Alquezar, foll camping sp. Med, mkd, hdstg, pt shd, terr, EHU (10A) inc; bbq; twin axles; Eng spkn; adv bkg acc; ccard acc. *"Tricky access; hard 2km walk up hill to old town; interesting town & selection of walking rtes; gd."* **€28.00** **2016**

ALTEA *4F2* (4km S Coastal) *38.57751, -0.06440* **Camping Cap-Blanch,** Playa de Albir, 03530 Altea (Alicante) **965-84 59 46; info@camping-capblanch.com; www.camping-capblanch.com**

12 👥 🆆 ♨ ♨ 🔥 🚐 ♪ MSP 🦋 ℘ 🍴 ⓘ 🚻 nr ⛺ 🐾shgl adj

Exit AP7/E15 junc 64 Altea-Collosa onto N332, site bet Altea & Benidorm, dir Albir. 'No entry' sps on prom rd do not apply to access to site. 1*, Lge, hdstg, pt shd, EHU (5-10A) €3.50; gas; red long stay; TV; 10% statics; Eng spkn; ccard acc; car wash; golf 5km; watersports; tennis. *"V cr in winter with long stay campers; lge pitches; Altea mkt Tues; buses to Benidorm & Altea; handy for lovely beach; most pitches hdstg on pebbles; excel loc; excel walking/cycling."* **€38.00** **2019**

AMETLLA DE MAR, L' *3C2* (3km S Coastal) *40.86493, 0.77860* **Camping L'Ametlla Village Platja,** Paratge de Santes Creus s/n, 43860 L'Ametlla de Mar (Tarragona) **977-26 77 84; info@campingametlla.com; www.campingametlla.com**

12 🐕 👥 (htd) 🆆 ♨ ♨ 🔥 🚐 ♪ MSP ℘ 🍴 ⓘ 🏧 🚻 ⛺ 🏊 ⚓ 🛁 🐾shgl 400m

Exit AP7 junc 39, fork R as soon as cross m'way. Foll site sp for 3km - 1 v sharp, steep bend. Lge, hdstg, mkd, hdg, pt shd, terr, EHU (5-10A) inc; gas; bbq; red long stay; TV; 10% statics; phone; Eng spkn; adv bkg acc; ccard acc; games rm; bike hire; fitness rm; games area; CKE. *"Conv Port Aventura & Ebro Delta National Park; excel site & facs; can cycle into vill with mkt; dogs free; diving cent; delightful site."* **€41.50** **2016**

AMPOLLA, L' *3C2* (2km SW Coastal) *40.79940, 0.69974* **Camping L'Ampolla Playa,** Playa Arenal s/n, 43895 L'Ampolla **977-46 05 35; reservas@campingampolla.es; reservas@campingampolla.es**

🐕 👥 🆆 ♨ ♨ 🔥 🚐 ♪ ℘ 🍴 ⓘ 🚻 🐾50m

Exit AP7 at junc 39A twds S on N340 to km 1098. Turn L onto TV3401 sp L'Ampolla. At rndabt after1 km go L twds L'Ampolla and at next rndabt take 1st exit alongside campsite to ent. Med, hdg, mkd, hdstg, shd, EHU (5-10A); bbq; twin axles; train/bus 1km; Eng spkn; adv bkg acc; CCI. *"Kite surfing; natural park of Ebro Delta; cycling; historic ctrs; vg."* **€34.00, 4 Mar-1 Nov.** **2016**

ARANDA DE DUERO *1C4* (3km N Rural) *41.70138, -3.68666* **Camping Costajan,** Ctra A1/E5, Km 164-165, 09400 Aranda de Duero (Burgos) **947-50 20 70;** campingcostajan@camping-costajan.com; https://guiacampingfecc.com/campings/costajan/
12 🐕 €2 ♥♦(htd) 🚾 ♨ ▤ ⅃ MSP 🦋 ♈ ⓘ 🎣 🏊

Sp on A1/E5 Madrid-Burgos rd, N'bound exit km 164 Aranda Norte, S'bound exit km 165 & foll sp to Aranda & site 500m on R. 3*, Med, shd, pt sl, EHU (10A) €5 (poss rev pol &/or no earth); gas; bbq; 10% statics; phone; Eng spkn; adv bkg acc; tennis; games area; CKE. *"Lovely site under pine trees; poultry farm adj; diff pitch access due trees & sandy soil; friendly, helpful owner; site poss clsd LS - phone ahead to check; many facs clsd LS & gate clsd o'night until 0800; recep poss open evening only LS; poss cold/tepid shwrs LS; gd winter NH; vg site for dogs."* **€20.00**
2019

ARANJUEZ *1D4* (2.5km NE Rural) *40.04222, -3.59944* **Camping International Aranjuez,** Calle Soto del Rebollo s/n, 28300 Aranjuez (Madrid) **918-91 13 95;** info@campingaranjuez.com; www.campingaranjuez.com
12 🐕 ♥♦(htd) 🚾 ♨ ♿ ▤ ⅃ MSP 🦋 ♈ ⓘ 🎣 🏊

Fr N (Madrid) turn off A4 exit 37 onto M305. After ent town turn L bef rv, after petrol stn on R. Take L lane & watch for site sp on L, also mkd M305 Madrid. Site in 500m on R. (If missed cont around cobbled rndabt & back twd Madrid.) Fr S turn off A4 for Aranjuez & foll Palacio Real sp. Join M305 & foll sp for Madrid & camping site. Site on Rv Tajo. Warning: rd surface rolls, take it slowly on app to site & ent gate tight. 3*, Lge, hdg, mkd, unshd, pt sl, serviced pitches; EHU (16A) €4 (poss no earth, rev pol); gas; red long stay; 10% statics; phone; ccard acc; rv fishing; bike hire; games area; canoe hire; CKE. *"Well-maintained site; gd san facs; rest vg value; some lge pitches - access poss diff due trees; hypmkt 3km; some uneven pitches - care req when pitching; pleasant town - World Heritage site; conv Madrid by train; excel site; free train to Royal Palace each morning; shop & rest clsd Tuesdays."* **€35.00** 2016

See advertisement

ARBIZU *3B1* (2km S Rural) *42.89860, -2.03444* **Camping Arbizu eko,** NA 7100 km 5, 31839 Arbizu **848-47 09 22;** info@campingarbizu.com; www.campingarbizu.com
🐕 ♥♦ 🚾 ♨ ▤ ⅃ 🦋 ♈ 🍴 ⓘ 🎣 🚵 ⚓ 🐕 sand

Fr A10 Irurtzun to Altsasu exit 17 onto NA-7100. Site on R in 1km. Med, EHU (16A); bbq; twin axles; TV; Eng spkn; adv bkg acc; ccard acc; fishing; games rm. *"Stunning views of mountains fr site; excel, clean shwr block; v helpful, friendly staff; lots to do in area; gd size pitches; best site."* **€28.00, 7 Jan-23 Dec.** 2015

ARENAS, LAS *1A4* (1km E Rural) *43.29973, -4.80321* **Camping Naranjo de Bulnes,** Ctra Cangas de Onís-Panes, Km 32.5, 33554 Arenas de Cabrales (Asturias) **985-84 65 78;** info@campingnaranjodebulnes.com; www.campingnaranjodebulnes.com
♥♦ 🚾 ♨ ♿ ▤ ⅃ ♈ 🍴 ⓘ 🎣 🚵

Fr Unquera on N634, take N621 S to Panes, AS114 23km to Las Arenas. Site E of vill of Las Arenas de Cabrales, both sides of rd. 2*, V lge, mkd, pt shd, pt sl, terr, EHU (10A) €3.50 (poss rev pol); gas; TV; bus 100m; ccard acc. *"Beautifully-situated site by rv; delightful vill; attractive, rustic-style, clean san facs; wcs up steps; poss poor security; conv Picos de Europa; mountain-climbing school; excursions; walking; excel cheese festival last Sun in Aug; excel rest, bars in vill; lovely."* **€32.00, 2 Apr-9 Oct.** 2017

ARNES *3C2* (1km NE Rural) *40.91860, 0.26780* **Camping Els Ports,** Ctra Tortosa T330, Km 2, 43597 Arnes (Tarragona) **977-43 55 60;** info@camping-elsports.com; www.camping-elsports.com
12 🐕 ♥♦(htd) ♨ ♿ ▤ ⅃ 🦋 🍴 ⓘ 🎣 🚵 🏊

Exit AP7 at junc Tortosa onto C12 sp Gandesa. Turn W onto T333 at El Pinell de Brai, then T330 to site. 2*, Med, pt shd, EHU (6A) €5.20; TV; 10% statics; phone; bus 1km; ccard acc; bike hire; games area; horseriding 3km. *"Nr nature reserve & many sports activities; excel walking/mountain cycling; rock pegs req; nice site; great views; elc kept tripping fuses so low amps; excel san facs, poss stretched in hg ssn."* **€30.00** 2019

AURITZ *3A1* (3km SW Rural) *42.97302, -1.35248*
Camping Urrobi, Ctra Pamplona-Valcarlos, Km 42,
31694 Espinal-Aurizberri (Navarra) **948-76 02 00;**
info@campingurrobi.com; www.campingurrobi.com
🛉🛉 ⬚ ⚓ ⬚ 🛁 ⬚ / 🌀 ▾ ⬚ 🍴 🛒 ⬚

NE fr Pamplona on N135 twd Valcarlos thro Erro;
1.5km after Auritzberri (Espinal) turn R on N172.
Site on N172 at junc with N135 opp picnic area.
Med, pt shd, EHU (5A) €4.90; gas; bbq; 20% statics;
phone; Eng spkn; ccard acc; horseriding; tennis; bike
hire; CKE. *"Excel, busy site & facs; solar htd water - hot
water to shwrs only; walks in surrounding hills; ltd facs
LS; poss youth groups; overprices; poor wifi; clean; gd
local walks."* **€29.00, 1 Apr-1 Nov.**   **2017**

AYERBE *3B2* (10km NE Rural) *42.31989, -0.61848*
Camping Castillo de Loarre, Ctra del Castillo
s/n, 22809 Loarre (Huesca) **974-38 27 22;** info@
camplingloarre.com; www.campingloarre.com
⬚ 🐕 🛉🛉 ⬚ ⚓ ⬚ 🛁 ⬚ / 🌀 ▾ ⬚ 🍴 🛒 ⬚

NW on A132 fr Huesca, turn R at ent to Ayerbe to
Loare sp Castillo de Loarre. Pass 1st site on R (La
Banera) & foll sp to castle past Loarre vill on L; site
on L. App rd steep & twisting. Med, pt shd, pt sl, EHU
(6A) €4.50; gas; 10% statics; phone; Eng spkn; ccard
acc; bike hire; CKE. *"Elevated site in almond grove;
superb scenery & views, esp fr pitches on far L of site;
excel birdwatching - many vultures/eagles; site open
w/end in winter; busy high ssn & w/ends; pitching poss
diff lge o'fits due low trees; worth the journey; site
clsd Feb; v pleasant, well maint site; san facs clean but
dated."* **€16.00**   **2015**

BAIONA *1B2* (1km E Coastal) *42.11416, -8.82611*
Camping Bayona Playa, Ctra Vigo-Baiona, Km 19,
Sabarís, 36393 Baiona (Pontevedra) **986-35 00 35;**
campingbayona@campingbayona.com;
www.campingbayona.com
⬚ 🐕 🛉🛉 ⬚ ⚓ ⬚ 🛁 ⬚ / 🌀 ▾ ⬚ 🍴 🛒 ⬚ 🏖 sand adj

Fr Vigo on PO552 sp Baiona. Or fr A57 exit Baiona
& foll sp Vigo & site sp. Lge, mkd, pt shd, EHU (3A)
€4.80; gas; red long stay; 50% statics; phone; adv bkg
req; waterslide; CKE. *"Area of outstanding natural
beauty with sea on 3 sides; well-organised site; excel,
clean san facs; avoid access w/end as v busy; ltd
facs LS; tight access to sm pitches high ssn; gd cycle
track to town; replica of ship 'La Pinta' in harbour."*
€33.00   **2017**

BAIONA *1B2* (8km SW Coastal) *42.08642, -8.89129*
Camping Mougás (Naturist), As Mariñas 20B, Ctra
Baiona-A Guarda, Km 156, 36309 Mougás
(Pontevedra) **986-38 50 11;** info@campingmuino.com
🛉🛉 ⬚ ⚓ ⬚ 🛁 ⬚ / 🌀 ▾ ⬚ 🍴 ⬚ ⬚

Fr Baiona take coastal rd PO552 S; site sp. Med, mkd,
pt shd, EHU €4.65; bbq; 80% statics; phone; Eng spkn;
ccard acc; fishing; games area; tennis; CKE. *"Excel
staff; lovely site on rocky coast; gd for watching
sunsets; gd NH; o'looks beach; vg."*
€29.00, 18 Mar-27 Mar & 15 May-15 Sep.   **2016**

BALAGUER *3C2* (8km N Rural) *41.86030, 0.83250*
Camping La Noguera, Partida de la Solana s/n, 25615
Sant Llorenç de Montgai (Lleida) **973-42 03 34;** info@
camplinglanoguera.com; www.campinglanoguera.com
⬚ 🐕 €3.50 🛉🛉 ⬚ ⚓ ⬚ 🛁 ⬚ / 🌀 ▾ ⬚ 🍴 🛒 ⬚

Fr Lleida, take N11 ring rd & exit at km 467 onto C13
NE dir Andorra & Balaguer. Head for Balaguer town
cent, cross rv & turn R onto LV9047 dir Gerb. Site on
L in 8km thro Gerb. App fr Camarasa not rec.
Lge, hdstg, mkd, pt shd, terr, EHU (6A) €5.15; gas;
bbq; red long stay; TV; 80% statics; phone; Eng spkn;
adv bkg acc; ccard acc; games area; CKE. *"Next to lake
& nature reserve; gd cycling; poss diff lge o'fits; friendly
warden; gd facs."* **€35.50**   **2017**

BALERMA *2H4* (1km S Coastal) *36.72202, -2.87838*
Camping Mar Azul, Ctra de Guardias Viejas, S/N 04712
Balerma **950-93 76 37;** info@campingbalerma.com;
www.campingbalerma.com
⬚ 🐕 €2.60 🛉🛉 ⬚ ⚓ ⬚ 🛁 ⬚ / 🌀 ▾ 🍴 🛒 ⬚ 🏖 ⬚ 🐟 100m

Exit junc 403 off A7/E15 for Balerma. Site in 6 km.
Lge, hdg, mkd, hdstg, shd, EHU (16A) €0.35 per kw;
bbq; twin axles; red long stay; TV; 4% statics; bus 1km;
Eng spkn; adv bkg acc; games area. *"Lge car park;
excel."* **€28.60**   **2016**

BANYOLES *3B3* (2km W Rural) *42.12071, 2.74690*
Camping Caravaning El Llac, Ctra Circumvallació de
l'Estany s/n, 17834 Porqueres (Gerona) **972-57 03 05;**
info@campingllac.com; www.campingllac.com
⬚ 🐕 €2.30 🛉🛉 (htd) ⬚ ⚓ ⬚ 🛁 ⬚ / 🌀 ▾ 🍴 🛒 ⬚

Exit AP7 junc 6 to Banyoles. Go strt thro town (do
not use by-pass) & exit town at end of lake in 1.6km.
Use R-hand layby to turn L sp Porqueres. Site on
R in 2.5km. Lge, mkd, pt shd, EHU €4.60; sw; red
long stay; 80% statics; bus 1km; site clsd mid-Dec to
mid-Jan. *"Immac, ltd facs LS & stretched high ssn; sm
pitches bet trees; pleasant walk around lake to town;
site muddy when wet."* **€30.00**   **2016**

SPAIN

BEAS DE GRANADA *2G4* (0.8km N Rural) *37.22416, -3.48805* **Camping Alto de Viñuelas,** Ctra de Beas de Granada s/n, 18184 Beas de Granada (Granada) **958-54 60 23; info@campingaltodevinuelas.com; www.campingaltodevinuelas.com**

12 🐕 � (htd) 🅦 ⏚ ♨ ⊟ ⩣ ⸝ 🅼🅿 ⍦ 𝕐 ⊕⩩ 🌡 ⚒ /⩗ ⚓

E fr Granada on A92, exit junc 256 & foll sp to Beas de Granada. Site well sp on L in 1.5km. Sm, mkd, pt shd, terr, EHU (5A) €3.50; bbq; red long stay; 10% statics; bus to Granada at gate; Eng spkn; CKE. *"In beautiful area; views fr all pitches; 4X4 trip to adj natural park; gd; conv for night halt."* **€26.00**   **2019**

BECERREA *1D2* (16km E Rural) *42.83315, -7.06112* **Camping Os Ancares,** Ctra NV1, Liber, 27664 Mosteiro-Cervantes (Lugo) **982-36 45 56**

12 🐕 €1 ♦♦ ⏚ ⊟ ⩣ ⸝ 🦋 𝕐 ⊕⩩ /⩗ ⚓

Fr A6 exit Becerreá S onto LU722 sp Navia de Suarna. After 10km in Liber turn R onto LU723 sp Doiras, site in 7km just beyond Mosteiro hamlet; site sp. Site ent steep & narr - diff lge o'fits & lge m'vans. 2*, Med, shd, terr, EHU (6A) €3; gas; 10% statics; fishing; horseriding; CKE. *"Isolated, scenic site; gd rest & san facs; ltd facs LS; low trees some pitches; gd walking; friendly owner; 17km fr nearest town."* **€21.00**   **2015**

BEJAR *1D3* (15km SW Rural) *40.28560, -5.88182* **Camping Las Cañadas,** Ctra N630, Km 432, 10750 Baños de Montemayor (Cáceres) **927-48 11 26; info@campinglascanadas.com; www.campinglascanadas.com**

12 🐕 ♦♦ (htd) 🅦 ⏚ ♨ ⊟ ⩣ ⸝ 🦋 𝕐 ⊕⩩ 🌡 ⚒ /⩗ ⚓ 🛝

Fr S turn off A630 m'way at 437km stone to Heruns then take old N630 twd Béjar. Site at 432km stone, behind 'Hervas Peil' (leather goods shop). Fr N exit A66 junc 427 thro Baños for 3km to site at km432 on R. 3*, Lge, mkd, shd, pt sl, EHU (5A) €4; gas; red long stay; TV; 60% statics; Eng spkn; ccard acc; fishing; bike hire; games area; tennis; CKE. *"Gd san facs but poss cold shwrs; high vehicles take care o'hanging trees; gd walking country; NH/sh stay."* **€25.00**   **2016**

BENAJARAFE *2H4* (3km E Coastal) *36.71962, -4.16467* **Camping Valle Niza Playa,** Ctra N340, km 264,1 ES-29792 Benajarafe **952-51 31 81; info@campingvalleniza.es; www.campingvalleniza.es**

12 ♦♦ 🅦 ⏚ ♨ ⊟ ⩣ ⸝ 🅼🅿 ⍦ 𝕐 ⊕⩩ 🌡 ⚒ /⩗ ⚓ (htd) 𝑇 50 mtrs

On N340 (old coast rd), bet Torre Del Mar and Benajarafe. Lge, hdg, mkd, hdstg, pt shd, EHU (10-16A); bbq; twin axles; red long stay; TV; 20% statics; phone; bus 100m; Eng spkn; adv bkg acc; bike hire; games rm. *"Gd site; gymnasium; free yoga twice a week."* **€33.00**   **2017**

BENICARLO *3D2* (2.6km NE Urban/Coastal) *40.42611, 0.43777* **Camping La Alegría del Mar,** Ctra N340, Km 1046, Calle Playa Norte, 12580 Benicarló (Castellón) **964-47 08 71; info@camping alegria.com; www.campingalegria.com**

12 🐕 ♦♦ (htd) 🅦 ⏚ ♨ ⊟ ⩣ ⸝ 🅼🅿 ⍦ 𝕐 ⊕⩩ 🌡 ⚒ /⩗ ⚓ 🛝 𝑇 adj

Sp off main N340 app Benicarló. Take slip rd mkd Service, go under underpass, turn R on exit & cont twd town, then turn at camp sp by Peugeot dealers. Sm, hdstg, mkd, hdg, pt shd, EHU (16A) €4.90; gas; bbq; red long stay; twin axles; 40% statics; phone; bus 800m; Eng spkn; ccard acc; games rm; CKE. *"Friendly British owners; access to pitches variable, poss diff in ssn; vg, clean san facs; Xmas & New Year packages; phone ahead to reserve pitch; excel; well run site."* **€30.00**   **2016**

BENICASSIM *3D2* (0.9km E Coastal) *40.05709, 0.07429* **Camping Bonterra Park,** Avda de Barcelona 47, 12560 Benicàssim (Castellón) **964 30 00 07; info@bonterrapark.com; www.bonterrapark.com**

12 🐕 €2.20 ♦♦ (htd) 🅦 ⏚ ♨ ⊟ ⩣ ⸝ 🅼🅿 ⍦ 𝕐 ⊕⩩ 🌡 ⚒ /⩗ ⚓ (covrd, htd) 🛝 𝑇 sand 300m

Fr N exit AP7 junc 45 onto N340 dir Benicàssim. In approx 7km turn R to Benicàssim/Centro Urba; strt ahead to traff lts, then turn L, site on L 500m after going under rlwy bdge. 4*, Lge, hdstg, mkd, shd, pt sl, serviced pitches; EHU (6-10) inc; gas; bbq; red long stay; TV; 15% statics; phone; train; Eng spkn; adv bkg acc; gym; games rm; tennis; bike hire; games area; CKE. *"Fabulous, excel site in gd location; excel cycle tracks & public trans; lovely beach; reasonable sized pitches; no o'fits over 10m; no dogs Jul/Aug; well-kept & well-run; clean modern san facs; access to some pitches poss diff due to trees; sun shades some pitches; winter festival 3rd wk Jan; Harley Davidson rallies Jan & Sep, check in adv; highly rec; flat rd to town; excel facs; sep car park; ACSI card acc; site organises trips out; gd rest; excel."* **€60.00, E19.**   **2018**

BENICASSIM *3D2* (4.5km NW Coastal) *40.05908, 0.08515* **Camping Azahar,** Ptda Villaroig s/n, 12560 Benicàssim (Castellón) **964-30 35 51 or 964-30 31 96; campingazahar.benicasim@gmail.com; www.campingazahar.es**

12 🐕 €4.07 ♦♦ (htd) 🅦 ⏚ ♨ ⊟ ⩣ ⸝ 𝕐 ⊕⩩ 🌡 ⚒ /⩗ ⚓ 𝑇 sand 300m

Fr AP7 junc 45 take N340 twd València; in 5km L at top of hill (do not turn R to go-karting); foll sp. Turn R under rlwy bdge opp Hotel Voramar. Lge, mkd, unshd, pt sl, terr, EHU (4-6A) €2.90 (long leads poss req); gas; red long stay; 25% statics; phone; bus adj; Eng spkn; adv bkg acc; ccard acc; bike hire; CKE. *"Popular site, esp in winter; access poss diff for m'vans & lge o'fits; poss uneven pitches; organised events; tennis at hotel; gd walking & cycling; gd touring base."* **€38.00**   **2017**

BENIDORM *4F2* (5.6km N Coastal) *38.56926, -0.09328*
Camping Almafrá, Partida de Cabut 25, 03503
Benidorm (Alicante) **965-88 90 75; info@camping
almafra.es; www.campingalmafra.es**

🔟2️⃣ 🐕 ♿ (htd) ⬚ ▲ ♨ ♿ 🖥 ∥ ⓂⓈⓅ ⛹ 🍴 ⓦ 🍴 🔥 ⏟ ✎
⛷ (covrd, htd) 🏖

Exit AP7/E15 junc 65 onto N332 N. Foll sp Alfaz del
Pi, site sp. 5*, V lge, mkd, hdstg, hdg, pt shd, EHU
(16A); bbq; twin axles; red long stay; TV (pitch);
20% statics; bus; Eng spkn; adv bkg acc; games rm;
jacuzzi; sauna; gym; games area; tennis; CKE. *"Tennis,
Alfaz del Pi a sh walk away; private san facs avail;
wellness/fitness cent; reg bus into Benidorm; excel."*
€15.00   **2016**

BENIDORM *4F2* (3.6km NE Urban) *38.55564,
-0.09754* **Camping Villamar,** Ctra del Albir, Km 0.300,
03503 Benidorm (Alicante) **966-81 12 55; camping@
campingvillamar.com; www.campingvillamar.com**

🔟2️⃣ ♿ ⬚ ▲ ♿ 🖥 ∥ ⛹ 🍴 ⓦ 🔥 ⏟
✎ ⛷ (covrd, htd) ☂ sand 2km

Exit AP7 junc 65. Down hill twd town, turn L at traff
lts into Ctra Valenciana, turn R where 2 petrol stns
either side of rd, site on L. V lge, mkd, pt shd, terr,
serviced pitches; EHU (16A) €3.50; gas; red long stay;
TV (pitch); 60% statics; phone; adv bkg acc; games
rm. *"Excel site, esp winter; gd security; v welcoming; gd
walking area; excel food; spotless san facs; great value;
excel food; bus to town."* **€28.00**   **2019**

BENQUERENCIA *2E3* (2km SW Rural) *39.29626,
-06.10109* **Camping Las Grullas (Naturist),** Camino
Valdefuentes 4, 10185 Benquerencia **34 634 264 504;
info@lasgrullas.es; www.campinglasgrullas.es**

♿ ⓦ ▲ ∥ ⛹ ⓦ ☂ (htd)

Take EX-206 to Miajadas. After 30km take 2nd
turning to Benquerencia (close to Valdefuentes vill).
Site on R after 2.5 km. 1*, Sm, hdg, mkd, pt shd, EHU
(4-6A) inc; twin axles; Eng spkn; adv bkg acc. *"Over
16's only; close historic town; no childrens facs; v
helpful owners; gd walks fr site; vg."*
€25.00, 1 Apr-16 Oct.   **2016**

BIELSA *3B2* (8km W Rural) *42.65176, 0.14076*
Camping Pineta, Ctra del Parador, Km 7,
22350 Bielsa (Huesca) **974-50 10 89; info@
campingpineta.com; www.campingpineta.com**

🏔 €2.50 ♿ ⓦ ▲ ♨ ♿ ∥ ⓂⓈⓅ 🍴 ⓦ 🔥 ⏟ ⛷

Fr A138 in Beilsa turn W & foll sp for Parador Monte
Perdido & Valle de Pineta. Site on L after 8km
(ignore previous campsite off rd). 2*, Lge, pt shd,
pt sl, terr, EHU (6A) €5 (poss rev pol); gas; bbq;
10% statics; phone; ccard acc; bike hire; games area;
CKE. *"Well-maintained site; clean facs; glorious location
in National Park."* **€27.00, 25 Mar-2 Oct.**   **2016**

BIESCAS *3B2* (3km SE Rural) *42.61944, -0.30416*
Camping Gavín, Ctra N260, Km 502.5, 22639 Gavín
(Huesca) **974-48 50 90 or 659-47 95 51; info@
campinggavin.com; www.campinggavin.com**

🔟2️⃣ 🐕 ♿ (htd) ⓦ ▲ ♨ ♿ 🖥 ∥ ⓂⓈⓅ 🍴 ⓦ 🍴 🔥 ⏟ ⛷

Take N330/A23/E7 N fr Huesca twd Sabiñánigo
then N260 twd Biescas & Valle de Tena. Ignore all sp
to Biescas on N260 until R turn at g'ge. Drive over
blue bdge & foll sp Gavin & site. Site is at km 502.5
fr Huesca, bet Biescas & Gavín. Lge, mkd, pt shd, terr,
EHU (10A) inc; gas; TV; phone; bus 1km; Eng spkn; adv
bkg acc; tennis; CKE. *"Wonderful, scenic site nr Ordesa
National Park; poss diff access to pitches for lge o'fits &
m'vans; superb htd san facs; bike hire in National Park;
immac kept, excel, superb site; pitches with views, gd
for walking."* **€37.00**   **2016**

BILBAO *1A4* (18km N Coastal) *43.38916, -2.98444*
Camping Sopelana, Ctra Bilbao-Plentzia, Km 18,
Playa Atxabiribil 30, 48600 Sopelana (Vizcaya)
**946-76 19 81 or 649-11 57 51; recepcion@
campingsopelana.com; www.campingsopelana.com**

🔟2️⃣ ♿ ⓦ ▲ ♨ ♿ 🖥 ∥ 🍴 ⓦ 🔥 ⏟ ⛷ ☂ sand 200m

In Bilbao cross rv by m'way bdge sp to airport, foll
637/634 N twd & Plentzia. Cont thro Sopelana & foll
sp on L. 1*, Med, hdg, sl, EHU (10A) €4.50; own san
req; gas; red long stay; 70% statics; Eng spkn; adv bkg
req; CKE. *"Poss strong sea winds; ltd space for tourers;
pitches sm, poss flooded after heavy rain & poss diff
due narr, steep site rds; ltd facs LS; helpful manager;
site used by local workers; poss clsd LS - phone ahead
to check; gd NH/sh stay only."* **€36.00**   **2016**

BILBAO *1A4* (2.5km W Urban) *43.25960, -2.96351*
Motorhome Parking Bilbao, Monte Kobeta 31, 48001
Bilbao **688 809 399 or 944 655 789; kobetamendi@
suspertu.net; Bilbao.net**

♿ ⓦ ∥ ⓂⓈⓅ ⓦ

A8 m'way, Balmaseda exit, dir Altamira - Alto de
Kastrexana. Med, unshd, terr, EHU inc; bus adj; ccard
acc. *"MH's only; on hill o'looking Bilbao; ehu & water to
each pitch; v conv for visiting city by bus (every 1/2 hr);
max stay 2 days; clsd 1st week of Jul; vg; full security."*
€15.00, 17 Mar-9 Jan.   **2017**

BLANES *3C3* (1km S Coastal) *41.65933, 2.77000*
Camping Blanes, Avda Vila de Madrid 33, 17300 Blanes
(Gerona) **972-33 15 91; info@campingblanes.com;
www.campingblanes.com**

🔟2️⃣ 🐕 ♿ ⓦ ▲ ♿ ∥ ⓂⓈⓅ ⛹ 🍴 ⓦ 🍴 🔥 ⏟ ✎ ⛷ ☂ sand

Fr N on AP7/E15 exit junc 9 onto NII dir Barcelona
& foll sp Blanes. Fr S to end of C32, then NII dir
Blanes. On app Blanes, foll camping sps & Playa
S'Abanell - all campsites are sp at rndabts; all sites
along same rd. Site adj Hotel Blau-Mar. Lge, mkd,
shd, EHU (5A) inc; gas; phone; bus; Eng spkn; ccard
acc; solarium; bike hire; watersports; games rm. *"Excel
site, espec LS; helpful owner; narr site rds; easy walk to
town cent; dir access to beach; trains to Barcelona &
Gerona."* **€37.00**   **2017**

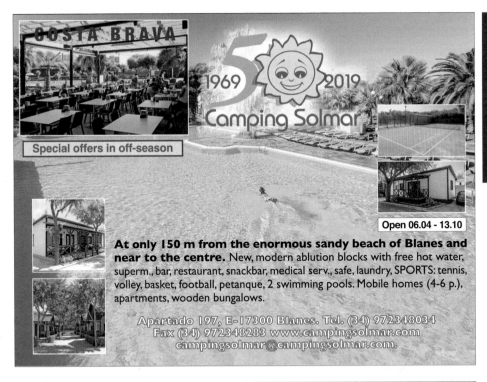

Camping Solmar

COSTA BRAVA

1969 2019

Camping Solmar

Special offers in off-season

Open 06.04 - 13.10

At only 150 m from the enormous sandy beach of Blanes and near to the centre. New, modern ablution blocks with free hot water, superm., bar, restaurant, snackbar, medical serv., safe, laundry, SPORTS: tennis, volley, basket, football, petanque, 2 swimming pools. Mobile homes (4-6 p.), apartments, wooden bungalows.

Apartado 197, E-17300 Blanes. Tel. (34) 972348034
Fax (34) 972348283 www.campingsolmar.com
campingsolmar@campingsolmar.com

BLANES 3C3 (1.5km SW Coastal) *41.66206, 2.78046*
Camping Solmar, Calle Cristòfor Colom 48, 17300 Blanes (Gerona) 972-34 80 34; campingsolmar@ campingsolmar.com; www.campingsolmar.com

Fr N on AP7/E15 exit junc 9 onto NII dir Barcelona & foll sp Blanes. Fr S to end of C32, then NII dir Blanes. On app Blanes, foll camping sps. Lge, mkd, hdg, shd, EHU (6A) inc; bbq; red long stay; 10% statics; bus 100m; adv bkg acc; ccard acc; games area; games rm; tennis; CKE. "*Excel site & facs; dogs free.*" **€39.40, 2 Apr-12 Oct.** 2017

See advertisement

BOSSOST 3B2 (3km SE Rural) *42.74921, 0.70071*
Camping Prado Verde, Ctra de Lleida a Francia, N230, Km 173, 25551 Era Bordeta/La Bordeta de Vilamòs (Lleida) 973-64 71 72; info@campingpradoverde.es; www.campingpradoverde.es

On N230 at km 173 on banks of Rv Garona. Med, shd, EHU (6A) €5.50; TV; 10% statics; bus; ccard acc; bike hire; fishing; CKE. "*V pleasant NH.*" **€22.00** 2016

BROTO 3B2 (7km W Rural) *42.61576, -0.15432*
Camping Viu, Ctra N260, Biescas-Ordesa, Km 484.2, 22378 Viu de Linás (Huesca) 974-48 63 01; info@ campingviu.com; www.campingviu.com

Lies on N260, 4km W of Broto. Fr Broto, N for 2km on rd 135; turn W twd Biesca at junc with Torla rd; site approx 4km on R. Med, pt shd, sl, EHU (5-8A) €4.20; gas; bbq; phone; adv bkg acc; ccard acc; games rm; bike hire; horseriding; CKE. "*Friendly owners; gd home cooking; walking adj; skiing adj; car wash; fine views; highly rec; climbing adj; clean, modern san facs; poss not suitable for lge o'fits.*" **€17.40** 2016

SPAIN

BURGOS *1B4* (4km E Rural) *42.34111, -3.65777*
Camp Fuentes Blancas, Ctra Cartuja Miraflores,
Km 3.5, 09193 Burgos **947-48 60 16;** info@
campingburgos.com; www.campingburgos.com
🎫 €2.17 ♔♟ (htd) 🆆🅾 ♨ ⚓ 🅳 ✎ 🅼🆂🅿 🦋 ♈ ▽ ⓓ🍴🎿 ⚠ ♒

E or W on A1 exit junc 238 & cont twd Burgos. Strt
over 1st rndabt, turn R sp Cortes & then L. Look for
yellow sps to site. Fr N (N627 or N623) on entering
Burgos keep in R hand lane. Foll signs Cartuja
miraflores & yellow camp signs. 3*, Lge, mkd, shd,
EHU (6A) inc; gas; 10% statics; phone; bus at gate;
Eng spkn; ccard acc; games area. *"Neat, roomy, adj
woodland; some sm pitches; ltd facs LS; poss v muddy
in wet; easy access town car parks or cycle/rv walk;
Burgos lovely town; gd NH; San Rafael dated; gd bus to
town; excel, well maintained busy site; gd shd; gd facs."*
€28.00 2018

CABRERA, LA *1D4* (1km SW Rural) *40.85797,
-3.61580* **Camping Pico de la Miel,** Ctra A-1 Salida 57,
28751 La Cabrera (Madrid) **918-68 80 82 or 918-68 95
07;** info@picodelamiel.com; www.picodelamiel.com
🎫 🐕 ♔♟ (htd) 🆆🅾 ♨ ⚓ 🅳 ✎ 🦋 ♈ ▽ ⓓ🍴🎿 ⚠ 🎿⛵

Fr Madrid on A1/E5, exit junc 57 sp La Cabrera.
Turn L at rndabt, site sp. Lge, mkd, pt shd, pt sl, EHU
(10A) €4.45; gas; red long stay; 75% statics; phone;
Eng spkn; adv bkg acc; ccard acc; tennis; games area;
sailing; windsurfing; squash; fishing; CKE. *"Attractive
walking country; conv Madrid; mountain-climbing; car
wash; ltd touring area not v attractive; some pitches
have low sun shades; excel san facs; ltd facs LS."*
€33.50 2017

CACERES *2E3* (6km NW Urban) *39.48861, -6.41277*
Camp Municipal Ciudad de Cáceres, Ctra N630,
Km 549.5, 10005 Cáceres **927-23 31 00;** reservas@
campingcaceres.com; www.campingcaceres.com
🎫 🐕 ♔♟ 🆆🅾 ♨ ⚓ 🅳 ✎ 🅼🆂🅿 ♈ ▽ ⓓ🍴🎿 ⚠ 🎿⛵

Fr Cáceres ring rd take N630 dir Salamanca. At
1st rndbt turn R sp Via de Servicio with camping
symbol. Foll sp 500m to site. Or fr N exit A66 junc
545 onto N630 twd Cáceres. At 2nd rndabt turn L sp
Via de Servicio, site on L adj football stadium. Med,
mkd, hdstg, unshd, terr, EHU (10A) €4.50; gas; bbq;
TV; 15% statics; bus 500m over footbdge; Eng spkn;
adv bkg acc; ccard acc; games area; CKE. *"Vg, well-run
site; excel facs; ACSI acc; vg value rest; gd bus service
to and fr interesting old town with many historical
bldgs; excel site with ensuite facs at each pitch;
individual san facs each pitch; location not pretty adj
to football stadium & indus est; town too far to walk; v
lush, free use of spa; Lydl 1.6km."* **€26.00** 2019

CALATAYUD *3C1* (15km N Rural) *41.44666, -1.55805*
Camping Saviñan Parc, Ctra El Frasno-Mores, Km 7,
50299 Saviñan (Zaragoza) **976-82 54 23;** info@
campingsavinan.com; www.campingsavinan.com
🎫 €2.70 ♔♟ 🆆🅾 🅳 ✎ 🅼🆂🅿 🦋 🎿

Exit A2/E90 (Zaragoza-Madrid) at km 255 to T-junc.
Turn R to Saviñan for 6km, foll sps to site 1km S.
2*, Lge, hdstg, pt shd, terr, EHU (6-10A) €4.60; gas;
15% statics; phone; ccard acc; site clsd Jan; tennis;
horseriding; CKE. *"Beautiful scenery & views; some sm
narr pitches; rec identify pitch location to avoid stop/
start on hill; terr pitches have steep, unfenced edges;
many pitches with sunscreen frames & diff to
manoeuvre long o'fits; modern facs block but cold in
winter & poss stretched high ssn; hot water to some
shwrs only; gates poss clsd LS - use intercom; site poss
clsd Feb."* **€20.00** 2017

CALIG *3D2* (1km NW Rural) *40.45183, 0.35211*
Camping L'Orangeraie, Camino Peniscola-Calig,
12589 Càlig **34 964 765 059;** info@camping-
lorangeraie.es
🐕 €2.50 ♔♟ 🆆🅾 ♨ ⚓ 🅳 ✎ 🅼🆂🅿 🦋 ♈ ▽ 🍴🎿 ⚠ 🎿⛵🐟

On AP7 exit 43 Benicarlo-Peniscola. 1st R at rndabt
to Calig then foll sp to campsite. Fr N340 exit N232
to Morella, then after 1.5km turn L to Calig CV135,
foll sp to campsite. 5*, Med, hdg, mkd, pt shd, terr,
EHU (10A); bbq; twin axles; 15% statics; bus 1km; Eng
spkn; adv bkg acc; waterslide; games area. *"Excel site."*
€33.00, 1 Apr-31 Dec. 2019

CALPE *4F2* (0.3km NE Urban/Coastal) *38.64488,
0.05604* **Camping Calpe Mar,** Calle Eslovenia 3,
03710 Calpe (Alicante) **965-87 55 76;** info@camp-
ingcalpemar.com; www.campingcalpemar.com
🎫 🐕 ♔♟ (htd) 🆆🅾 ♨ ⚓ 🅳 ✎ 🦋 ♈ ▽ ⓓ🍴🎿nr ⚠ ✎
🎿☂ sand 300m

Exit AP7/E15 junc 63 onto N332 & foll sp, take
slip rd sp Calpe Norte & foll dual c'way CV746
round Calpe twd Peñón d'Ifach. At rndabt nr
police stn with metal statues turn L, then L at
next rndabt, over next rndabt, site 200m on R.
Med, hdstg, mkd, hdg, unshd, serviced pitches; EHU
(10A) inc (metered for long stay); bbq; red long
stay; TV; 3% statics; phone; bus adj; Eng spkn; adv
bkg acc; ccard acc; ice; games area; games rm; dog
wash; CKE. *"High standard site; well-kept & laid out;
Spanish lessons; gd security; excel; extra lge pitches
avail at additional charge; car wash; gd for long stay,
friendly staff; sep car park; close to beach and Lidl."*
€34.00 2018

See advertisement opposite

CAMBRILS *3C2* (1.5km N Urban/Coastal) *41.06500, 1.08361* **Camping Playa Cambrils Don Camilo,** Carrer Oleastrum 2, Ctra Cambrils-Salou, Km 1.5, 43850 Cambrils (Tarragona) **977-36 14 90; camping@ playacambrils.com; www.playacambrils.com**

🛉 €4.35 ♥♦ ⓌⒸ 🛁 🚽 ⚑ 🖥 🖊 🏮 ⍦ ⑭ 🦯
🛖 ⋀ 🎿 🛥 (htd) 🏖 🛶 sand adj

Exit A7 junc 37 dir Cambrils & N340. Turn L onto N340 then R dir port then L onto coast rd. Site sp on L at rndabt after rv bdge 100m bef watch tower on R, approx 2km fr port. V lge, mkd, hdg, shd, EHU (6A) inc; gas; red long stay; TV; 25% statics; bus 200m; Eng spkn; adv bkg req; ccard acc; tennis; watersports; games rm; bike hire; boat hire; CKE. *"Helpful, friendly staff; children's club; cash machine; doctor; cinema; sports activities avail; Port Aventura 5km; 24-hr security; vg site."* **€46.00,** 15 Mar-16 Oct. 2018

CAMBRILS *3C2* (11km SW Coastal) *41.02512, 0.95906* **Camping Miramar,** Ctra N340, km 1134 43892 Mont-roig del Camp **977-81 12 03; recepcio@ camping-miramar.com; www.camping-miramar.es**

🛉 🐕 ♥♦ ⓌⒸ 🛁 🚽 ⚑ 🖊 🏮 ⍦ 🖥 🛖 ⋀ 🛶

Fr the AP7 take exit 37 to the N340. Turn L at KM134 to campsite. Sm, pt shd, EHU (6A) €5.20; bbq; twin axles; red long stay; 75% statics; bus; Eng spkn; adv bkg acc. *"Site on beach, walking, sw, snorkelling; vg."* **€35.00,** 1 Jan-30 Nov. 2017

CAMBRILS *3C2* (8km SW Coastal) *41.03333, 0.96777* **Playa Montroig Camping Resort,** N340, Km1.136, 43300 Montroig (Tarragona) **977 810 637; info@playamontroig.com; www.playamontroig.com**

♥♦ (htd) ⓌⒸ 🛁 🚽 ⚑ 🖥 🖊 MSP 🏮 ⍦ ⑭ 🦯 🛖 ⋀ 🎿 🛥 (htd)
🛶 sand adj

Exit AP7 junc 37, W onto N340. Site has own dir access onto N340 bet Cambrils & L'Hospitalet de L'Infant, well sp fr Cambrils. 5*, V lge, mkd, shd, pt sl, serviced pitches; EHU (10A) inc; gas; 30% statics; phone; Eng spkn; adv bkg acc; ccard acc; games rm; games area; golf 3km; tennis; bike hire; CKE. *"Magnificent, clean, secure site; private, swept beach; skateboard track; some sm pitches & low branches; cash machine; doctor; 4 grades pitch/price; highly rec."* **€53.00,** 1 Apr-30 Oct. 2017

See advertisement above

CAMBRILS *3C2* (8km W Coastal) *41.03717, 0.97622*
Camping La Torre del Sol, Ctra N340, Km 1.136, Miami-Playa, 43300 Montroig Del Camp (Tarragona) **977 810 486; info@latorredelsol.com; www. latorredelsol.com**

♦♦♦ ⓦ ▲ ♿ ⛁ ∅ ▥ ♔ ⓣ ♈ ⑪ ä ੬ ⋒ ♪ ≋ (htd) 🏊
↑2 sand

Leave A7 València/Barcelona m'way at junc 37 & foll sp Cambrils. After 1.5km join N340 coast rd S for 6km. Watch for site sp 4km bef Miami Playa. Fr S exit AP7 junc 38, foll sp Cambrils on N340. Site on R 4km after Miami Playa. Site ent narr, alt ent avail for lge o'fits. 4*, V lge, mkd, hdg, shd, EHU (6A) inc (10A avail); gas; bbq; TV; 40% statics; Eng spkn; adv bkg acc; ccard acc; squash; games rm; gym; tennis; sauna; bike hire; golf 4km. *"Attractive well-guarded site for all ages; sandy pitches; gd, clean san facs; steps to facs for disabled; whirlpool; jacuzzi; access to pitches poss diff lge o'fits due trees & narr site rds; skateboard zone; radios/TVs to be used inside vans only; conv Port Aventura, Aquaparc, Aquopolis; cinema; disco; highly rec, can't praise site enough; excel."* **€52.00, 15 Mar-30 Oct, E14.**
2017

See advertisement opposite

CANGAS DE ONIS *1A3* (16km E Rural) *43.33527, -4.94777* **Camping Picos de Europa,** Avin-Onís, 33556 Avín, **985-84 40 70; info@picos-europa.com; www.picos-europa.com**

⓬ ♦♦♦ ⓦ ▲ ♿ ⛁ ∅ ♔ ⓣ ⑪ ä ੬ ≋

E80, exit 307. Dir Posada A5-115. Loc on the rd Onis-Carrena, 15 km fr Cangas de Onis and 10 km fr Carrena, foll sps. 2*, Med, hdg, mkd, pt shd, terr, EHU (6A) €3.80; gas; 10% statics; phone; Eng spkn; adv bkg acc; horseriding; CKE. *"Owners v helpful; beautiful, busy, well-run site; vg value rest; modern san facs; poss diff access due narr site rds & cr; some sm pitches, lge o'fits may need 2; canoeing on local rvs; conv local caves, mountains, National Park, beaches; highly rec."* **€27.00**
2019

CANGAS DE ONIS *1A3* (3km SE Rural) *43.34715, -5.08362* **Camping Covadonga,** 33589 Soto de Cangas (Asturias) **985-94 00 97; campingcovadonga@ hotmail.es; www.camping-covadonga.com**

♦♦♦ ⓦ ▲ ⛁ ∅ ♔ ⓣ ⑪ ä ੬

N625 fr Arriondas to Cangas de Onis, then AS114 twds Covadonga & Panes, cont thro town sp Covadonga. At rndabt take 2nd exit sp Cabrales, site on R in 100m. Access tight. 1*, Med, mkd, pt shd, EHU (10A) €3.50 (no earth); red long stay; bus adj; adv bkg acc; CKE. *"Sm pitches; take care with access; site rds narr; 17 uneven steps to san facs; conv for Picos de Europa."* **€21.00, Holy Week & 15 Jun-30 Sep.**
2017

CARBALLO *1A2* (15km N Coastal) *43.29556, -8.65528* **Camping Baldayo,** San Salvador de Rebordelos, 15105 Carballo **981-73 95 29; campingbaldayo@ yahoo.es; www.campingbaldayo.com**

⓬ ♠ ♦♦♦ ⓦ ▲ ੬ ⛁ ∅ ♔ ♈ ⓣ ä ੬ ⋒ ↑ sand 200m

Access via DP-1916 fr Carballo. Turn L in vill and foll sp. App rds are unmade. On site access rds are narr with sharp corners, diff for long o'fits. 2*, Med, hdg, mkd, hdstg, pt shd, pt sl, terr, EHU (3A) €1.50; bbq; twin axles; 75% statics; phone; adv bkg acc. *"Sm pitches & narr camp rds poss diff lge o'fits; poss unkempt LS; nrby lagoon with boardwalk and bird hides; beach popular for surfing & watersports."* **€15.00**
2017

CARRION DE LOS CONDES *1B4* (0.4km W Rural) *42.33506, -04.60447* **Camping El Edén,** Ctra Vigo-Logroño, Km 200, 34120 Carrión de los Condes (Palencia) **979-88 07 14**

♠ ♦♦♦ ▲ ♿ ੬ ∅ ▥ ♔ ⓣ ♈ ⑪ ⋒

Fr N231 take junc 85, go S then L at 3rd rndabt to ctr. Site sp on L. 2*, Med, mkd, pt shd, EHU (6A) €3.50; gas; bus 500m; Eng spkn. *"Pleasant walk to town; basic rvside site; recep in bar/rest; site open w/ ends only LS; fair NH; quite lively in high ssn; nice site in interesting town on pilgrim rte; no lts in san block."* **€19.80, 1 Apr-30 Oct.**
2017

CASTELLO D'EMPURIES *3B3* (4km NE Rural) *42.26460, 3.10160* **Camping Mas Nou,** Ctra Mas Nou 7, Km 38, 17486 Castelló d'Empúries (Gerona) **972-45 41 75; info@campingmasnou.com; www.camping masnou.com**

♠ €2.35 ♦♦♦ (htd) ⓦ ▲ ♿ ੬ ⛁ ∅ ▥ ♔ ⓣ ⑪ ä ੬ nr ⋒ ♪ ≋ ↑ 2.5km

On m'way A7 exit 3 if coming fr France & exit 4 fr Barcelona dir Roses (E) C260. Site on L at ent to Empuriabrava - use rndabt to turn. 3*, Lge, mkd, shd, EHU (10A) €4.90; bbq; red long stay; TV; 5% statics; phone; Eng spkn; ccard acc; tennis; games area; CKE. *"Aqua Park 4km, Dali Museum 10km; gd touring base; helpful staff; well-run site; excel, clean san facs; sports activities & children's club; gd cycling; excel; vg rest."* **€47.50, 8 Apr-24 Sep.**
2017

For a guide to symbols see the fold out on the rear cover

CATALUNYA

Catalunya Sud

SEA, WELLNESS AND ANIMATION

ANIMATION NON-STOP
15.03/31.10

TROPICAL OPEN AIR JACUZZI
JACUZZIS WITH WARM SEA WATER

CAMPING RESORTS

soleil VILLAGE

✉ **E-43892 MIAMI PLATJA (TARRAGONA)**
Tel.: +34 977 810 486 · Fax: +34 977 811 306
www.latorredelsol.com · info@latorredelsol.com

SPAIN

CASTELLO D'EMPURIES *3B3* (4km SE Coastal) *42.20725, 3.10026* **Camping Nautic Almatá,** Aiguamolls de l'Empordà, 17486 Castelló d'Empúries (Gerona) **972-45 44 77; info@almata.com; www. almata.com**

🐕 €6.40 ♟️ WD ⚓ ♿ 🚿 ✉ 🦋 🍷 ⑪ 🏊 ⛺ ♨ 🏄 🛥️ ⛵ sand adj

Fr A7 m'way exit 3; foll sp to Roses. After 12km turn S for Sant Pere Pescador & site on L in 5km. Site clearly sp on rd Castelló d'Empúries-Sant Pere Pescador. Lge, pt shd, EHU (10A) inc; gas; TV; adv bkg acc; sailing school; tennis; bike hire; horseriding; games area. *"Excel, clean facs; ample pitches; sports facs inc in price; disco bar on beach; helpful staff; direct access to nature reserve; waterside pitches rec."* **€59.00, 16 May-20 Sep.** 2016

See advertisement

CASTRO URDIALES *1A4* (1km N Coastal) *43.39000, -3.24194* **Camping de Castro,** Barrio Campijo, 39700 Castro Urdiales (Cantabria) **942-94 48 97; info@campingdecastro.com; http://campingdecastro.es/en/**

🐕 ♟️ ⚓ ♿ 🚿 ✉ 🦋 🍷 ⑪ 🏊 ⛺ 🏄 🛥️ sand 1km

Fr Bilbao turn off A8 at 2nd Castro Urdiales sp, km 151. Camp sp on R by bullring. V narr, steep lanes to site - no passing places, great care req. 2*, Lge, unshd, pt sl, terr, EHU (6A) €3; 90% statics; phone; bus; Eng spkn; adv bkg acc; CKE. *"Gd, clean facs; conv NH for ferries; ltd touring pitches; narr, long, steep single track ent; great views over Bilbao bay."* **€27.00, 13 Feb-10 Dec.** 2019

> ## "There aren't many sites open at this time of year"
>
> If you're travelling outside peak season remember to call ahead to check site opening dates – even if the entry says 'open all year'.

CASTROJERIZ *1B4* (1km NE Rural) *42.29102, -4.13165* **Camping Camino de Santiago,** Calle Virgen del Manzano s/n, 09110 Castrojeriz (Burgos) **947-37 72 55 or 658-96 67 43 (mob);** info@campingcamino. com; www.campingcamino.com

🛒 ⛽€2 � ⯑wo ⚕ ♿ 🛁 ∥ ⯑ ⛲ ⛱ ⓘ 🍴 🛟 nr

Fr N A62/E80 junc 40 dir Los Balbases, Vallunquera & Castrojeriz - narr, uneven rd. In 16 km ent Castrojeriz, sp fr BU400 where you turn onto BU404. Once on BU404 proceed for approx 500yds to next rndabt, take 2nd exit. Site 1m on the L. Fr S A62, exit 68 twds Torquemada, then take P412, then BU4085 to Castrojeriz. Do not go thro town, as rd are narr. Med, mkd, hdg, shd, pt sl, EHU (5-10A) €4 (poss no earth); TV; bus 200m; Eng spkn; games area; games rm; CKE. *"Lovely site; helpful owner; pilgrims' refuge on site; some diff sm pitches; vg; site ent narr; excel bird watching tours on req; san facs dated."* **€32.00, 15 Mar-15 Nov.** 2019

"That's changed – Should I let the Club know?"

If you find something on site that's different from the site entry, fill in a report and let us know. See camc.com/europereport.

CERVERA DE PISUERGA *1B4* (0.5km W Rural) *42.87135, -4.50332* **Camping Fuentes Carrionas,** La Bárcena s/n, 34840 Cervera de Pisuerga (Palencia) **979-87 04 24;** campingfuentescarrionas@hotmail.com; campingfuentescarrionas.com

♟ ⯑wo ⚕ ♿ 🛁 ∥ ⯑ ⛲ ⓘ nr 🛟 nr

Fr Aguilar de Campóo on CL626 pass thro Cervera foll sp CL627 Potes. Site sp on L bef rv bdge. Med, mkd, pt shd, EHU €3.50; 80% statics; bus 100m; games area; tennis; CKE. *"Gd walking in nature reserve; conv Casa del Osos bear info cent; rest/bar area busy at wkend; new gd clean san facs; site busy with wkenders in statics or cabins; owners v helpful and pleasant; well maintained."* **€21.00, Holy Week-30 Sep.** 2017

CIUDAD RODRIGO *1D3* (1.5km S Rural) *40.59206, -6.53445* **Camping La Pesquera,** Ctra Cáceres-Arrabal, Km 424, Huerta La Toma, 37500 Ciudad Rodrigo (Salamanca) **923-48 13 48;** campinglapesquera@ hotmail.com; www.campinglapesquera.es

12 🛒 ♟ ⯑wo ⚕ ♿ 🛁 ∥ ⯑ ⛲ 🍴

Fr Salamanca on A62/E80 exit junc 332. Look for tent sp on R & turn R, then 1st L & foll round until site on rvside. 2*, Med, mkd, pt shd, EHU (6A) inc; sw nr; TV; phone; ccard acc; fishing adj; CKE. *"Medieval walled city worth visit - easy walk over Roman bdge; gd san facs; vg, improved site; friendly nice sm site next to rv, gd for NH; lovely town; v helpful staff."* **€17.00** 2017

CLARIANA *3B3* (6km NE Rural) *41.95900, 1.60384* **Camping La Ribera,** Pantà de Sant Ponç, 25290 Clariana de Cardener (Lleida) **973-48 25 52 or 973-48 15 57;** info@campinglaribera.com; www.camping laribera.com

12 🛒 ♟ ⯑wo ⚕ ♿ 🛁 ∥ ⯑ ⛲ 🍴 🛟 ⛰ ⛱ 🏊

Fr Solsona S on C55, turn L onto C26 at km 71. Go 2.7km, site sp immed bef Sant Ponç Dam. 2*, Lge, mkd, hdstg, pt shd, EHU (4-10A) €4.60-8.45; sw nr; TV; 95% statics; phone; games area; tennis. *"Excel facs; gd site; narr pitches, can be diff to site o'fit."* **€38.00** 2016

COLOMBRES *1A4* (3km SW Rural) *43.37074, -4.56799* **Camping Colombres,** Ctra El Peral A Noriega Kml - 33590 Colombres (Ribadedeva) **985 412 244;** campingcolombres@hotmail.com; www.camping colombres.com

12 🛒 ♟ (htd) ⯑wo ⚕ ♿ 🛁 ∥ ⯑mp ⯑ ⛲ ⛱ ⓘ 🍴 🛟 ⛰ ⛱ 🐾
🐾 sand 3km

Turn off A8/E70 at J277. 3rd exit then 2nd exit fr rndabts. East on N634 then R opp petrol stn. Site to L 1km. Med, mkd, pt shd, terr, EHU (6A) €4.20; bbq (sep area); twin axles; 10% statics; Eng spkn; ccard acc; games area; CKE. *"Quiet, peaceful site in rural setting with fine mountain views; v helpful owners; nice pool; excel san facs; well kept & clean; immac, modern san facs; dogs free; gd walking."* **€31.50** 2017

COLUNGA *1A3* (12km E Coastal) *43.47160, -5.18434* **Camping Arenal de Moris,** Ctra de la Playa s/n, 33344 Caravia Alta (Asturias) **985-85 30 97;** camoris@des deasturias.com; www.arenaldemoris.com

♟ ⯑wo ⚕ 🛁 ∥ ⯑ ⛲ 🍴 ⓘ 🛟 ⛰ ⛱ 🐾 sand 500m

Fr E70/A8 exit junc 337 onto N632 to Caravia Alta, site clearly sp. Lge, mkd, pt shd, terr, EHU (5A) €4.50; 10% statics; adv bkg acc; ccard acc; tennis; CKE. *"Lovely views to mountains & sea; well-kept, well-run site; excel, clean san facs."* **€35.00, 23 Mar-15 Sep.** 2015

COMILLAS *1A4* (1km E Coastal) *43.38583, -4.28444* **Camping de Comillas,** 39520 Comillas (Cantabria) **942-72 00 74;** info@campingcomillas.com; www.campingcomillas.com

🛒 ♟ ⯑wo ⚕ 🛁 ∥ ⯑ ⛲ 🍴 ⓘ nr 🛟 ⛰ ⛱ 🐾 sand 800m

Site on coast rd CA131 at E end of Comillas by-pass. App fr Santillana or San Vicente avoids town cent & narr rds. Lge, hdg, mkd, pt shd, pt sl, EHU (5A) €3.85; TV; phone; adv bkg acc; CKE. *"Clean, ltd facs LS (hot water to shwrs only); vg site in gd position on coast with views; easy walk to interesting town; gd but rocky beach across rd; helpful owner; pitches inbetween 2 rds."* **€29.50, Holy Week & 1 Jun-30 Sep.** 2017

COMILLAS *1A4* (5km E Rural) *43.38328, -4.24689*
Camping El Helguero, 39527 Ruiloba (Cantabria)
942-72 21 24; reservas@campingelhelguero.com;
www.campingelhelguero.com

🐕 🏕(htd) 🆆 ⚓ 👥 ♿ 🚿 🗑 ⚟ 🆖 👣 🍽 ⑪ 🛒 💈 🏪 🏊 ⛵

🏖 sand 3km

**Exit A8 junc 249 dir Comillas onto CA135 to km 7.
Turn dir Ruiloba onto CA359 & thro Ruiloba & La
Iglesia, fork R uphill. Site sp.** Lge, mkd, pt shd, pt sl,
EHU (6A) €4.35; 80% statics; Eng spkn; ccard acc;
tennis 300m; bike hire; CKE. *"Attractive site, gd touring
cent; clean facs but some in need of refurb; helpful
staff; night security; sm pitches poss muddy in wet; v
gd."* **€30.00, 1 Apr-30 Sep.**   2016

CONIL DE LA FRONTERA *2H3* (3km NE Rural)
36.31061, -6.11276 **Camping Roche,** Carril de Pilahito
s/n, N340 Km 19.2, 11149 Conil de la Frontera (Cádiz)
956-44 22 16; info@campingroche.com; www.camping
roche.com

12 🐕 €3.75 🏕 🆆 ♿ 🗑 ⚟ 🆖 🦋 🍽 ⑪ 🛒 💈 🏪 🏊 ⛵

🏖 sand 2.5km

**Exit A48 junc 15 Conil Norte. Site sp on N340 dir
Algeciras.** Lge, mkd, hdstg, pt shd, EHU (10A) €5; red
long stay; TV; 20% statics; Eng spkn; adv bkg acc;
ccard acc; games area; games rm; tennis. *"V pleasant,
peaceful site in pine woods; all-weather pitches;
friendly, helpful staff; special monthly rates; clean san
facs; superb beaches nr; excel facs; lack of adequate
management."* **€30.00, W02.**   2019

CORDOBA *2F3* (2km NW Urban) *37.89977, -04.78725*
Camp Municipal El Brillante, Avda del Brillante 50,
14012 Córdoba 957-40 38 36; elbrillante@campings.
net; www.campingelbrillante.com

12 🐕 🏕 🆆 ⚓ 👥 ♿ 🚿 🗑 ⚟ 🆖 ⑪ 🛒 💈 🏪

**Fr N1V take Badajoz turning N432. Take rd
Córdoba N & foll sp to Parador. Turn R into Paseo
del Brilliante which leads into Avda del Brilliante;
white grilleblock wall surrounds site. Alt, foll sp
for 'Macdonalds Brilliante.' Site on R 400m beyond
Macdonalds on main rd going uphill away fr town
cent. Site poorly sp.** 3*, Med, mkd, hdstg, hdg, pt
shd, serviced pitches; EHU (6-10A) €5.50 (poss no
earth); gas; bbq; phone; bus adj; Eng spkn; CKE.
*"Well-run, busy, clean site; rec arr bef 1500; friendly
staff; easy walk/gd bus to town; quiet but traff noise
& barking dogs off site; poss cramped pitches - diff lge
o'fits; poss travellers LS (noisy); pool adj in ssn; gd for
wheelchair users; highly rec; easy walk to beautiful city;
pitches easier to access with motor mover; Aldi nrby."*
€32.50   2018

CORUNA, LA *1A2* (11km E Rural) *43.348194,
-8.335745* **Camping Los Manzanos,** Olieros, 15179
Santa Cruz (La Coruña) 981-61 48 25; informacion@
campinglosmanzanos.com; www.campinglos
manzanos.com

🐕 🏕 🆆 🚿 🗑 ⚟ 🆖 ⑪ 🛒 💈 🏪 🏊

**App La Coruña fr E on NVI, bef bdge take AC173 sp
Santa Cruz. Turn R at 2nd traff lts in Santa Cruz cent
(by petrol stn), foll sp, site on L. Fr AP9/E1 exit junc
3, turn R onto NVI dir Lugo. Take L fork dir Santa
Cruz/La Coruña, then foll sp Meiras. Site sp.**
3*, Lge, pt shd, EHU (6A) €4.80; gas; TV; 10% statics;
phone; Eng spkn; adv bkg req; ccard acc; CKE. *"Lovely
site; steep slope into site, level exit is avail; helpful
owners; hilly 1km walk to Santa Cruz for bus to La
Coruña; gd rest; conv for Santiago de Compostela;
excel."* **€32.00, 22 Mar-30 Sep.**   2018

COTORIOS *4F1* (2km E Rural) *38.05255, -2.83996*
Camping Llanos de Arance, Ctra Sierra de Cazorla/
Beas de Segura, Km 22, 23478 Cotoríos (Jaén) 953-71
31 39; arancel@inicia.es; www.llanosdearance.com

12 🏕 ⚓ ⚟ 🦋 🍽 ⑪ 🛒 💈 nr 🏪 🏊

**Fr Jaén-Albecete rd N322 turn E onto A1305 N of
Villanueva del Arzobispo sp El Tranco. In 26km to
El Tranco lake, turn R & cross over embankment.
Cotoríos at km stone 53, approx 25km on shore of
lake & Río Guadalaquivir. App fr Cazorla or Beas
definitely not rec if towing.** Lge, shd, EHU (5A) €3.21;
gas; bbq; 2% statics; phone; ccard acc; CKE. *"Lovely
site; excel walks & bird life, boar & wild life in Cazorla
National Park."* **€18.50**   2019

CREIXELL *3C3* (3km E Coastal) *41.16512, 1.45800*
Camping La Plana, Ctra N340, Km 1182, 43839
Creixell (Tarragona) 977-80 03 04; info@camping
laplana.com; www.campinglaplana.com

🐕 €1.10 🏕 🆆 🚿 🗑 ⚟ 🍽 ⑪ 🛒 💈 🏖 sand adj

Site sp at Creixell off N340. Med, hdstg, shd, EHU €6;
gas; Eng spkn; adv bkg acc. *"Vg, v clean site; v helpful &
pleasant owners."* **€23.25, 3 Mar-30 Sep.**   2017

CREIXELL *3C3 (3km SW Coastal) 41.14851, 1.41821*
Camping La Noria, Passeig Miramar 278, 43830
Torredembarra **977-64 04 53; info@camping-lano-ria.com; www.camping-lanoria.com**

♞ ♦ ♦ 🚳 🛒 🛁 🛗 ⚲ 🍴 ♱ 🍴 ⑪ 🛒 🏧 ⋔ ✎ ☂ adj

**Just outside Torredembarra, going N on the old
coastal N340 rd.** Lge, hdg, mkd, hdstg, pt shd,
EHU (6A) €5; bbq; twin axles; red long stay; TV;
60% statics; bus adj; Eng spkn; adv bkg rec; games
area; games rm. *"Adj to Els Muntanyans Nature
reserve, with walks & birdwatching; rail 1.6km; beach
has naturist area; some noise fr train line bet beach &
site; vg; conv for town; sep beach area for naturist."*
€41.00, 1 Apr-1 Oct. 2018

See advertisement

CREVILLENT *4F2 (8km S Rural) 38.17770, -0.80876*
Marjal Costa Blanca Eco Camping Resort, AP-7
Salida 730, 03330 Crevillent (Comunidad Valenciana)
**965-48 49 45; camping@marjalcostablanca.com;
www.marjalcostablanca.com**

12 ♞ €2.20 ♦ ♦ 🚳 🛒 🛁 🛗 ⚲ 🍴 ♱ 🍴 ⑪ 🛒 🏧 ⋔ ✎ ☂ (htd)

**Fr A7/E15 merge onto AP7 (sp Murcia), take exit
730; site sp fr exit.** 4*, V lge, hdstg, mkd, hdg, pt
shd, serviced pitches; EHU (16A) inc; gas; bbq; sw;
twin axles; TV; 30% statics; phone; Eng spkn; adv bkg
acc; ccard acc; tennis; bike hire; games area; games
rm; CCI. *"Superb site; car wash; hairdresser; doctor's
surgery; gd security; excel facs; wellness cent with
fitness studio, htd pools, saunas, physiotherapy & spa;
tour ops; new site, trees and hedges need time to
grow; lge pitches extra charge; excel, immac san facs;
nr to Elfondo birdwatching; v helpful staff."* **€47.50,
W05.** 2016

CUBILLAS DE SANTA MARTA *1C4 (4km S Rural)
41.80511, -4.58776* **Camping Cubillas,** Ctra N620,
Km 102, 47290 Cubillas de Santa Marta (Valladolid)
**983-58 50 02 or 983-58 51 74; info@campingcubillas.
com; www.campingcubillas.com**

12 ♞ €2 ♦ ♦ 🚳 🛁 🛗 ⚲ 🍴 nr ⑪ 🛒 🏧 ⋔ ✎ 🏊

**A-62 Exit 102 Cubillas de Santa Marta. Fr N foll slip
rd and cross rd to Cubillas de Santa Marta the site is
on the R in 200m. Fr S take exit 102 take 5th exit off
rndabt, cross over m'way and then 1st L. Site on R
in 200m.** Lge, hdg, mkd, unshd, pt sl, EHU (6-10A) inc;
gas; bbq; red long stay; 50% statics; phone; ccard acc;
site clsd 18 Dec-10 Jan; CKE. *"Ltd space for tourers;
conv visit Palencia & Valladolid; rd & m'way, rlwy &
disco noise at w/end until v late; v ltd facs LS; NH only;
2.5h fr Santander; adequate o'night stop."* **€26.00**
2019

CUDILLERO *1A3 (2.7km SE Rural) 43.55416, -6.12944*
Camping Cudillero, Ctra Playa de Aguilar, Aronces,
33150 El Pito (Asturias) **985-59 06 63; info@
campingcudillero.com; www.campingcudillero.com**

♞ €2.15 ♦ ♦ 🚳 🛁 🛗 ⚲ 🦋 🍴 ♱ 🍴 🛒 🏧 ⋔ ✎ 🏊 (htd)
☂ sand 1.2km

**Exit N632 (E70) sp El Pito. Turn L at rndabt sp
Cudillero & in 300m at end of wall turn R at site sp,
cont for 1km, site on L. Do not app thro Cudillero;
rds v narr & steep; much traff.** Med, mkd, hdg, pt
shd, EHU (6A) €4.50; gas; TV; phone; bus 1km; adv
bkg acc; games area; CKE. *"Excel, well-maintained,
well laid-out site; some generous pitches; gd san
facs; stccp walk to beach & vill, v helpful staff; excel
facs; vill worth a visit, parking on quay but narr rds;
diff to get to vill, very steep; sm crowded pitches."*
€18.00, 18 Mar-27 Mar & 30 Apr-15 Sep. 2016

SPAIN

CUDILLERO *1A3* (2km S Rural) *43.55555, -6.13777*
Camping L'Amuravela, El Pito, 33150 Cudillero
(Asturias) **985-59 09 95; camping@lamuravela.com;**
www.lamuravela.com

€1 ♛♛ wo ♨ ♫ msp ⛱ ⛱ ♨ ♨ ♨ 🏊 ⚓ sand 2km

Exit N632 (E70) sp El Pito. Turn L at rndabt sp
Cudillero & in approx 1km turn R at site sp. Do not
app thro Cudillero; rds v narr & steep; much traff.
Med, mkd, unshd, pt sl, EHU €4.10; gas; 50% statics;
ccard acc. *"Pleasant, well-maintained site; gd clean facs;*
hillside walks into Cudillero, attractive fishing vill with
gd fish rests; red facs LS & poss only open w/ends,
surroundings excel."
€22.00, Holy Week & 1 Jun-30 Sep. 2017

DEBA *3A1* (5.7km W Coastal) *43.30577, -2.37789*
Camping Aitzeta, Ctra Deba-Guernica, Km. 3.5, C6212,
20930 Mutriku (Guipúzkoa) **943-60 33 56; aitzeta@**
hotmail.com; www.campingseuskadi.com/aitzeta

♛ ♛♛ wo ♨ ♨ ♨ ♫ ⛱ ⛱ ⛱ nr ♨ ⛰ 🏊 sand 1km

On N634 San Sebastián-Bilbao rd thro Deba & on
o'skts turn R over rv sp Mutriku. Site on L after 3km
on narr & winding rd up sh steep climb. Med, mkd,
pt shd, terr, EHU (4A) €3; gas; phone; bus 500m; CKE.
"Easy reach of Bilbao ferry; sea views; gd, well-run,
clean site; not suitable lge o'fits; ltd pitches for tourers;
helpful staff; walk to town; basic facs but gd NH."
€20.00, 1 May-31 Oct. 2016

DELTEBRE *3D2* (8km E Coastal) *40.72041, 0.84849*
Camping L'Aube, Afores s/n, 43580 Deltebre
(Tarragona) **977-26 70 66; campinglaube@hotmail.**
com; www.campinglaube.com

♛♛ wo ♨ ♨ ♨ ♫ msp ⛱ ♨ ♨ 🏊 ⚓ sand adj

Exit AP7 junc 40 or 41 onto N340 dir Deltebre.
Fr Deltebre foll T340 sp Riumar for 8km. At info
kiosk branch R, site sp 1km on R. 2*, Lge, hdstg, mkd,
pt shd, EHU (3-10A) €2.80-5; red long stay;
40% statics; phone; CKE. *"At edge of Ebro Delta*
National Park; excel birdwatching; ltd facs in winter;
sm pitches; pricey; interesting local rest."
€26.00, 1 Mar-31 Oct. 2018

DENIA *4E2* (3.5km SE Coastal) *38.82968, 0.14767*
Camping Los Pinos, Ctra Dénia-Les Rotes, Km 3, Les
Rotes, 03700 Dénia (Alicante) **965-78 26 98; lospinos-**
denia@gmail.com; www.lospinosdenia.com

12 ♛ €3 ♛♛ wo ♨ ♨ ♫ ⛱ ♨ nr ⛰ ⚓ shgl adj

Fr N332 foll sp to Dénia in dir of coast. Turn R sp
Les Rotes/Jávea, then L twrds Les Rotes. Foll site
sp turn L into narr access rd poss diff lge o'fits.
2*, Med, mkd, pt shd, EHU (6-10A) €3.20; gas; bbq;
cooking facs; red long stay; TV; 25% statics; phone;
bus 100m; Eng spkn; adv bkg acc; ccard acc; CKE.
"Friendly, well-run, clean, tidy site but san facs tired
(Mar 09); excel value; access some pitches poss diff due
trees - not suitable lge o'fits or m'vans; many long-stay
winter residents; cycle path into Dénia; social rm with
log fire; naturist beach 1km, private but rocky shore."
€26.40 2019

DENIA *4E2* (7km W Coastal) *38.87264, -0.02031*
Camping Los Patos, Playa de Les Deveses, Vergel,
03700 Dénia (Alicante) **965-75 52 93; info@camping-**
lospatos.com; www.camping-lospatos.com

12 ♛ ♛♛ (htd) wo ♨ ♨ ♫ msp ✿ ⛱ ⛱ ⛰ ♨ ♨ ♨ ⛰ ⚓ sand adj

Exit A7/E15 junc 61 onto N332. Foll site sp.
Med, hdg, mkd, pt shd, EHU (6A); gas; bbq; twin axles;
red long stay; Eng spkn; adv bkg acc; golf 1km. *"Gd*
site." **€14.50** 2015

DOS HERMANAS *2G3* (3km SW Urban) *37.27731,*
-5.93722 **Camping Villsom**, Ctra Sevilla/Cádiz A4,
Km 554.8, 41700 Dos Hermanas (Sevilla) **954-72 08 28;**
campingvillsom@hotmail.com; campingvillsom.
blogspot.co.uk

♛ ♛♛ wo ♨ ♨ ♨ ♫ ⛱ ⛱ ♨ ♨ ⛰ 🏊

On main Seville-Cádiz NIV rd travelling fr Seville
take exit at km. 555 sp Dos Hermanos-Isla Menor.
At the rndabt turn R (SE-3205 Isla Menor) to site
80 m. on R. 3*, Lge, hdstg, mkd, hdstg, pt shd, pt sl,
EHU (8A) inc (poss no earth); gas; bus to Seville 300m
(over bdge & rndabt); Eng spkn; adv bkg acc; ccard
acc; CKE. *"Adv bkg rec Holy Week; helpful staff; clean,*
tidy, well-run site; vg, san facs; ltd LS; height barrier
at Carrefour hypmkt - ent via deliveries; no twin axles;
wifi only in office & bar area; pitches long but narr, no
rm for awnings; dusty, rough, tight turns; c'vans parked
too cls." **€29.00, 10 Jan-23 Dec.** 2018

EL BARRACO *1D4* (6.6km SW Rural) *40.428630,*
-4.616408 **Camping Pantano del Burguillo**, AV-902
Km 16 400, El Barraco **678-48 20 69; info@pantano**
delburguillo.com; www.pantanodelburguillo.com

♛ €2 ♛♛ wo ♨ ♨ ♫ ✿ ⛱ ♨

31km S of Avila on N403, take AV902 W for 5km.
Site on L beside reservoir. Sm, hdstg, mkd, pt shd,
EHU inc; bbq (sep area); ccard acc. *"Mainly residential*
c'vans, but staff very welcoming; as bit scruffy; open hg
ssn & w'ends only; fair." **€27.00, 22 Jun-10 Sep.** 2018

ELCHE *4F2* (10km SW Urban) *38.24055, -0.81194*
Camping Las Palmeras, Partida Deula 75, 03330
Crevillent (Alicante) **966-68 06 30; laspalmeras@**
laspalmeras-sl.com; www.laspalmeras-sl.com

12 ♛ ♛♛ wo ♨ ♨ ♫ ⛱ ♨ ♨ ♨ nr 🏊 ⚓

Exit A7 junc 726/77 onto N340 to Crevillent. Immed
bef traff lts take slip rd into rest parking/service area.
Site on R, access rd down side of rest. Med, mkd, hdstg,
pt shd, EHU (6A) inc; 10% statics; ccard acc; CKE.
"Useful NH; report to recep in hotel; helpful staff; gd
cent for touring Murcia; dogs free; gd rest in hotel; gd,
modern san facs; excel." **€28.00** 2019

ESCALA, L' *3B3* (3km S Coastal) *42.10512, 3.15843*
Camping Neus, Cala Montgó, 17130 L'Escala (Gerona)
638-65 27 12; info@campingneus.com; www.camping
neus.com

🛉 €2 ♗ ⊞ ⚠ ☗ ⊘ ✦ ☸ 🦋 ☂ ⊤ ⊿ ☲ ⚒ ⬿ ⚲ ⛴

⛵ sand 850m

**Exit AP7 junc 5 twd L'Escala then turn R twd Cala
Montgó & foll sp.** Med, mkd, shd, pt sl, terr, EHU (6A)
€4; gas; red long stay; TV; 15% statics; phone; bus
500m; Eng spkn; adv bkg acc; ccard acc; fishing; tennis;
car wash; CKE. *"Pleasant, clean site in pine forest; gd
san facs; lge pitches; vg."* **€48.00, 14 May-18 Sep.**
2016

ESCORIAL, EL *1D4* (6km NE Rural) *40.62630, -4.09970*
Camping-Caravaning El Escorial, Ctra Guadarrama a
El Escorial, Km 3.5, 28280 El Escorial (Madrid) **918 90
24 12 or 02 01 49 00**; info@campingelescorial.com;
www.campingelescorial.com

⒓ 🛉 ♗ (htd) ⊞ ⚠ ☗ ⚸ ⊘ ✦ ☸ ⊤ ⊕ ⊿ ☲ ⚒ ⚲ ⛴

**Exit AP6 NW of Madrid junc 47 El Escorial/
Guadarrama, onto M505 & foll sp to El Escorial,
site on L at km stone 3,500 - long o'fits rec cont to
rndabt (1km) to turn & app site on R.** V lge, hdstg,
mkd, pt shd, EHU (5A) inc (long cable rec); gas; bbq;
TV; 80% statics; Eng spkn; adv bkg acc; ccard acc;
tennis; games rm; horseriding 7km. *"Excel, busy site;
mountain views; o'fits over 8m must reserve lge pitch
with elec, water & drainage; helpful staff; clean facs;
gd security; sm pitches poss diff due trees; o'head
canopies poss diff for tall o'fits; facs ltd LS; trains &
buses to Madrid nr; Valle de Los Caídos & Palace at El
Escorial well worth visit; cash machine; easy parking
in town for m'vans if go in early; mkt Wed; stunning
scenery, nesting storks; well stocked shop; v well run;
20min walk to bus stop for El Escorial or Madrid; rec; gd
for families; gd pool."* **€39.00** **2017**

SPAIN

ESPOT *3B2 (0.9km SE Rural) 42 57223, 1.09677* **Camping Sol I Neu,** Ctra Sant Maurici s/n, 25597 Espot (Lleida) **973-62 40 01**; camping@solineu.com; www.solineu.com

🛉 👫 wo ♨ ☼ ☐ ⊘ ❦ ⅋ 🐾 🍸 🏊 /🛂 ⚓ 👙

N fr Sort on C13 turn L to Espot on rd LV5004, site on L in approx 6.5km by rvside. 2*, Med, mkd, pt shd, EHU (6-10A) €5.80; gas; TV; ccard acc; CKE. *"Excel facs; beautiful site nr National Park (Landrover taxis avail - no private vehicles allowed in Park); suitable sm o'fits only; poss unrel opening dates; 10 mins walk to vill, many bars & rest."* €25.60, 1 Jul-31 Aug.   **2015**

ESTARTIT, L' *3B3 (1km S Coastal) 42.04972, 3.18416* **Camping El Molino,** Camino del Ter, 17258 L'Estartit (Gerona) **972-75 06 29**

👫 🛉 ♨ ☐ ⊘ mbf ⅋ 🍸 ⑪ 🏊 /🛂 ⚓ 👙 sand 1km

Fr N11 junc 5, take rd to L'Escala. Foll sp to Torroella de Montgri, then L'Estartit. Ent town & foll sp, site on rd GI 641. V lge, hdg, pt shd, pt sl, EHU (6A) €3.60; gas; bus 1km; adv bkg rec; games rm. *"Site in 2 parts - 1 in shd, 1 at beach unshd; gd facs; quiet location outside busy town."* €28.00, 1 Apr-30 Sep.   **2018**

See advertisement below

ESTARTIT, L' *3B3 (2km S Coastal) 42.04250, 3.18333* **Camping Les Medes,** Paratge Camp de l'Arbre s/n, 17258 L'Estartit (Gerona) **972-75 18 05**; info@campinglesmedes.com; www.campingles-medes.com

12 🐾 €2.60 👫🛉 (htd) wo ♨ ☼ ⅋ ☐ ⊘ ❦ mbf 🐾 ⅋ 🍸 ⑪ 👙 🛂 /🏊 🏊 (htd, indoor) ☀ sand 800m

Fr Torroella foll sp to L'Estartit. In vill turn R at town name sp (sp Urb Estartit Oeste), foll rd for 1.5km, turn R, site well sp. Lge, mkd, shd, serviced pitches; EHU (6A) €4.60; gas; red long stay; TV; 7% statics; phone; Eng spkn; adv bkg acc; sauna; games area; tennis; horseriding 400m; car wash; games rm; watersports; solarium; bike hire; CKE. *"Excel, popular, family-run & well organised site; helpful, friendly staff; gd clean facs & constant hot water; gd for children; no dogs high ssn; no twin axle vans high ssn - by arrangement LS; conv National Park; well mkd foot & cycle paths; ACSI acc."* €47.00   **2017**

See advertisement above

ESTEPAR *1B4* (2km NE Rural) *42.29233, -3.85097*
Quinta de cavia, A62, km 17, 09196 Cavia, Burgos
947-41 20 78; reservas@quintadecavia.es

🕧 🐕 🛉🏃 �📶 🚿 ⁄ 🍽 ⅊ ⊕ ⟁

Site 15km SW of Burgos on N side of A62/E80,
adj Hotel Rio Cabia. Ent via Campsa petrol stn,
W'bound exit 17, E'bound exit 16, cross over &
re-join m'way. Ignore camp sp at exit 18 (1-way).
Site at 17km stone. 2*, Med, pt shd, EHU (6A) inc;
10% statics; ccard acc; CKE. *"Friendly, helpful owner;
gd rest; conv for m'way for Portugal but poorly sp fr
W; poss v muddy in winter; NH only; food in rest vg and
cheap; can get to Bilbao ferry in morn if ferry is mid-aft;
elec security gate; lit at night; gd NH; new san facs
(2018); site 2723 feet abv sea level, cold at night; gem
of a site; site being improved (2019)."* **€20.00** **2019**

ESTEPONA *2H3* (7km E Coastal) *36.45436, -5.08105*
Camping Parque Tropical, Ctra N340, Km 162, 29680
Estepona (Málaga) **952-79 36 18; parquetropical
camping@hotmail.com; www.campingparque
tropical.com**

🕧 🐕 🚐₂ 🛉🏃 ⌷ 🚿 🕹 ⁄ 🍽 ⅊ ⊕🚱🛒 ⟁ 🏊 (covrd, htd)

🎣 shgl 1km

On N side of N340 at km 162, 200m off main rd.
2*, Med, mkd, hdg, pt shd, terr, serviced pitches; EHU
(10A) €4; gas; red long stay; 10% statics; phone; bus
400m; Eng spkn; adv bkg acc; golf nr; horseriding nr;
CKE. *"Tropical plants thro out; clean facs; tropical
paradise swimming pool; wildlife park 1km; helpful
owners."* **€27.00** **2017**

"I need an on-site restaurant"

We do our best to make sure site information
is correct, but it is always best to check any
must-have facilities are still available or will
be open during your visit.

ETXARRI ARANATZ *3B1* (2km N Rural) *42.91255,
-2.07919* **Camping Etxarri,** Parase Dambolintxulo,
31820 Etxarri-Aranatz (Navarra) **948-46 05 37; info@
campingetxarri.com; www.campingetxarri.com**

🕧 🚐₂.₁₅ 🛉🏃 �📶 ⌷ 🚿 ⁄ 🕹 ⅊ ⊕ 🛒 ⟁ 🏄 🏊

Fr N exit A15 at junc 112 to join A10 W dir Vitoria/
Gasteiz. Exit at junc 19 onto NA120; go thro Etxarri
vill, turn L & cross bdge, then take rd over rlwy. Turn
L, site sp. Med, hdg, pt shd, EHU (6A) €5.50; gas; bbq;
90% statics; phone; Eng spkn; ccard acc; games area;
archery; cycling; horseriding; CKE. *"Gd, wooded site;
gd walks; interesting area; helpful owner; conv NH to/
fr Pyrenees; youth hostel & resident workers on site;
san facs gd; various pitch sizes & shapes, some diff lge
o'fits; NH only."* **€32.00, 1 Mar-1 Nov.** **2019**

FIGUERES *3B3* (8km NE Rural) *42.33902, 3.06758*
Camping Vell Empordà, Ctra Roses-La Jonquera s/n,
17780 Garriguella (Gerona) **972-53 02 00 or
972-57 06 31 (LS); vellemporda@vellemporda.com;
www.vellemporda.com**

🕇€4.50 🛉🏃 (htd) �📶 ⌷ 🚿 🕹 🍽 ⁄ 🗺 🦋 🕹 ⅊ ⊕🚱🛒 ⟁
⁄ 🏊 🏖

On A7/E11 exit junc 3 onto N260 NE dir Llançà. Nr
km 26 marker, turn R sp Garriguella, then L at T-junc
N twd Garriguella. Site on R shortly bef vill.
Lge, hdstg, mkd, hdg, shd, terr, EHU (6-10A) inc; gas;
bbq; red long stay; TV; 20% statics; phone; Eng spkn;
adv bkg acc; ccard acc; games rm; games area; CKE.
*"Conv N Costa Brava away fr cr beaches & sites; 20
mins to sea at Llançà; o'hanging trees poss diff high
vehicles; excel."* **€40.00, 1 Feb-15 Dec.** **2018**

FIGUERUELA DE ARRIBA *1B3* (2km E Rural)
41.86563, -6.41937 **Camping Sierra de la Culebra,**
Carretera Riomanzanas, S/N 49520 Figueruela de
Arriba **980-68 30 20 or 630-66 13 29 (mob); info@
campingsierradelaculebra.com; www.campingsierra
delaculebra.com**

🕇 🛉🏃 �📶 ⌷ 🚿 🕹 ⁄ 🦋 🕹 ⅊ ⊕ 🛒 ⟁ 🏊 🏖

Fr S: At Alcanices on the N122 (E82) Zamora-
Braganca rd, turn N onto ZA9112. In 21km at
Mahide turn L. Site sp on L in 3km. Fr N: Exit A52 at
junc 49 onto N631 dir Zamora. In 4km turn R onto
ZA912. In 28km at Mahide turn R. Site sp. Med, pt
shd, EHU (6A) €4.10; bbq; twin axles; TV; 10% statics;
Eng spkn; adv bkg acc; games area. *"Fam owned;
many interesting old vill; gd bird-watching; tennis;
gd walking; gd for Braganca in Portugal; excel."*
€26.60, 5 Mar-2 Nov. **2016**

FORTUNA *4F1* (3km N Rural) *38.20562, -1.10712*
Camping Fuente, Camino de la Bocamina s/n, 30709
Baños de Fortuna (Murcia) **968-68 50 17; info@
campingfuente.com; www.campingfuente.com**

🕧 🕇€1.10 🛉🏃 (htd) �📶 ⌷ 🕹 🍽 ⁄ 🕹 ⅊ ⊕🚱🛒 ⟁ 🏊 (htd)

Fr Murcia on A7/E15 turn L onto C3223 sp Fortuna.
After 19km turn onto A21 & foll sp Baños de
Fortuna, then sp 'Complejo Hotelero La Fuente'.
Avoid towing thro vill, if poss. Med, mkd, hdstg,
unshd, pt sl, EHU (10-16A) €2.20 or metered; poss rev
pol; gas; bbq; red long stay; 10% statics; phone; bus
200m; adv bkg acc; ccard acc; CKE. *"Gd san facs; excel
pool & rest; secure o'flow parking area; many long-stay
winter visitors - adv bkg rec; private san facs some
pitches; ltd recep hrs LS; spa; jacuzzi; poss sulphurous
smell fr thermal baths."* **€19.00** **2015**

FOZ *1A2* (11km E Coastal) *43.56236, -7.20761*
Camping Poblado Gaivota, Playa de Barreiros, 27790
Barreiros Lugo **982-12 44 51; www.campingpoblado
gaivota.com**

🛉🏃 ⁄ 📶 ⌷ 🕹 ⁄ 🍽 🕹 ⅊ ⊕🚱🛒 ⟁ ⁄ 🎣 opp

Junc 516 on A8, on to N634 to Barreiros. Foll sp to
the R in Barreiros. Rd winds down to coast for 2km.
Site on L, parallel with sea. Sm, hdg, shd, EHU (6A);
bbq; Eng spkn. *"Excel."* **€30.00, 21 Mar-15 Oct.** **2016**

FRANCA, LA *1A4* (1km NW Coastal) *43.39250, -4.57722* **Camping Las Hortensias,** Ctra N634, Km 286, 33590 Colombres/Ribadedeva (Asturias) **985-41 24 42; lashortensias@campinglashortensias.com; www.campinglashortensias.com**

🛏 €5 ♦♦ WD ♨ ♨ ♨ ⚏ ⅄ nr ⓗ nr 🔋 🏛 ⵣ sand adj

Fr N634 on leaving vill of La Franca, at km286 foll sp 'Playa de la Franca' & cont past 1st site & thro car park to end of rd. Med, mkd, pt shd, pt sl, terr, EHU (6-10A) €5; gas; phone; bus 800m; Eng spkn; adv bkg acc; ccard acc; bike hire; tennis; CKE. *"Beautiful location nr scenic beach; sea views fr top terr pitches; vg."* **€28.50, 5 Jun-30 Sep.** **2017**

"Satellite navigation makes touring much easier"

Remember most sat navs don't know if you're towing or in a larger vehicle – always use yours alongside maps and site directions.

FUENTE DE PIEDRA *2G4* (0.7km S Rural) *37.12905, -4.73315* **Camping Fuente de Pedra,** Calle Campillos 88-90, 29520 Fuente de Piedra (Málaga) **952-73 52 94; info@campingfuentedepiedra.com; www.camping-rural.com**

12 🐕 €3 ♦♦ ♨ ♨ ⚏ ⅄ ⅄ ⓗ ♨ 🔋 🏛 ⵣ

Turn off A92 at km 132 sp Fuente de Piedra. Sp fr vill cent. Or to avoid town turn N fr A384 just W of turn for Bobadilla Estación, sp Sierra de Yeguas. In 2km turn R into nature reserve, cont for approx 3km, site on L at end of town. 2*, Sm, mkd, hdstg, pt shd, pt sl, terr, EHU (10A) €5; gas; bbq; red long stay; 25% statics; phone; Eng spkn; ccard acc; CKE. *"Mostly sm, narr pitches, but some avail for o'fits up to 7m; gd rest; san facs dated & poss stretched; poss noise fr adj public pool; adj lge lake with flamingoes (visible but access is 4.8km away); gd."* **€26.00** **2017**

FUENTEHERIDOS *2F3* (0.6km SW Rural) *37.9050, -6.6742* **Camping El Madroñal,** Ctra Fuenteheridos-Castaño del Robledo, Km 0.6, 21292 Fuenteheridos (Huelva) **959-50 12 01; castillo@campingel madronal.com; www.campingelmadronal.com**

12 🐕 ♦♦ WD ♨ ⚏ ⅄ 🦋 ⅄ 🔋 ⵣ

Fr Zafra S on N435n turn L onto N433 sp Aracena, ignore first R to Fuenteheridos vill, camp sp R at next x-rd 500m on R. At rndabt take 2nd exit. Avoid Fuenteheridos vill - narr rds. 2*, Med, mkd, pt shd, pt sl, EHU €3.20; gas; bbq; 80% statics; phone; bus 1km; horseriding; car wash; bike hire; CKE. *"Tranquil site in National Park of Sierra de Aracena; pitches among chestnut trees - poss diff lge o'fits or m'vans & poss sl & uneven; o'hanging trees on site rds; scruffy, pitches not clearly mkd; beautiful vill 1km away, worth a visit."* **€13.00** **2019**

GALLARDOS, LOS *4G1* (4km N Rural) *37.18448, -1.92408* **Camping Los Gallardos,** 04280 Los Gallardos (Almería) **950-52 83 24; reception@ campinglosgallardos.com; www.campinglos gallardos.com**

12 🐕 €2.25 ♦♦ WD ♨ ♨ ♨ ⚏ ⅄ MSP ⅄ ⓗ ♨ 🔋 ⵣ

Fr N leave A7/E15 at junc 525; foll sp to Los Gallardos; take 1st R after approx 800m pass under a'route; turn L into site ent. Med, mkd, hdstg, pt shd, serviced pitches; EHU (10A) €3; gas; red long stay; 40% statics; adv bkg acc; ccard acc; CKE. *"British owned; 90% British clientele LS; gd social atmosphere; sep drinking water supply nr recep; prone to flooding wet weather; 2 grass bowling greens; facs tired; poss cr in winter; friendly staff."* **€23.50** **2017**

GANDIA *4E2* (4km NE Coastal) *38.98613, -0.16352* **Camping L'Alqueria,** Avda del Grau s/n; 46730 Grao de Gandía (València) **962-84 04 70; lalqueria@ lalqueria.com; www.lalqueria.com**

12 🐕 €1.90 ♦♦ (htd) WD ♨ ♨ ⚏ ⅄ MSP 🦋 ⅄ ⅄ ⓗ nr 🔋 🏛 ⚡ ⵣ (covrd, htd) ⵣ sand 1km

Fr N on A7/AP7 exit 60 onto N332 dir Grao de Gandía. Site sp on rd bet Gandía & seafront. Fr S exit junc 61 & foll sp to beaches. 3*, Lge, hdstg, mkd, pt shd, EHU (10A) €5.94; gas; red long stay; 30% statics; phone; bus; adv bkg acc; ccard acc; games area; jacuzzi; bike hire; CKE. *"Pleasant site; helpful, friendly family owners; lovely pool; easy walk to town & stn; excel beach nrby; bus & train to Valencia; shop & snacks not avail in Jul; gd biking; no dogs over 10kg; m'van friendly; site scruffy but san facs gd; gd location; rec; gd location bet old town & beach; gd cycling & walking."* **€42.00** **2019**

GARGANTILLA DEL LOZOYA *1C4* (2km SW Rural) *40.9503, -3.7294* **Camping Monte Holiday,** Ctra C604, Km 8.8, 28739 Gargantilla del Lozoya (Madrid) **918-69 52 78; monteholiday@monteholiday.com; www.monteholiday.com**

12 ♦♦ WD ♨ ♨ ⚏ ⅄ MSP 🦋 ⅄ ⓗ ⵣ

Fr N on A1/E5 Burgos-Madrid rd turn R on M604 at km stone 69 sp Rascafría; in 8km turn R immed after rlwy bdge & then L up track in 300m, foll site sp. Do not ent vill. Lge, pt shd, pt sl, terr, EHU (7A) €4.30 (poss rev pol); 80% statics; phone; bus 500m; Eng spkn; adv bkg acc; ccard acc; CKE. *"Interesting, friendly site; vg san facs; gd views; easy to find; some facs clsd LS; lovely area but site isolated in winter & poss heavy snow; conv NH fr m'way & for Madrid & Segovia; excel wooded site; v rural but well worth the sh drive fr the N1 E5; clean; lovely surroundings."* **€35.40, E04.** **2019**

GIJON *1A3* (9.5km NW Coastal) *43.58343, -5.75713* **Camping Perlora,** Ctra Candás, Km 12, Perán, 33491 Candás (Asturias) **985-87 00 48; recepcion@ campingperlora.com; www.campingperlora.com**

🐎 ♨ wc ♨ ☕ ⚙ 🚿 ⛱ 🍴 Ⓗ 🛒 ⚠ ♨ sand 1km

Exit A8 dir Candás; in 9km at rndabt turn R sp Perlora (AS118). At sea turn L sp Candás, site on R. Avoid Sat mkt day. 2*, Med, mkd, unshd, pt sl, terr, serviced pitches; EHU (10A) €3.50; gas; red long stay; 80% statics; phone; bus adj; Eng spkn; ccard acc; watersports; fishing; tennis. *"Excel; helpful staff; attractive, well-kept site on dramatic headland o'looking Candas Bay; ltd space for tourers; easy walk to Candás; gem of a site; train (5 mins); excel fish rests; no mob signal; facs gd & clean, ltd LS; rec."* **€27.50, 18 Jan-10 Dec.** 2019

GORLIZ *1A4* (1km N Coastal) *43.41782, -2.93626* **Camping Arrien,** Uresarantze Bidea, 48630 Gorliz (Bizkaia) **946-77 19 11; recepcion@campinggorliz.com** or **campingarrien@gmail.com; www.camping gorliz.com**

🐎 €1 ♨ wc ☕ ⚙ 🚿 🍴 Ⓗ 🛒 ⚠ ♨ sand 700m

Fr Bilbao foll m'way to Getxo, then 637/634 thro Sopelana & Plentzia to Gorliz. In Gorliz turn L at 1st rndabt, foll sps for site, pass TO on R, then R at next rndabt, strt over next, site on L adj sports cent/ running track. Not sp locally. Lge, pt shd, pt sl, EHU (6A) inc; gas; bbq; red long stay; 60% statics; phone; bus 150m; Eng spkn; ccard acc; CKE. *"Useful base for Bilbao & ferry (approx 1hr); bus to Plentzia every 20 mins, fr there can get metro to Bilbao; friendly, helpful staff; poss shortage of hot water; very cramped; no mkd pitches."* **€36.00, 1 Mar-31 Oct.** 2016

"There aren't many sites open at this time of year"

If you're travelling outside peak season remember to call ahead to check site opening dates – even if the entry says 'open all year'.

GRANADA *2G4* (10km SE Urban) *37.12444, -3.58611* **Camping Reina Isabel,** Calle de Laurel de la Reina, 18140 La Zubia (Granada) **958-59 00 41; info@ campingreinaisabel.com; www.campingreina isabel.es**

12 🐎 ♨ (htd) wc ☕ ⚙ 🚿 ♨ MSP 🦋 🍴 🛒 ⚠ ☕ 🍴

Exit A44 nr Granada at junc sp Ronda Sur, dir Sierra Nevada, Alhambra, then exit 2 sp La Zubia. Foll site sp approx 1.2km on R; narr ent set back fr rd. 2*, Med, hdstg, hdg, pt shd, EHU (6A) poss rev pol €4.20; gas; red long stay; TV; phone; bus; Eng spkn; adv bkg rec; ccard acc; CKE. *"Well-run, busy site; poss shwrs v hot/cold - warn children; ltd touring pitches & sm; poss student groups; conv Alhambra (order tickets at site); shwr block not htd; tight site; elec unrel."* **€29.00** 2017

GUARDAMAR DEL SEGURA *4F2* (4km N Rural/ Coastal) *38.10916, -0.65472* **Camping Marjal,** Ctra N332, Km 73.4, 03140 Guardamar del Segura (Alicante) **965-48 49 45; camping@marjal.com; www.campingmarjal.com**

12 🐎 €2.20 ♨ wc ☕ ⚙ ☕ 🚿 ♨ 🦋 🍴 Ⓗ 🛒 ⚠ 🏊 (covrd, htd) ♨ sand 1km

Fr N exit A7 junc 72 sp Aeropuerto/Santa Pola; in 5km turn R onto N332 sp Santa Pola/Cartagena, U-turn at km 73.4, site sp on R at km 73.5. Fr S exit AP7 at junc 740 onto CV91 twd Guardamar. In 9km join N332 twd Alicante, site on R at next rndabt. 5*, Lge, hdstg, mkd, hdg, pt shd, serviced pitches; EHU (16A) €3 or metered; gas; bbq; red long stay; TV; 50% statics; phone; Eng spkn; adv bkg rec; ccard acc; bike hire; tennis; sauna; CKE. *"Fantastic facs; friendly, helpful staff; excel family entmnt & activities; recep 0800-2300; sports cent; tropical waterpark; excel; well sign-posted; lge shwr cubicles; highly rec."* **€67.00** 2018

HARO *1B4* (0.5km N Urban) *42.57824, -2.85421* **Camping de Haro,** Avda Miranda 1, 26200 Haro (La Rioja) **941-31 27 37; campingdeharo@fer.es; www.campingdeharo.com**

🐎 €3 ♨ (htd) wc ☕ ⚙ 🚿 ♨ MSP 🍴 🛒 ⚠ 🏊 (htd)

Fr N or S on N124 take exit sp A68 Vitoria/Logrono & Haro. In 500m at rndabt take 1st exit, under rlwy bdge, cont to site on R immed bef rv bdge. Fr AP68 exit junc 9 to town; at 2nd rndabt turn L onto LR111 (sp Logroño). Immed after rv bdge turn sharp L & foll site sp. Avoid cont into town cent. 2*, Med, hdg, mkd, pt shd, EHU (6A) inc; gas; bbq; 70% statics; phone; bus 800m; Eng spkn; adv bkg acc; ccard acc; site clsd 9 Dec-13 Jan; car wash; CKE. *"Clean, tidy, well run, lovely site - peaceful LS; friendly owner; some sm pitches & diff turns; excel facs; statics busy at w/ends; conv Rioja 'bodegas' & Bilbao & Santander ferries; recep clsd 1300-1500 no entry then due to security barrier; excel & conv NH for Santander/Bilbao; lge o'night area with electric; big, busy, vg site; easy walk to lovely town; san facs constantly cleaned!"* **€30.00, 27 Jan-10 Dec, E02.** 2017

HARO *1B4* (10km SW Rural) *42.53017, -2.92173* **Camping De La Rioja,** Ctra de Haro/Santo Domingo de la Calzada, Km 8.5, 26240 Castañares de la Rioja (La Rioja) **941-30 01 74; info@campingdelarioja.com**

🐎 ♨ (htd) wc ☕ ⚙ ♨ 🍴 Ⓗ 🛒 ♨ 🏊

Exit AP68 junc 9, take rd twd Santo Domingo de la Calzada. Foll by-pass round Casalarreina, site on R nr rvside just past vill on rd LR111. 3*, Lge, hdg, pt shd, EHU (4A) €3.90 (poss rev pol); gas; 90% statics; bus adj; adv bkg acc; ccard acc; bike hire; tennis; clsd 10 Dec-8 Jan; site clsd 9 Dec-11 Jan. *"Fair site but fairly isolated; basic san facs but clean; ltd facs in winter; sm pitches; conv for Rioja wine cents; Bilbao ferry."* **€36.00, 10 Jan-10 Dec.** 2016

SPAIN

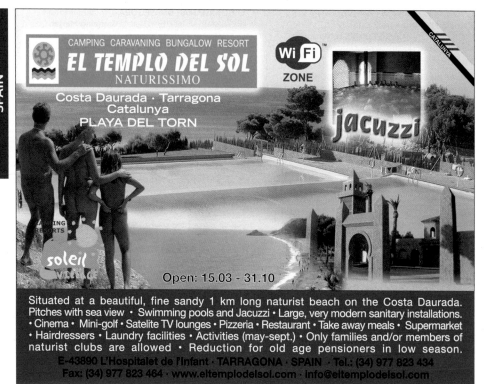

HECHO *3B1* (1km S Rural) *42.73222, -0.75305*
Camping Valle de Hecho, Ctra Puente La Reina-
Hecho s/n, 22720 Hecho (Huesca) **974-37 53 61;**
campinghecho@campinghecho.com; www.camping
hecho.com

12 🐕 ♦️♦️ (htd) WD ⬆️ 🖥️ / MSP 🦋 ⵜ ⵚ 🦞 ⛰️ 🛶

**Leave Jaca W on N240. After 25km turn N on A176
at Puente La Reina de Jaca. Site on W of rd, o'skts
of Hecho/Echo.** 1*, Med, mkd, pt shd, pt sl, EHU
(5-15A) €4.20; gas; 40% statics; phone; bus 200m;
ccard acc; games area; CKE. *"Pleasant site in foothills
of Pyrenees; excel, clean facs but poss inadequate hot
water; gd birdwatching area; Hecho fascinating vill;
shop & bar poss clsd LS except w/end; v ltd facs LS; not
suitable lge o'fits; gd rest in vill."* **€27.00**   2016

HOSPITAL DE ORBIGO *1B3* (1.3km N Urban)
42.4664, -5.8836 **Camp Municipal Don Suero,** 24286
Hospital de Órbigo (León) 987-36 10 18; camping@
hospitaldeorbigo.com; www.hospitaldeorbigo.com

🐕 ♦️♦️ ⬆️ 🖥️ / ⵜ ⵚ nr 🦞

**N120 rd fr León to Astorga, km 30. Site well sp
fr N120. Narr rds in Hospital.** Med, hdg, pt shd, EHU
(6A) €1.90; bbq; 50% statics; phone; bus to León 1km;
Eng spkn; ccard acc; poss open w/end only mid Apr-May;
CKE. *"Statics v busy w/ends, facs stretched; pool adj;
phone ahead to check site open if travelling close to
opening/closing dates."* **€15.00, Easter-1 Oct.**   2016

HOSPITALET DE L'INFANT, L' *3C2* (2km S Coastal)
40.97722, 0.90083 **Camping El Templo del Sol (Naturist),** Polígon 14-15, Playa del Torn, 43890 L'Hospitalet de l'Infant (Tarragona) 977-82 34 34; info@
eltemplodelsol.com; www.eltemplodelsol.com

♦️♦️ WD ⬆️ 🖥️ & 🖥️ / ⵜ 🦞 ⛰️ 🛶

**Leave A7 at exit 38 or N340 twds town cent. Turn
R (S) along coast rd for 2km. Ignore 1st camp sp
on L, site 200m further on L.** Lge, hdg, mkd, pt shd,
pt sl, serviced pitches; EHU (6A) inc; gas; red long
stay; TV; 5% statics; Eng spkn; adv bkg req; ccard
acc; INF card. *"Excel naturist site; no dogs, radios or
TV on pitches; cinema/theatre; solar-energy park;
jacuzzi; official naturist sand/shgl beach adj; lge
private wash/shwr rms; pitches v tight - take care
o'hanging branches; conv Port Aventura; mosquito
problem; poss strong winds - take care with awnings."*
€43.00, 1 Apr-22 Oct.   2016

See advertisement

SPAIN

HUMILLADERO *2G4* (0.5km S Rural) *37.10750, -4.69611* **Camping La Sierrecilla,** Avda de Clara Campoamor s/n, 29531 Humilladero (Málaga) **951-19 90 90;** info@lasierrecilla.com; www.camping lasierrecilla.com

12 ⛺ €1.50 �100 (htd) ⊌ ♨ ⚓ & ▣ ∥ ᴹˢᴾ 🦋 ⍦ ⍟ ⊕ ⚓ ⚓nr ⚏ ⚐ ⚐ (htd) ⚑

Exit A92 junc 138 onto A7280 twd Humilladero. At vill ent turn L at 1st rndabt, site visible. Med, hdstg, mkd, pt shd, pt sl, terr, serviced pitches; EHU (10A) €3.50; bbq; 10% statics; Eng spkn; adv bkg acc; CKE. *"Excel new site; gd modern, san facs; vg touring base; gd walking; horseriding, caving, archery high ssn; Fuentepiedra lagoon nrby; lots of facs clsd until Jun/ Jul."* **€24.00** 2019

"That's changed – Should I let the Club know?"

If you find something on site that's different from the site entry, fill in a report and let us know. See camc.com/europereport.

IRUN *3A1* (2km N Rural) *43.36638, -1.80436* **Camping Jaizkibel,** Ctra Guadalupe Km 22, 20280 Hondarribia (Guipúzkoa) **943-64 16 79;** recepcion@ campingjaizkibel.com; www.campingjaizkibel.com

�100 ♨ ⚓ ▣ ∥ 🦋 ⍦ ⍟ ⊕ ⚏ ⚐ sand 1.5km

Fr Hondarribia/Fuenterrabia inner ring rd foll sp to site below old town wall. Do not ent town. Med, hdg, hdstg, pt shd, terr, EHU (6A) €4.35 (check earth); bbq; 90% statics; phone; bus 1km; Eng spkn; adv bkg acc; ccard acc; tennis; CKE. *"Easy 20 mins walk to historic town; scenic area; gd walking; gd touring base but ltd turning space for tourers; clean facs; gd rest & bar; helpful staff; gd lndry facs."* **€34.00, 28 Mar-15 Nov.** 2017

IRUN *3A1* (6km W Coastal) *43.37629, -1.79939* **Camping Faro de Higuer,** Ctra. Del Faro, 58, 20280 Hondarribia **943 64 10 08;** faro@campingseuskadi.com; www.campingseuskadi.com

12 ⛺ €1.20 �100 ⊌ ♨ ⚓ & ▣ ∥ ᴹˢᴾ ⍦ ⍟ ⊕ ⚓ ⚓ ⚏ ⚐ ⚐ ⚑ ⚐adj

Fr AP8 exit at junc 2 Irun. Foll signs for airport. At rndabt after airport take 2nd exit, cross two more rndabts. 2nd exit at next 2 rndabts. Cont uphill to lighthouse & foll signs for Faro. Med, mkd, hdg, unshd, pt sl, terr, EHU (10A) €5.20; bbq; cooking facs; TV; 50% statics; phone; Eng spkn; adv bkg acc; bike hire; games rm; waterslide; games area. *"Vg site on top of winding rd, is v busy outside; sep ent & exit; exit has low stone arch, be careful when leaving."* **€23.00** 2019

ISABA *3B1* (13km E Rural) *42.86618, -0.81247* **Camping Zuriza,** Ctra Anso-Zuriza, Km 14, 22728 Ansó (Huesca) **974-37 01 96; contacto@camping zuriza.es;** www.campingzuriza.es

�100 ♨ ⚓ ▣ ∥ 🦋 ⍟ ⊕ ⚓ ⚏

On NA1370 N fr Isaba, turn R in 4km onto NA2000 to Zuriza. Foll sp to site. Fr Ansó, take HUV2024 N to Zuriza. Foll sp to site; narr, rough rd not rec for underpowered o'fits. 1*, Lge, pt shd, pt sl, serviced pitches; EHU €6; 50% statics; phone; ccard acc; CKE. *"Beautiful, remote valley; no vill at Zuriza, nearest vills Isaba & Ansó; no direct rte to France; superb location for walking; best to call prior to journey to check opening dates."* **€18.00, 1 Jul-31 Oct.** 2018

ISLA CRISTINA *2G2* (4km E Coastal) *37.20555, -7.26722* **Camping Playa Taray,** Ctra La Antilla-Isla Cristina, Km 9, 21430 La Redondela (Huelva) **959-34 11 02;** info@campingplayataray.es; www.camping taray.com

12 ⛺ �100 ♨ ⚓ & ▣ ∥ ᴹˢᴾ 🦋 ⍟ ⊕ ⚓ ⚏ ⚐ sand adj

Fr W exit A49 sp Isla Cristina & go thro town heading E. Fr E exit A49 at km 117 sp Lepe. In Lepe turn S on H4116 to La Antilla, then R on coast rd to Isla Cristina & site. 2*, Lge, pt shd, EHU (10) €4.28; gas; red long stay; 10% statics; phone; bus; ccard acc; CKE. *"Gd birdwatching, cycling; less cr than other sites in area in winter; poss untidy LS & ltd facs; poss diff for lge o'fits; friendly, helpful owner."* **€19.00** 2016

"I like to fill in the reports as I travel from site to site"

You'll find report forms at the back of this guide, or you can fill them in online at camc.com/europereport.

ISLARES *1A4* (1km W Coastal) *43.40361, -3.31027* **Camping Playa Arenillas,** Ctra Santander-Bilbao, Km 64, 39798 Islares (Cantabria) **942-86 31 52 or 609-44-21-67 (mob);** cueva@mundivia.es; www.campingplayaarenillas.es

�100 ⊌ ♨ ⚓ ▣ ∥ ᴹˢᴾ ⍟ ⊕nr ⚓ ⚏ ⚐ sand 100m

Exit A8 at km 156 Islares. Turn W on N634. Site on R at W end of Islares. Steep ent & sharp turn into site, exit less steep. 1*, Lge, mkd, pt shd, EHU (5A) €4.63 (poss no earth); gas; bbq; TV; 40% statics; phone; bus 500m; adv bkg rec; ccard acc; bike hire; horseriding; games area; CKE. *"Facs ltd LS & stretched in ssn; facs constantly cleaned; hot water to shwrs and washing up; rec arr early for choice of own pitch, and avoid Sat & Sun due to parked traff; conv Guggenheim Museum; excel NH for Bilbao ferry; beautiful setting."* **€30.60, 24 Mar-30 Sep.** 2016

JACA *3B2* (10km N Rural) *42.624191, -0.543496*
Solopuent Camping, Ctra Bescos de la Garcipollera s/n 22710, Castiello de Jaca **974 35 00 46 or 644 54 51 38;** info@solopuent.com; www.solopuent.com

🐕 ♟️(htd) ⓦ 🏊 ♿ 🗑️ ⚡ 🦋 🐾 ♟️ 🍴 Ⓤ nr 🍴 🪜 nr 🏔️

🏊(htd) ⚓ 🌴 shgl

Fr N240 take N330A/N330 to Castiello de Jaca. Turn R and cross bdge over rv and take rd to site 450m on R. Sm, mkd, pt shd, EHU (10A) inc; gas; bbq (charcoal, elec, gas, sep area); cooking facs; twin axles; TV; 50% statics; phone; bus/train; Eng spkn; adv bkg acc; ccard acc; games area & rm. *"Excel loc beside rv & vill; clean facs; flat pitches; min 10A supply for aldi heating, c'van shwr & cooking; wonderful mountain views, rv walks, wildlife; gd cycle rtes; excel."* €35.00, 1 Jan-5 Nov, 4 Dec-31 Dec. **2019**

JACA *3B2* (2km W Urban) *42.56416, -0.57027*
Camping Victoria, Avda de la Victoria 34, 22700 Jaca (Huesca) **974-35 70 08;** campingvictoria@ eresmas.com; www.campingvictoria.es

12 🐕 ♟️ ⓦ 🏊 ⚡ 🦋 🍴 🪜 🏔️ 🏊(htd)

Fr Jaca cent take N240 dir Pamplona, site on R. Med, mkd, pt shd, EHU (10A) €5; bbq; 80% statics; bus adj. *"Basic facs, but clean & well-maintained; friendly staff; conv NH/sh stay Somport Pass."* **€18.50** **2017**

JAVEA/XABIA *4E2* (1km S Rural) *38.78333, 0.17294*
Camping Jávea, Camí de la Fontana 10, 03730 Jávea (Alicante) **965-79 10 70;** info@campingjavea. es; www.campingjavea.es

12 🐕 €2 ♟️ ⓦ 🏊 ♿ 🗑️ ⚡ 🦋 🍴 🍴 Ⓤ 🍴 🪜 nr 🏔️ 🏊

⚓ 🌴 sand 1.5km

Exit N332 for Jávea on A132, cont in dir Port on CV734. At rndabt & Lidl supmkt, take slip rd to R immed after rv bdge sp Arenal Platjas & Cap de la Nau. Strt on at next rndabt to site sp & slip rd 100m sp Autocine. If you miss slip rd go back fr next rndabt. Lge, mkd, pt shd, EHU (8A) €4.56 (long lead rec); gas; bbq; red long stay; 15% statics; adv bkg acc; ccard acc; games area; tennis; CKE. *"Excel site & rest; variable pitch sizes/prices; some lge pitches - lge o'fits rec phone ahead; gd, clean san facs; mountain views; helpful staff; m'vans beware low trees; gd cycling; site a bit tired but gd."* **€35.00** **2017**

See advertisement

JAVEA/XABIA *4E2* (3km S Coastal) *38.77058, 0.18207*
Camping El Naranjal, Cami dels Morers 15, 03730 Jávea (Alicante) **965-79 29 89;** info@campingel naranjal.com; www.campingelnaranjal.com

12 🐕 ♟️(htd) ⓦ 🏊 ♿ 🗑️ ⚡ 🦋 🍴 🍴 🪜 🏔️ 🏊

⚓ 🌴 sand 500m

Exit A7 junc 62 or 63 onto N332 València/Alicante rd. Exit at Gata de Gorgos to Jávea. Foll sp Camping Jávea/Camping El Naranjal. Access rd by tennis club, foll sp. Med, hdstg, mkd, pt shd, EHU (10A) inc (poss rev pol); gas; bbq; red long stay; TV; 35% statics; phone; bus 500m; Eng spkn; adv bkg acc; ccard acc; bike hire; tennis 300m; games rm; golf 3km; CKE. *"Gd scenery & beach; pitches poss tight lge o'fits; dogs free; excel rest; immac facs; tourist info - tickets sold; rec; ACSI rate."* **€33.50** **2017**

LAREDO *1A4* (3km W Coastal) *43.41176, -3.45329* **Camping Playa del Regatón,** El Sable 8, 39770 Laredo (Cantabria) **942-60 69 95; info@camping playaregaton.com; www.campingplayaregaton.com**
🛉🛉 [wc] ♨ ⚷ 🗑 ∅ [MSP] 👕 ♈ 🍴 ⑪ 🐕 🎣 �🏊 sand adj

Fr W leave A8 junc 172, under m'way to rndabt & take exit sp Calle Rep Colombia. In 800m turn L at traff lts, in further 800m turn L onto tarmac rd to end, passing other sites. Fr E leave at junc 172, at 1st rndabt take 2nd exit sp Centro Comercial N634 Colindres. At next rndabt take exit Calle Rep Colombia, then as above. 2*, Lge, mkd, pt shd, EHU (6-10A) €4.30; gas; red long stay; 75% statics; bus 600m; Eng spkn; adv bkg acc; ccard acc; horseriding nr; CKE. "Clean site; sep area for tourers; wash up facs (cold water) every pitch; gd, modern facs; gd NH/sh stay (check opening times of office for EHU release); gd bird watching." **€26.70, 18 Mar-25 Sep.** 2016

LEKEITIO *3A1* (3km S Coastal) *43.35071, -2.49260* **Camping Leagi,** Calle Barrio Leagi s/n, 48289 Mendexa (Vizcaya) **946-84 23 52; leagi@campingleagi.com; www.campingleagi.com**
🐕 🛉🛉 [wc] ♨ 🗑 ∅ [MSP] 🍴 ⑪ 🐕 🎣 ⚲ 🏊 sand 1km

Fr San Sebastian leave A8/N634 at Deba twd Ondarroa. At Ondarroa do not turn into town, but cont on BI633 beyond Berriatua, then turn R onto BI3405 to Lekeitio. Fr Bilbao leave A8/N634 at Durango & foll B1633 twd Ondarroa. Turn L after Markina onto BI3405 to Lekeitio - do not go via Ondarroa, foll sp to Mendexa & site. Steep climb to site & v steep tarmac ent to site. Only suitable for o'fits with v high power/weight ratio. Med, mkd, unshd, pt sl, serviced pitches; EHU (5A) €3.90 (rev pol); 80% statics; ccard acc; CKE. "Ltd facs LS; tractor tow avail up to site ent; beautiful scenery; excel local beach; lovely town; gd views; gd walking; san facs under pressure due to many tents; bus to Bilbao & Gurnika." **€39.00, 1 Mar-1 Nov.** 2019

LEON *1B3* (7km SE Urban) *42.5900, -5.5331* **Camping Ciudad de León,** Ctra N601, 24195 Golpejar de la Sobarriba **987-26 90 86; campingleon@yahoo.es; sites.google.com/site/campingleon/**
🐕 €1.50 🛉🛉 [wc] ♨ ⚷ 🗑 ∅ 👕 ♈ 🍴 ⑪ 🐕 🎣 ⚲ 🏊 ⛵

SE fr León on N601 twds Valladolid, L at top of hill at rndabt & Opel g'ge & foll site sp Golpejar de la Sobarriba; 500m after radio masts turn R at site sp. Narr track to site ent. Sm, shd, pt sl, EHU inc (6A) €3.60; gas; bus 200m; Eng spkn; adv bkg acc; bike hire; tennis; CKE. "Clean, pleasant site; helpful, welcoming staff; access some sm pitches poss diff; easy access to León; shwrs need refurb (2015)." **€19.00, 1 Jun-20 Sep.** 2019

LINEA DE LA CONCEPCION, LA *2H3* (3.6km N Urban/ Coastal) *36.19167, -5.3350* **Camping Sureuropa,** Camino de Sobrevela s/n, 11300 La Línea de la Concepción (Cádiz) **956-64 35 87; info@camping sureuropa.es; www.campingsureuropa.es**
[12] 🛉🛉 [wc] ♨ ⚷ 🗑 ∅ 🍴 ⑪ 🎣 🏊 sand 500m

Fr AP7, ext junc 124. Use junc124 fr both dirs. Just bef Gibraltar turn R up lane, in 200m turn L into site. Fr N on AP7, exit junc 124 onto A383 dir La Línea; foll sp Santa Margarita thro to beach. Foll rd to R along sea front, site in approx 1km - no advance sp. App rd to site off coast rd poss floods after heavy rain. Med, hdg, mkd, hdstg, pt shd, EHU €4.30; phone; Eng spkn; adv bkg acc; site clsd 20 Dec-7 Jan; CKE. "Clean, flat, pretty site; vg, modern san facs; sm pitches & tight site rds poss diff twin axles & l'ge o'fits; sports club adj; quiet but noise fr adj sports club; ideal for Gibraltar 4km; stay ltd to 4 days; wifi in recep only; sh stay only." **€20.00** 2016

LLANES *1A4* (8km E Coastal) *43.39948, -4.65350*
Camping La Paz, Ctra N634, Km 292, 33597 Playa de Vidiago (Asturias) **985-41 12 35; delfin@campinglapaz.com; www.campinglapaz.eu**

🏕 €2.50 ♦♦♦ WD ♨ ♿ ⊟ ♦ / MSP 🦋 ♗ Ⴇ ⓗ 🝙 ⚠ 🏊 sand adj

Take Fr A8/N634/E70 turn R at sp to site bet km stone 292 & 293 bef Vidiago.Site access via narr 1km lane. Stop bef bdge & park on R, staff will tow to pitch. Narr site ent & steep access to pitches. Lge, mkd, shd, terr, EHU (9A) €4.82 (poss rev pol); gas; bbq; TV; phone; Eng spkn; adv bkg acc; ccard acc; fishing; golf 4km; watersports; games rm; horseriding; CKE. *"Exceptionally helpful owner & staff; sm pitches; gd, modern san facs; mountain sports; excel views; cliff top rest; superb beaches in area."* **€42.00, Easter-30 Sep.** **2017**

See advertisement on previous page

LLANES *1A4* (3km W Coastal) *43.42500, -4.78944*
Camping Las Conchas de Póo, Ctra General, 33509 Póo de Llanes (Asturias) **985-40 22 90 or 674-16 58 79 (mob); campinglasconchas@gmail.com; www.campinglasconchas.com**

🏕 ♦♦♦ WD ♨ ♿ ⊟ ♦ / 🦋 ♗ Ⴇ ⓗ 🝙 ⚠ 🏊 sand adj

Exit A8/E70 at Llanes West junc 307 & foll sp. Site on rd AS263. 2*, Med, pt shd, sl, terr, EHU (6A) €3.20; 50% statics; phone; bus adj. *"Pleasant site; footpath to lovely beach; lovely coastal walk to Celorio; stn in Póo vill; gd pitches for tourers; gd clean san facs; gd WiFi at recep."* **€20.00, 1 Jun-15 Sep.** **2019**

LLORET DE MAR *3B3* (1km SW Coastal) *41.6984, 2.8265* **Camping Santa Elena-Ciutat,** Ctra Blanes/ Lloret, 17310 Lloret de Mar (Gerona) **972-36 40 09; santaelana@betsa.es; www.betsa.es**

12 ♦♦♦ ♨ ♿ ⊟ ♦ / 🦋 Ⴇ ⓗ 🝙 ⚠ ⚓ 🏄 🏊 shgl 600m

Exit A7 junc 9 dir Lloret. In Lloret take Blanes rd, site sp at km 10.5 on rd GI 682. V lge, pt sl, EHU (5A) €3.90; gas; phone; Eng spkn; games area; CKE. *"Ideal for teenagers; cash machine."* **€34.60** **2016**

LOGRONO *3B1* (2km N Urban) *42.47122, -2.45493*
Camping La Playa, Avda de la Playa 6, 26006 Logroño (La Rioja) **941-25 22 53; info@campinglaplaya.com; www.campinglaplaya.com**

12 🏕 €2 ♦♦♦ ♨ ♿ ⊟ ♦ / MSP 🝙 ⚠ 🏄

Leave Logroño by bdge 'Puente de Piedra' on N111, then turn L at rndabt into Camino de las Norias. Site well sp in town & fr N111, adj sports cent Las Norias, on N side of Rv Ebro. 1*, Med, hdg, shd, EHU (5A) €4.80; gas; sw nr; 80% statics; tennis; CKE. *"Sh walk to town cent; ltd facs LS & site poss clsd; vg; nr rest."* **€25.00** **2016**

LUARCA *1A3* (1km NE Coastal) *43.54914, -6.52426*
Camping Los Cantiles, Ctra N634, Km 502.7, 33700 Luarca (Asturias) **985-64 09 38; cantiles@campingloscantiles.com; www.campingloscantiles.com**

12 🏕 €1 ♦♦♦ WD ♨ ♿ ⊟ ♦ / MSP 🦋 ♗ Ⴇ ⓗ 🝙 🝙 🏊 shgl

On A8 exit junc 467 (sp Luarca/Barcia/Almuña), At rndabt foll sp to Luarca, after petrol stn turn R, foll sp to site. Not rec to ent town fr W. Not rec to foll sat nav as may take you up v steep & narr rd. On leaving site, retrace to main rd - do not tow thro Luarca. 3*, Med, hdg, pt shd, EHU inc (3-6A) €2-2.50; gas; red long stay; phone; Eng spkn; adv bkg acc; CKE. *"Site on cliff top; some narr site rds; pitches soft after rain; steep climb down to beach; 30 min walk to interesting town & port; pool 300m; wonderful setting; san fac's OK, water in shwrs v hot."* **€23.00** **2017**

LUMBIER *3B1* (1.3km S Rural) *42.65111, -1.30222*
Camping Iturbero, Ctra N240 Pamplona-Huesca, 31440 Lumbier (Navarra) **948-88 04 05; iturbero@campingiturbero.com; www.campingiturbero.com**

🏕 ♦♦♦ WD ♨ ⊟ ♦ / 🦋 Ⴇ ⓗ 🝙 🝙 nr ⚠

SE fr Pamplona on N240 twds Yesa Reservoir. In 30km L on NA150 twds Lumbier. In 3.5km immed bef Lumbier turn R at rndabt then over bdge, 1st L to site, adj sw pool. Well sp fr N240. 2*, Med, hdg, mkd, hdstg, pt shd, EHU (5A) €4.95; gas; bbq; 25% statics; bus 1km; tennis; CKE. *"Beautiful, well-kept site; clean, basic facs; pool 100m; excel touring base; open w/end only Dec-Easter (poss fr Sep) but clsd 19 Dec-19 Feb; eagles & vultures in gorge & seen fr site; hang-gliding; helpful staff; Lumbier lovely sm town."* **€27.40, 15 Mar-15 Dec.** **2019**

MADRID *1D4* (13km NE Urban) *40.45361, -3.60333*
Camping Osuna, Jardines de Aranjuez 1, 28042 Madrid **917-41 05 10; camping.osuna.madrid@microgest.es**

12 🏕 ♦♦♦ WD ♨ ♿ ⊟ ♦ / 🝙 nr ⚠

Fr M40, travelling S clockwise (anti-clockwise fr N or E) exit junc 8 at Canillejas sp 'Avda de Logroño'. Turn L under m'way, then R under rlwy, immed after turn R at traff lts. Site on L corner - white painted wall. Travelling N, leave M40 at junc 7 (no turn off at junc 8) sp Avda 25 Sep, U-turn at km 7, head S to junc 8, then as above. 2*, Med, hdg, mkd, pt shd, pt sl, EHU (6A) €4.85 (long lead rec); 10% statics; phone; Eng spkn; CKE. *"Sm pitches poss diff lge o'fits; poss neglected LS & facs tired (June 2010); poss travellers; conv city cent; busy; gd basic facs; metro to town 600m; easy walk to metro with frequent svr into Madrid."* **€33.00** **2015**

MADRID *1D4* (13km S Urban) *40.31805, -3.68888*
Camping Alpha, Ctra de Andalucía N-IV, Km 12.4,
28906 Getafe (Madrid) **916-95 80 69; info@camping
alpha.com; www.campingalpha.com**

12 🛖 ♦♦♦ [wc] ♨ 🗑 ⁄ [MSP] ⵎ Y ⊕ ⓐ 🛒 /◸\ 🏊

Fr S on A4/E5 twd Madrid, leave at km 12B to W
dir Ocaña & foll sp. Fr N on A4/E5 at km 13B to
change dir back onto A4; then exit 12B sp 'Polígono
Industrial Los Olivos' to site. 2*, Lge, hdstg, hdg, pt
shd, EHU (15A) €5.90 (poss no earth); 20% statics;
phone; Eng spkn; adv bkg acc; ccard acc; games area;
tennis; CKE. *"Lorry depot adj; poss vehicle movements
24 hrs but minimal noise; bus & metro to Madrid 30-40
mins; sm pitches poss tight for space; vg, clean facs;
helpful staff; NH or sh stay."* **€28.00**   **2016**

MANGA DEL MAR MENOR, LA *4G2* (3.5km W
Urban) *37.6244, -0.7447* **Caravaning La Manga,**
Autovia Cartagena - La Manga, exit 11, E-30370 La
Manga del Mar Menor **968-56 30 19; lamanga@
caravaning.es; www.caravaning.es**

12 🛖 €1.45 ♦♦♦ [wc] ♨ ♒ 🗑 ⁄ [MSP] ⵎ Y ⊕ ⓐ 🛒 /◸\ 🏊 🚴 🏊 🛶

Take Autovia CT-32 fr Cartagena to La Manga;
take exit 800B twds El Algar/Murcia; keep L,
merge onto Autovia MU312; cont to foll MU-312;
cont onto Ctra a La Manga & cont onto Av Gran
Via; site clearly sp. Lge, hdg, hdstg, pt shd, serviced
pitches; EHU (10A) inc; bbq; 10% statics; bus to
Murcia and Cartagena; Eng spkn; adv bkg acc; ccard
acc; watersports; tennis; games rm. *"Immac, busy,
popular site; Mar Menor shallow & warm lagoon; open
air cinema & children's programme high ssn; lovely
location & gd for golfers; horseridng nrby; recep open
24 hrs; Mar Menor well worth visiting; vg rest; gd for
families; outdoor fitness; some narr site rds & trees
- rec park in car park on arr & walk to find pitch; gd
walking; gym; sauna; jacuzzi; mountain biking; bird
sanctuary; poss lge rallies on site Dec-Mar; excel;
friendly, helpful staff; immac facs."* **€38.00**   **2016**

See advertisement

MARBELLA *2H3* (14km E Coastal) *36.48881, -4.74294*
Kawan Village Cabopino, Ctra N340/A7, Km 194.7,
29600 Marbella (Málaga) **952-83 43 73; info@
campingcabopino.com; www.campingcabopino.com**

12 🛖 €2 ♦♦♦ [wc] ♨ 🚻 ♿ 🗑 ⁄ [MSP] ⵎ Y ⊕ ⓐ 🛒 /◸\ 🏊 (covrd)

🏖 sand 200m

Fr E site is on N side of N340/A7; turn R at km 195
'Salida Cabopino' past petrol stn, site on R at rndabt.
Fr W on A7 turn R at 'Salida Cabopino' km 194.7, go
over bdge to rndabt, site strt over. NB Do not take
sm exit fr A7 immed at 1st Cabopino sp. Lge, mkd,
pt shd, pt sl, EHU (6-10A) inc (poss long lead req);
bbq (elec, gas); TV; 50% statics; bus 100m; Eng spkn;
ccard acc; golf driving range; archery; games area;
games rm; watersports; CKE. *"V pleasant site set in
pine woodland; rd noise & lge groups w/enders; marina
300m; busy, particularly w/end; varied pitch size, poss
diff access lge o'fits, no o'fits over 11m high ssn; blocks
req some pitches; gd, clean san facs; feral cats on site
(2009)."* **€36.00, E21.**   **2016**

MARBELLA *2H3* (7km E Coastal) *36.50259, -4.80413*
Camping La Buganvilla, Ctra N340, Km 188.8,
29600 Marbella (Málaga) **952-83 56 21 or 952-83 19 73;
info@campingbuganvilla.com; www.camping
buganvilla.com**

12 🛖 €4 ♦♦♦ [wc] ♨ ♿ 🗑 ⁄ ⵎ Y ⊕ 🛒 /◸\ 🏊 🏖 sand 350m

E fr Marbella for 6km on N340/E15 twds Málaga.
Pass site & cross over m'way at Elviria & foll site sp.
Fr Málaga exit R off autovia immed after 189km
marker. Lge, shd, pt sl, terr, EHU (16A) inc; gas; bbq;
red long stay; TV; 40% statics; phone; Eng spkn; adv
bkg acc; ccard acc; fishing; tennis; games rm; CKE.
*"Relaxed, conv site; helpful staff; excel beach; no dogs
Jul/Aug; bus stop to Marbella at ent; 20min walk to
nice beach; bigger & more shaded pitches at top of
site."* **€25.00**   **2016**

SPAIN

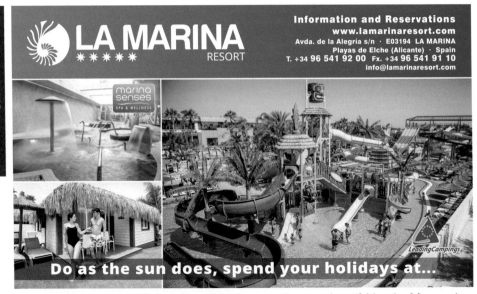

LA MARINA RESORT
★★★★★

Information and Reservations
www.lamarinaresort.com
Avda. de la Alegría s/n · E03194 LA MARINA
Playas de Elche (Alicante) · Spain
T. +34 96 541 92 00 Fx. +34 96 541 91 10
info@lamarinaresort.com

marina senses
SPA & WELLNESS

LeadingCampings

Do as the sun does, spend your holidays at...

Located at the Elche coastline, in the middle of nature. Close to a beautiful beach of fine sand. Distinguished with the EEC blue flag for optimal water quality. We offer luxurious installations: 3000 m² thematic swimming-pool complex, 3.000 m² Spa&Wellness, 2.500 m² New Water Park, very high quality sanitary, entertainment to the highest level for children, young and adults. Prices in accordance with season and duration of the stays. Open all year.

MARIA *4G1* (8km W Rural) *37.70823, -2.23609*
Camping Sierra de María, Ctra María a Orce, Km 7, Paraje La Piza, 04838 María (Málaga) **620-23 22 23;** info@campingsierrademaria.com; www.camping sierrademaria.es

12 🐕 ♦♦ wⓄ ♨ ᕤ ⅃ ✿ ♈ 🍽 Ⓗ 🛴

Exit A92 at junc 408 to Vélez Rubio, Vélez Blanco & María. Foll A317 to María & cont dir Huéscar & Orce. Site on R. Med, mkd, pt shd, pt sl, EHU (16A) €3.75; 10% statics; adv bkg acc; ccard acc; bike hire; horseriding; CKE. *"Lovely, peaceful, ecological site in mountains; much wildlife; variable pitch sizes; facs poss stretched high ssn; v cold in winter; v helpful mgrs, gd food in rest."* **€23.00**   **2016**

MARINA, LA *4F2* (1.5km S Coastal) *38.12972, -0.65000* **Camping Internacional La Marina,** Ctra N332a, Km 76, 03194 La Marina (Alicante) **965-41 92 00;** info@campinglamarina.com; www.lamarin-aresort.com

12 🐕 €2.14 ♦♦ (htd) wⓄ ♨ ♨ ᕤ 🖥 ✿ 🖥 ♈ 🍽 Ⓗ 🛴 🛴 🏛

🛵 🏊 (covrd, htd) ☂ sand 500m

Fr N332 S of La Marina turn E twd sea at rndabt onto Camino del Cementerio. At next rndabt turn S onto N332a & foll site sp along Avda de l'Alegría. 5*, V lge, hdstg, mkd, hdg, shd, terr, serviced pitches; EHU (10A) €3.21; gas; red long stay; TV; 10% statics; phone; bus 50m; Eng spkn; adv bkg acc; ccard acc; watersports; games rm; solarium; fishing; sauna; tennis; games area; waterslide; CKE. *"Popular winter site - almost full late Feb; v busy w/end; disco; clean, high quality facs; various pitch sizes/prices; fitness cent; bus fr gate; gd security; car wash; security; excel rest; gd site; v helpful; hire cars avail; fantastic site."* **€65.00**   **2017**

See advertisement

MASNOU, EL *3C3* (0.8km W Coastal) *41.4753, 2.3033*
Camping Masnou, Ctra NII, Km 633, Carrer de Camil
Fabra 33, 08320 El Masnou (Barcelona) **935-55 15 03;**
masnou@campingsonline.es; www.campingmasnou
barcelona.com

App site fr N on N11. Pass El Masnou rlwy stn on
L & go strt on at traff lts. Site on R on N11 after
km 633. Not clearly sp. 2*, Med, shd, pt sl, EHU
€5.88; bbq; phone; bus 300m, train to Barcelona nr;
Eng spkn; ccard acc; CKE. *"Gd pitches, no awnings;
some sm pitches, poss shared; facs vg, though poss
stretched when site busy; no restriction on NH vehicle
movements; well-run, friendly site but v tired; gd
service LS; rlwy line best site & excel beach - subway
avail; excel train service to Barcelona; excel pool."*
€35.00 2017

"There aren't many sites open at this time of year"

If you're travelling outside peak season
remember to call ahead to check site opening
dates – even if the entry says 'open all year'.

MAZAGON *2G2* (10km E Coastal) *37.09855, -6.72650*
Camping Doñana Playa, Ctra San Juan del Puerto-
Matalascañas, Km 34.6, 21130 Mazagón (Huelva)
959-53 62 81; info@campingdonana.com;
www.campingdonana.com

Fr A49 exit junc 48 at Bullullos del Condado onto
A483 sp El Rocio, Matalascañas. At coast turn R sp
Mazagón, site on L in 16km. V lge, mkd, hdstg, pt shd,
EHU (6A) €5.20; 10% statics; bus 500m; adv bkg acc;
games area; site clsd 14 Dec-14 Jan; watersports; bike
hire; tennis; CKE. *"Pleasant site amongst pine trees
but lack of site care LS; ltd LS; lge pitches but poss soft
sand; quiet but v noisy Fri/Sat nights; new (2014) lge
shwr block on lower pt of site."* **€35.00** 2019

MENDIGORRIA *3B1* (0.5km SW Rural) *42.62416,
-1.84277* **Camping El Molino,** Ctra Larraga, 31150
Mendigorría (Navarra) **948-34 06 04;** info@camping
elmolino.com; www.campingelmolino.com

Fr Pamplona on N111 turn L at 25km in Puente la
Reina onto NA601 sp Mendigorría. Site sp thro vill
dir Larraga. 1*, Med, mkd, pt shd, serviced pitches;
EHU (6A) inc; gas; bbq; TV; phone; adv bkg acc; ccard
acc; games area; canoe hire; waterslide; tennis; clsd
23 Dec-14 Jan & poss Mon-Thurs fr Nov to Feb, phone
ahead to check; CKE. *"Gd clean san facs; solar water
heating - water poss only warm; vg leisure facs; v ltd
facs LS; for early am dep LS, pay night bef & obtain
barrier key; friendly, helpful staff; statics (sep area);
lovely medieval vill."* **€29.60, 1 Feb-15 Dec.** 2018

MERIDA *2E3* (4km NE Urban) *38.93558, -6.30426*
Camping Mérida, Avda de la Reina Sofia s/n, 06800
Mérida (Badajoz) **924-30 34 53;** proexcam@jet.es

Fr E on A5/E90 exit junc 333/334 to Mérida, site
on L in 2km. Fr W on A5/E90 exit junc 346, site sp.
Fr N exit A66/E803 at junc 617 onto A5 E. Leave
at junc 334, site on L in 1km twd Mérida. Fr S on
A66-E803 app Mérida, foll Cáceres sp onto bypass
to E; at lge rndabt turn R sp Madrid; site on R after
2km. 2*, Med, mkd, pt shd, pt sl, EHU (6A) €3.30 (long
lead poss req & poss rev pol); gas; TV; 10% statics;
phone; CKE. *"Roman remains & National Museum of
Roman Art worth visit; poss diff lge o'fits manoeuvring
onto pitch due trees & soft grnd after rain; ltd facs
& run down in LS; conv NH; taxi to town costs 5-9
euros; grass pitches; bread can be ordered fr rest; poss
nightclub noise at w/end."* **€21.00** 2017

MIAJADAS *2E3* (14km SW Rural) *39.09599, -6.01333*
Camping-Restaurant El 301, Ctra Madrid-Lisbon,
Km 301, 10100 Miajadas (Cáceres) **927-34 79 14;**
camping301@hotmail.com; www.camping301.com

Leave A5/E90 just bef km stone 301 & foll sp 'Via de
Servicio' with rest & camping symbols; site in 500m.
Med, pt shd, EHU (8A) €5.50 (poss no earth); gas; TV;
phone; ccard acc; CKE. *"Well-maintained, clean site;
grass pitches; OK wheelchair users but steps to pool; gd
NH; gd bird life."* **€24.00** 2016

MOJACAR *4G1* (9km S Rural) *37.06536, -1.86864*
Camping Sopalmo, Sopalmo, 04638 Mojácar
(Almería) **950-47 84 13; 660-73 53 68;** camping
sopalmo@gmail.com; campingsopalmo.com

Exit A7/E15 at junc 520 onto AL6111 sp Mojácar.
Fr Mojácar turn S onto A1203/AL5105 dir
Carboneras, site sp on W of rd about 1km S of El
Agua del Medio. Sm, mkd, hdstg, pt shd, terr, EHU
(6A); gas; bbq; twin axles; 10% statics; Eng spkn; adv
bkg acc; CKE. *"Clean, pleasant, popular site; remote &
peaceful; friendly owner; gd walking in National Park;
lovely san facs; gd."* **€31.00** 2019

MONCOFA *3D2* (2km E Urban/Coastal) *39.80861,
-0.12805* **Camping Mon Mar,** Camino Serratelles s/n,
12593 Platja de Moncófa (Castellón) **964-58 85 92;**
campingmonmar@hotmail.com

Exit 49 fr A7 or N340, foll sp Moncófa Platja passing
thro Moncófa & foll sp beach & tourist info thro
1-way system. Site sp, adj Aqua Park. 2*, Lge, hdstg,
hdg, pt shd, serviced pitches; EHU (6A) inc; gas; bbq;
red long stay; 80% statics; phone; bus 300m; Eng
spkn; adv bkg acc; ccard acc; CKE. *"Helpful owner
& staff; rallies on site Dec-Apr; mini-bus to stn &
excursions; sunshades over pitches poss diff high o'fits;
excel clean, tidy site."* **€32.00** 2019

MONTBLANC *3C2* (1.5km NE Rural) *41.37743, 1.18511*
Camping Montblanc Park, Ctra Prenafeta, Km 1.8,
43400 Montblanc **977-86 25 44 or 492 28 38 48;**
montblancpark@capfun.com; www.montblancpark.com
12 🛉 €4.50 (htd) ♀♀♀ ♨ ♿ ⬛ ⁄ MSP ♔ ⟂ ⊕ 🍴 🎡 ⚠ ✦
🚊

**Exit AP2 junc 9 sp Montblanc; foll sp Montblanc/
Prenafeta/TV2421; site on L on TV2421.**
4*, Med, hdg, pt shd, pt sl, terr, EHU (10A) inc; bbq; red
long stay; 50% statics; phone; Eng spkn; adv bkg acc;
ccard acc; CKE. *"Excel site; excel facs; lovely area; many
static pitches only suitable for o'fits up to 7m; Cistercian
monasteries nrby; conv NH Andorra."* **€39.50**   **2019**

MONTERROSO *1B2* (1km S Rural) *42.78720, -7.84414*
Camp Municipal de Monterroso, A Peneda, 27560
Monterroso (Lugo) **982-37 75 01; campingmonterroso@
aged-sl.com; www.campingmonterroso.com**
🛉 ♀♀♀ ♨ ♿ ⁄ ♔ ⟂ nr ⊕ nr 🎡

**Fr N540 turn W onto N640 to Monterroso. Fr town
cent turn S on LU212. In 100m turn sharp R then
downhill for 1km; 2 sharp bends to site.** Sm, hdg,
mkd, pt shd, pt sl, EHU (10A) €3.50; Eng spkn; games
area; CKE. *"Helpful staff; v quiet & ltd facs LS; pool adj;
vg."* **€21.00, 30 Mar-24 Sep.**   **2017**

MOTILLA DEL PALANCAR *4E1* (10km NW Rural)
39.61241, -2.10185 **Camping Pantapino,** Paraje de
Hontanar, s/n, 16115 Olmedilla de Alarcón (Cuenca)
**969-33 92 33 or 676-47 85 40 (mob); pantapina@
hotmail.com; www.campingpantapino.eu**
12 🛉 €1.50 ♀♀♀ ♨ ♿ ⁄ MSP 🦋 ⟂ ⊕ 🎡 ⚠ 🚊

**Fr cent of Motilla foll NIII; turn NW onto rd CM2100
at sp for Valverde de Júcar; site on L just bef 12km
marker.** 2*, Med, mkd, pt shd, pt sl, serviced pitches;
EHU (6A) €4; gas; bbq; 40% statics; adv bkg acc; ccard
acc; tennis; bike hire; horseriding; games area; CKE.
*"Clean, attractive site but tatty statics; poor facs; gd
size pitches; resident owners hospitable; poss clsd in
winter - phone ahead to check; vg; san facs old but
clean; ltd facs LS; gd NH; poss problem with earth on
elec."* **€18.00**   **2019**

MOTRIL *2H4* (3km SW Urban/Coastal) *36.71833,
-3.54616* **Camping Playa de Poniente de Motril,**
18600 Motril (Granada) **958-82 03 03; info@camping
playadeponiente.com; www.campingplayade
poniente.com**
12 🛉 €1.50 ♀♀♀ (htd) ♨ ♿ ⬛ ⁄ MSP ♔ ⟂ ⊕ 🎡 ⚠ 🚊
🎯 adj

**Turn off coast rd N340 to port bef flyover; at rndabt
take rd for Motril. Turn R in town, site sp.** Lge, hdstg,
mkd, pt shd, EHU (6-10) €3.35; gas; bbq (elec, gas);
red long stay; 40% statics; bus; Eng spkn; adv bkg acc;
ccard acc; bike hire; games rm; horseriding; tennis;
golf; games area. *"Well-appointed site but surrounded
by blocks of flats; gd, clean facs; helpful recep; gd shop;
access diff for lge o'fits; poss lge flying beetles; excel
long stay winter; lovely promenade with dedicated
cycle track."* **€31.70**   **2017**

MUNDAKA *3A1* (1km S Coastal) *43.39915, -2.69620*
Camping Portuondo, Ctra Amorebieta-Bermeo,
Km 43, 48360 Mundaka (Bilbao) **946-87 77 01;
recepcion@campingportuondo.com; www.camping
portuondo.com**
12 🛉 ♀♀♀ ♨ ⬛ ⁄ ♔ ⟂ ⊕ 🍴 ⚠ 🚊 🎯500m

**Fr Bermeo pass Mundaka staying on main rd, do not
enter Mundaka. Stay on Bl-2235 sp Gernika. After
approx 1km site on L down steep slip rd.** Med, pt shd,
terr, EHU (6A) €4.20; 30% statics; train 800m; adv bkg
rec; ccard acc; site clsd end Jan-mid Feb. *"Excel clean,
modern facs; pitches tight not suitable for lge o'fits;
popular with surfers; conv Bilbao by train; site suitable
sm m'vans only; v ltd touring space; ent is very steep
single track."* **€35.00**   **2016**

MUROS *1B1* (7km W Coastal) *42.76100, 9.11100*
Camping Ancoradoiro, Ctra Corcubión-Muros,
Km.7.2, 15250 Louro (La Coruña) **981-87 88 97;
wolfgangh@hotmail.es or campingancora@
outlook.es; www.campingancoradoiro.com**
♀♀♀ ♨ ⬛ ⁄ 🦋 ⟂ nr ⊕ 🎡 nr ⚠ ✦ 🎯sand 500m

**Foll AC550 W fr Muros. Site on L (S), well sp. Immed
inside ent arch, to thro gate on L.** 1*, Med, hdg, mkd,
pt shd, terr, EHU (6-15A) €3.50; phone; bus 500m;
adv bkg acc; watersports; CKE. *"Excel, lovely, well-run,
well-kept site; superb friendly site on headland bet 2
sandy beaches; welcoming owner; excel rest; excel san
facs; poss diff for lge o'fits; beautiful beaches; scenic
area."* **€24.00, 25 Apr-16 Sep.**   **2019**

NAJERA *3B1* (0.6km S Urban) *42.41310, -2.73145*
Camping El Ruedo, San Julián 24, 26300 Nájera
(La Rioja) **941-36 01 02; www.campingslarioja.es**
♀♀♀ (htd) ⬛ ⁄ 🦋 ⟂ ⊕ 🎡 ⚠ ✦

**Take Nájera town dirs off N120. In town turn L bef
x-ing bdge. Site sp.** Sm, pt shd, EHU (10-16A) €3
(rev pol & poss no earth); gas; TV; phone; bus 200m;
adv bkg acc; ccard acc; CKE. *"Pleasant site in quiet
location, don't be put off by 1st impression of town;
monastery worth visit, some pitches in former bullring;
san facs tired; many trees, could be diff for lge o'fits."*
€26.00, 1 Apr-10 Sep.   **2016**

NAVAJAS *3D2* (1km W Rural) *39.87489, -0.51034*
Camping Altomira, Carretera, CV-213 Navajas Km. 1,
E-12470 Navajas (Castellón) **964-71 32 11; reservas@
campingaltomira.com; www.campingaltomira.com**
12 🛉 ♀♀♀ (htd) ⬛ ♨ ♿ ⬛ ⁄ ♔ ⟂ ⊕ 🍴 🎡 ⚠ 🚊 (htd) 🛁

**Exit A23/N234 at junc 33 to rndabt & take CV214 dir
Navajas. In approx 2km turn L onto CV213, site on
L just past R turn into vill, sp.** 4*, Med, hdstg, pt shd,
terr, serviced pitches; EHU (6A) inc; gas; bbq; red long
stay; TV; 70% statics; phone; bus 500m; Eng spkn; adv
bkg acc; ccard acc; games rm; tennis; bike hire; fishing;
CKE. *"Friendly welcome; panoramic views fr upper level
(steep app) but not rec for lge o'fits due tight bends &
ramped access/kerb to some pitches; gd birdwatching,
walking, cycling; vg, useful NH & longer; excel; stunnng
waterfall with sw nrby; site renovated; excel pitches,
fully serviced, new excel san facs (2019); gd loc."*
€32.50, E18.   **2019**

A NATURAL park

CAMPING URBASA
Navarre (SPAIN)
www.campingurbasa.com

SPAIN

NERJA *2H4* (4km E Rural) *36.76035, -3.83490* **Nerja Camping,** Ctra Vieja Almeria, Km 296.5, Camp de Maro, 29787 Nerja (Málaga) **952-52 97 14; info@nerjacamping.com; www.nerjacamping.com**

On N340, cont past sp on L for 200m around RH corner, bef turning round over broken white line. Foll partly surfaced rd to site on hillside. Fr Almuñécar on N340, site on R approx 20km. Med, pt shd, pt sl, terr, EHU (5A) €3.75 (check earth); gas; red long stay; Eng spkn; adv bkg rec; site clsd Oct; bike hire; CKE. *"5 mins to Nerja caves; mkt Tue; annual carnival 15 May; diff access lge o'fits; gd horseriding; site rds steep but gd surface; gd views; friendly owners."* **€24.00**   2016

"That's changed – Should I let the Club know?"

If you find something on site that's different from the site entry, fill in a report and let us know. See camc.com/europereport.

NOJA *1A4* (20km W Coastal) *43.46306, -3.72379* **Camping Derby Loredo,** Calle Bajada a lay Playa, 19 39160 Loredo **942 504106; info@campingloredo.com; campingloredo.com**

Fr Santander on S10 twrd Bilbao. L at J12, foll CA141 to Pedrena/Somo. After Somo L onto CA440 Loredo. On ent Loredo L sp @400m Playa Deloredo.' Med, mkd, pt shd, EHU; gas; twin axles; 70% statics; Eng spkn; ccard acc. *"Gd loc by beach; watersports; not suitable for lge o'fits; surf board hire; busy; friendly site with fams and surfers; gd."* **€27.00**   2017

NOJA *1A4* (1km NW Coastal) *43.49011, -3.53636* **Camping Playa Joyel,** Playa del Ris, 39180 Noja (Cantabria) **942-63 00 81; info@playayoyel.com; www.playajoyel.com**

Fr Santander or Bilbao foll sp A8/E70 (toll-free). Approx 15km E of Solares exit m'way junc 184 at Beranga onto CA147 N twd Noja & coast. On o'skirts of Noja turn L sp Playa del Ris, (sm brown sp) foll rd approx 1.5km to rndabt, site sp to L, 500m fr rndabt. Fr Santander take S10 for approx 8km, then join A8/E70. V lge, mkd, pt shd, pt sl, EHU (6A) €4.30; gas; bbq; TV; 40% statics; phone; Eng spkn; adv bkg acc; ccard acc; sailing; windsurfing; jacuzzi; tennis; games rm; CKE. *"Well-organised site on sheltered bay; cash dispenser; very busy high ssn; pleasant staff; hairdresser; car wash; no o'fits over 8m high ssn; gd, clean facs; superb pool & beach; recep 0800-2200; some narr site rds with kerbs; midnight silence enforced; highly rec."* **€49.00, 27 Mar-25 Sep, E05.**   2015

NUEVALOS *3C1* (1km N Rural) *41.21846, -1.79211* **Camping Lago Park,** Ctra De Alhama de Aragón a Cillas, Km 39, 50210 Nuévalos (Zaragoza) **976-84 90 38; lagoresort@gmail.com; www.lagoresort.com**

Fr E on A2/E90 exit junc 231 to Nuévalos, turn R sp Madrid. Site 1.5km on L when ent Nuévalos. Fr W exit junc 204, site well sp. Steep ent fr rd. 3*, V lge, hdg, mkd, pt shd, terr, EHU (10A) €5.40; gas; bbq; red long stay; 10% statics; bus 500m; adv bkg acc; fishing; games area; boating; CKE. *"Nr Monasterio de Piedra & Tranquera Lake; excel facs on top terr, but stretched high ssn & poss long, steepish walk; lake nrby; ltd facs LS; gd birdwatching; bar 500m; only site in area; gd; very friendly owner; an oasis en rte to Madrid in picturesque setting; vg rest; gd welcome; pool not open yet (2016); rec."* **€19.00**   2016

OCHAGAVIA *3A1* (0.5km S Rural) *42.90777, -1.0875U*
Camping Osate, Ctra Salazar s/n, 31680 Ochagavia
(Navarra) **948-89 01 84; info@campingosate.net;**
www.campingosate.net

On N135 SE fr Auritz, turn L onto NA140 & cont for
24km bef turning L twd Ochagavia on NA140. Site
sp in 2km on R, 500m bef vill. Med, mkd, pt shd,
serviced pitches; EHU (4A) €5.50; gas; bbq;
50% statics; Eng spkn. *"Attractive, remote vill; gd, well-
maintained site; touring pitches under trees, sep fr
statics; facs ltd & poss stretched high ssn; site clsd
3 Nov-15 Dec & rec phone ahead LS; facs require
maintenance (2018); TO v helpful; gd walks fr site."*
€22.00 2018

"I like to fill in the reports as I travel from site to site"

You'll find report forms at the back of this
guide, or you can fill them in online at
camc.com/europereport.

OCHAGAVIA *3A1* (7km S Rural) *42.85486, -1.09766*
Camping Murkuzuria, 31453 Esparza de Salazar
**948-89 01 90 or 661-08 87 35; campingesparza@
gmail.com; www.campingmurkuzuria.com**

Fr N or S on Pic d'Orhy rte thro Pyrenees, NA178
(Spain)/D26(France). Situated in vill. Pamplona
approx 80km. Med, mkd, pt shd, EHU; bbq; twin axles;
TV; phone; bus adj; Eng spkn; adv bkg acc. *"Discounted
forest passes avail for Foret d'Iraty; excel."*
€19.00, 15 May-30 Oct. 2015

OLIVA *4E2* (2km E Coastal) *38.93278, -0.09778*
Camping Kiko Park, Calle Assagador de Carro 2,
46780 Playa de Oliva (València) **962-85 09 05; info@
kikopark.com; www.kikopark.com**

Exit AP7/E15 junc 61; fr toll turn R at T-junc onto
N332.At rndabt turn L foll sp Platjas; next rdbt
take 1st exit sp Platja; next rndabt foll sp Kiko
Park. Do not drive thro Oliva. Access poss diff on
app rds due humps. Lge, hdstg, mkd, hdg, shd,
serviced pitches; EHU (16A) inc; gas; bbq; red long
stay; phone; Eng spkn; adv bkg acc; ccard acc;
horseriding nr; watersports; games rm; bike hire;
fishing; games area; tennis; windsurfing school; golf
nr; CKE. *"Gd, family-run site; whirlpool; spa; very
helpful staff; vg, clean san facs; excel rest in Michelin
Guide; pitch price variable (lge pitches avail); cash
machine; beauty cent; access tight to some pitches."*
€66.00, E20. 2019

See advertisement

OROPESA *3D2* (4.2km N Coastal) *40.12125, 0.15848*
Camping Didota, Avenida de la Didota s/n, 12594
Oropesa del Mar (Castellón) **964 31 95 51; info@
campingdidota.es; www.campingdidota.es**

N on rd E-15 fr València to Barcelona, bear L at exit
45 sp Oropesa del Mar. Turn L onto N-340. Turn R at
next exit, then cont strt at rndabt onto on Avenida
La Ratlla. Foll camping sp. Med, pt shd, EHU (6-10A)
€4.30; gas; 10% statics; adv bkg acc; ccard acc. *"Gd
site, helpful friendly staff; excel pool."* **€45.00** 2019

OROPESA *3D2* (3.5km NE Coastal) *40.1275, 0.15972*
Bravo Playa Camping Resort, Cami L'Atall s/n, 12595 Ribera de Cabanes (Castellón) **964-31 95 67;** camping@bravoplaya.com; www.bravoplaya.com
12 🏕 ⛵(htd) ⬜ ⚓ 🚿 🔥 ♨ 🚻 ⛲ 🍴 🏪 🛒 ⚡ 🔌
⚓(covrd, htd) 🎣 shgl adj

Leave AP7 at exit 45 & take N340 twd Tarragona. Foll camp sp fr km 1000 stone. Site adj Torre La Sal 1. 1*, Lge, hdstg, mkd, hdg, pt shd, serviced pitches; EHU (10A) inc; gas; red long stay; TV; 10% statics; Eng spkn; adv bkg acc; games area; tennis; sauna; CKE. *"Vg, clean, peaceful, well-run site; lger pitches nr pool; library; more mature c'vanners very welcome; many dogs; poss diff for lge o'fits & m'vans; excel rest; excel beach with dunes; excel site, spotless facs, highly rec."*
€60.00 **2019**

PALAFRUGELL *3B3* (5km E Coastal) *41.9005, 3.1893*
Kim's Camping, Calle Font d'en Xeco s/n, 17211 Llafranc (Gerona) **972-30 11 56;** info@campingkims.com; www.campingkims.com
🏕 ⛵ ⬜ ⚓ 🚿 🔥 ♨ 🚻 ⛲ 🍴 🏪 🛒 ⚡ 🔌 ⚓
🎣 sand 500m

Exit AP7 at junc 6 Gerona Nord if coming fr France, or junc 9 fr S dir Palamós. Foll sp for Palafrugell, Playa Llafranc. Site is 500m N of Llafranc. 3*, Lge, hdg, mkd, hdstg, shd, sl, terr, EHU (5A) inc; gas; bbq (gas); red long stay; TV; 10% statics; phone; Eng spkn; adv bkg acc; ccard acc; watersports; golf 10km; games area; excursions; tennis 500m; games rm; CKE. *"Fxcel, well-organised, friendly, fam run site; steep site rds, new 2nd ent fr dual c'way fr Palafrugell to llafranc for lge o'fits & steps to rd to beach; bike hire 500m; guarded; discount in high ssn for stays over 1 wk; excel, modern san facs; beautiful coastal area; mostly gd size pitches."* **€51.00, 14 Apr-24 Sep.** **2017**

PALAFRUGELL *3B3* (5km S Coastal) *41.88879, 3.17928* **Camping Moby Dick,** Carrer de la Costa Verda 16-28, 17210 Calella de Palafrugell (Gerona) **972-61 43 07;** info@campingmobydick.com; www.campingmobydick.com
🏕 €3.30 ⛵ ⬜ ⚓ 🚿 🔥 ♨ 🚻 🌳 ⛲ 🍴 🏪 nr 🛒 ⚡ 🔌 ⚓
🎣 shgl 100m

Fr Palafrugell foll sps to Calella. At rndabt just bef Calella turn R, then 4th L, site clearly sp on R. Med, hdstg, pt shd, sl, terr, EHU (10A); TV; 15% statics; phone; bus 100m; Eng spkn; adv bkg acc; ccard acc; CKE. *"Nice views fr upper terraces; gd rest; very friendly; very pretty sm resort; lovely coastal walks; gd value; excel; lovely sea views; great site."*
€35.00, 25 Mar-30 Sep. **2016**

PALAMOS *3B3* (2km NE Coastal) *41.87277, 3.15055*
Camping Benelux, Paratge Torre Mirona s/n, 17230 Palamós (Gerona) **972-31 55 75;** www.cbenelux.com
🏕 ⛵ ⬜ ⚓ 🚿 🔥 ♨ 🚻 ⛲ 🍴 🏪 🛒 ⚡ 🔌 ⚓ 🎣 sand 1km

Turn E off Palamós-La Bisbal rd (C66/C31) at junc 328. Site in 800m on minor metalled rd, twd sea at Playa del Castell. Lge, hdstg, mkd, pt shd, terr, EHU (10A) €6.90; gas; bbq; red long stay; TV; 30% statics; phone; Eng spkn; adv bkg acc; ccard acc; CKE. *"In pine woods; many long stay British/Dutch; friendly owner; safe dep; clean facs poss ltd LS; car wash; currency exchange; poss flooding in heavy rain; rough grnd; marvellous walking/cycling area; many little coves."*
€36.70, 24 Mar-25 Sep. **2016**

SPAIN

PALAMOS *3B3* (3km W Coastal) *41.84700, 3.09861* **Eurocamping,** Avda de Catalunya 15, 17252 Sant Antoni de Calonge (Gerona) **972-65 08 79; info@ euro-camping.com; www.euro-camping.com**

🐕 €4 ♐♐ wo 🔥 🚿 ♿ 🟦 ♦ msp 🦋 ⛵ 🍴 ⊕ 🍴 🛒 🏧 🏊 sand 300m

Exit A7 junc 6 dir Palamós on C66 & Sant Feliu C31. Take exit Sant Antoni; on ent Sant Antoni turn R at 1st rndabt. Visible fr main rd at cent of Sant Antoni. 1*, V lge, mkd, hdg, shd, serviced pitches; EHU (6A) inc; bbq; red long stay; TV; 15% statics; phone; Eng spkn; adv bkg acc; ccard acc; games area; games rm; tennis; golf 7km; waterpark *"Excel facs for families; fitness rm; doctor Jul & Aug; car wash; lots to do in area; excel; lots of ssnal pitches; immac san facs; generous flat pitches; waterpark 5km; helpful, friendly staff."* **€54.00, 28 Apr-17 Sep.** **2017**

PALS *3B3* (6km NE Coastal) *42.00120, 3.19388* **Camping Playa Brava,** Playa Pals, 17256 Pals (Gerona) **972-63 68 94; info@playabrava.com; www. playabrava.com**

♐♐ wo 🔥 🚿 ♿ 🟦 ♦ 🦋 🍴 ⊕ 🍴 🛒 nr 🏧 🏊 sand adj

App Pals on rd 650 fr N or S. Avoid Pals cent. Fr by-pass take rd E sp Playa de Pals at rndabt. In 4km turn L opp shops, in 400m turn L past golf course, site on L bef beach. Avoid Begur & coast rd. 3*, Lge, shd, EHU inc; gas; adv bkg acc; tennis; car wash; bike hire. *"Guarded; gd facs for children & families."* **€34.00, 15 May-12 Sep.** **2016**

See advertisement on previous page

"I need an on-site restaurant"

We do our best to make sure site information is correct, but it is always best to check any must-have facilities are still available or will be open during your visit.

PALS *3B3* (1km E Rural) *41.95541, 3.15780* **Camping Resort Mas Patoxas,** Ctra Torroella-Palafrugell, Km 339, 17256 Pals (Gerona) **972-63 69 28; info@ campingmaspatoxas.com; www.campingmas patoxas.com**

12 🐕 €3.60 ♐♐ (htd) wo 🔥 🚿 ♿ 🟦 ♦ msp 🦋 🍴 ⊕ 🍴 🛒 🏧 🏊 sand 4km

AP7 exit 6 onto C66 Palamós/La Bisbal, turn L via Torrent to Pals. Turn R & site on R almost opp old town of Pals on rd to Torroella de Montgri. Or fr Palafrugell on C31 turn at km 339. 3*, Lge, mkd, shd, terr, serviced pitches; EHU (5A) inc; gas; red long stay; TV; phone; Eng spkn; adv bkg req; ccard acc; bike hire; games area; tennis; site clsd 14 Dec-16 Jan; golf 4km; CKE. *"Excel; recep clsd Monday LS; gd security."* **€47.00** **2015**

PALS *3B3* (4km E Rural) *41.98555, 3.18194* **Camping Cypsela,** Rodors 7, 17256 Playa de Pals (Gerona) **972-66 76 96; info@cypsela.com; www.cypsela.com**

♐♐ wo 🔥 🚿 ♿ 🟦 ♦ msp 🍴 ⛵ ⊕ 🍴 🛒 🏧 🏊 🏊 sand 1.5km

Exit AP7 junc 6, rd C66 dir Palamós. 7km fr La Bisbal take dir Pals & foll sp Playa/Platja de Pals, site sp. 5*, V lge, hdg, mkd, hdstg, shd, serviced pitches; EHU (6-10A) inc; gas; bbq; red long stay; TV; 60% statics; Eng spkn; adv bkg acc; ccard acc; tennis; golf 1km; games rm; bike hire; CKE. *"Noise levels controlled after midnight; excel san facs; mini golf & other sports; free bus to beach; private bthrms avail; 4 grades of pitch/price (highest price shown); vg site."* **€56.00, 4 May-10 Sep.** **2016**

PAMPLONA *3B1* (7km N Rural) *42.85776, -1.62250* **Camping Ezcaba,** Ctra a Francia, km 2,5, 31194 Eusa-Oricain (Navarre) **948-33 03 15; info@camping ezcaba.com; www.campingezcaba.com**

12 ♐♐ €2.95 ♐♐ 🔥 🟦 ♦ 🍴 ⛵ 🍴 ⊕ 🍴 🛒 🏧 🏊

Fr N leave AP15 onto NA30 (N ring rd) to N121A sp Francia/Iruña. Pass Arre & Oricáin, turn L foll site sp 500m on R dir Berriosuso. Site on R in 500m - fairly steep ent. Or fr S leave AP15 onto NA32 (E by-pass) to N121A sp Francia/Iruña, then as above. Med, mkd, pt shd, pt sl, EHU (10A) €5.50; gas; phone; bus 1km; adv bkg acc; horseriding; tennis. *"Helpful, friendly staff; sm pitches unsuitable lge o'fits & poss diff due trees, esp when site full; attractive setting; gd pool, bar & rest; ltd facs LS & poss long walk to san facs; in winter use as NH only; phone to check open LS; excel cycle track to Pamplona; quiet rural site; gd facs not htd."* **€30.00** **2018**

PARADA DE SIL *1B2* (3km NW Rural) *42.38941, -7.58885* **Camping Cañón do Sil,** Lugar de Castro s/n, 32740 Parada de Sil **608 537 017; info@canondosil camping.com; www.canondosilcamping.com**

12 ♐♐ wo 🔥 ♦ 🍴 🛒 nr

OU-0604 to Ctra De Castro, turn R on OU-0605. Turn L to Ctra da Castro, site on L. Med, pt shd, terr, EHU €4. *"Amazing location on the edge of Rv Sil Gorge; gd walks fr site; vg."* **€23.00** **2016**

PENAFIEL *1C4* (1km SW Rural) *41.59538, -4.12811* **Camping Riberduero,** Avda Polideportivo 51, 47300 Peñafiel **983-88 16 37; camping@campingpenafiel. com; www.campingpenafiel.com**

🐕 €1.50 ♐♐ (htd) wo 🔥 🚿 ♿ 🟦 ♦ 🦋 🍴 ⊕ 🍴 🛒 🏧 🏊

Fr Valladolid 56km or Aranda de Duero 38km on N122. In Peñafiel take VA223 dir Cuéllar, foll sp to sports cent/camping. Med, mkd, hdstg, shd, EHU (5A) €5; gas; red long stay; TV; 20% statics; phone; bus 1km; Eng spkn; adv bkg acc; ccard acc; site open w/end only LS; bike hire. *"Excel, well-kept site; interesting, historical area; ideal for wheelchair users; sm pitches and access diff due to trees."* **€16.50, Holy Week & 1 Apr-30 Sep.** **2016**

PENISCOLA *3D2 (2km N Coastal) 40.37916, 0.38833*
Camping Los Pinos, Calle Abellars s/n, 12598 Peñíscola (Castellón) 964-48 03 79; info@campinglospinos.com; www.campinglospinos.com

12 🏕 ⚄ ⊞ ♨ ♦ ♿ ▣ ✎ ᴹᴾ ♔ ♈ ⏸ 🛒 📶 ⚓ 🚣 ♒ 1.5km

Exit A7 junc 43 or N340 sp Peñíscola. Site sp on L. 1*, Med, mkd, hdg, pt shd, EHU (10A) €5.95; gas; bbq; TV; 10% statics; phone; bus fr site; Eng spkn; adv bkg acc; games rm. *"Narr site rds, lots of trees; poss diff access some pitches; vg."* €30.00   2016

> ## "Satellite navigation makes touring much easier"
>
> Remember most sat navs don't know if you're towing or in a larger vehicle – always use yours alongside maps and site directions.

PENISCOLA *3D2 (3km NE Coastal) 40.37152, 0.40269*
Camping El Edén, Ctra CS501 Benicarló-Peñíscola Km 6, 12598 Peñíscola (Castellón) 964-48 05 62; camping@camping-eden.com; www.camping-eden.com

12 🏕 €0.75 ⚄ (htd) ⚄ ♨ ♦ ♿ ▣ ✎ ᴹᴾ ♔ ♈ ⏸ 🛒 nr 📶
♒ 🚣 ᴷ shgl adj

Exit AP7 junc 43 onto N340 then CV141 to Peñíscola ctr. Take 3rd exit off rndabt at seafront, after 1km turn L after Hotel del Mar. Rec avoid sat nav rte across marshes fr Peñíscola. 1*, Lge, hdg, mkd, pt shd, EHU (10A) inc; gas; red long stay; 40% statics; bus adj; ccard acc; ACSI acc. *"San facs refurbished & v clean; beach adj cleaned daily; gd security; excel pool; easy access to sandy/gravel pitches but many sm trees poss diff for awnings or high m'vans; cash dispenser; poss vicious mosquitoes at dusk; easy walk/cycle to town; 4 diff sizes of pitch (some with tap, sink & drain) with different prices; ltd facs LS; excel."* €53.00   2015

PILAR DE LA HORADADA *4F2 (4km NE Coastal) 37.87916, -0.76555* **Lo Monte Camping & Caravaning,** Avenida Comunidada Valenciana No 157 CP 03190 00 34 966 766 782; info@campinglomonte-alicante.es; www.campinglomonte-alicante.es

12 🏕 €1 ⚄ (htd) ⚄ ♨ ♦ ♿ ▣ ✎ 🦋 ♔ ♈ ⏸ 🛒 📶 ✎
♒ (covrd, htd) ᴷ 1km

Exit 770 of AP7 dir Pilar de la Horadada; take the 1st L. 4*, Med, hdg, mkd, serviced pitches; EHU (16A) €0.40; bbq; Eng spkn; adv bkg acc; ccard acc; bike hire; games rm; CKE. *"New site; superb facs, exceptionally clean; great location, lots of golf & gd for walks & cycling; rec; excel; gym/wellness cent; beautifully laid out; neat; gd pool; v gd rest; isolated, nothing around site."* €36.00   2018

PINEDA DE MAR *3C3 (1km SW Coastal) 41.61827, 2.67891* **Camping Bellsol,** Passeig Maritim 46, 08397 Pineda de Mar 937-67 17 78; info@campingbellsol.com; www.campingbellsol.com

🏕 ⚄ ⊞ ⚄ ♨ ♦ ♿ ▣ ✎ ♔ ♈ ⏸ 🛒 📶 ♒ ᴷ

Fr N, take exit AP7 Junc 9 & immed turn R onto N11 dir Barcelona. Foll sp Pineda de Mar and turn L twd Paseo Maritim at exit at rv x-ing. Fr S on C32, exit 122 dir Pineda de Mar & foll dir Paseo Maritim & Campings fr same rndabt. Beware narr rds at other turnings. Lge, hdstg, shd, EHU (4A); red long stay; twin axles; 15% statics; bus nrby, train 800m; Eng spkn; adv bkg acc; CKE. *"V friendly & helpful staff; walking; bike & moped hire; sea fishing trips; vg."* €34.60, 19 Mar-31 Dec.   2016

PLASENCIA *1D3 (4km NE Urban) 40.04348, -6.05751* **Camping La Chopera,** Ctra N110, Km 401.3, Valle del Jerte, 10600 Plasencia (Caceres) 927-41 66 60; lachopera@campinglachopera.com; www.campinglachopera.com

12 🏕 ⚄ ⊞ ⚄ ♨ ♦ ♿ ▣ ✎ ♔ ♈ ⏸ 🛒 nr 📶 ♒ 🚣

In Plasencia on N630 turn E on N110 sp Ávila & foll sp indus est & sp to site. 3*, Med, shd, serviced pitches; EHU (6A) inc; gas; bbq; ccard acc; tennis; bike hire; CKE. *"Peaceful & spacious; much birdsong; conv Manfragüe National Park (breeding of black/Egyptian vultures, black storks, imperial eagles); excel pool & modern facs; helpful owners; shop (Jul & Aug); Carrefour in town; 35 min walk to town."* €22.00   2016

> ## "There aren't many sites open at this time of year"
>
> If you're travelling outside peak season remember to call ahead to check site opening dates – even if the entry says 'open all year'.

PLASENCIA *1D3 (14km S Rural) 39.94361, -6.08444* **Camping Parque Natural Monfragüe,** Ctra Plasencia-Trujillo, Km 10, 10680 Malpartida de Plasencia (Cáceres) 927- 45 92 33 or 605 94 08 78 (mob); campingmonfrague@hotmail.com; www.camping monfrague.com

12 🏕 ⚄ (htd) ⚄ ♨ ♦ ♿ ▣ ✎ ᴹᴾ 🦋 ♔ ♈ ⏸ 🛒 📶 ♒

Fr N on A66/N630 by-pass town, 5km S of town at flyover junc take EXA1 (EX108) sp Navalmoral de la Mata. In 6km turn R onto EX208 dir Trujillo, site on L in 5km. 3*, Med, hdg, pt shd, pt sl, terr, EHU (10A) €4; gas; bbq; TV; 10% statics; phone; Eng spkn; ccard acc; tennis; archery; bike hire; horseriding; games area. *"Friendly, helpful staff; red ACSI; vg, gd rest; clean, tidy, busy site but poss dusty, hoses avail; 10km to National Park (birdwatching trips); rambling; 4x4 off-rd; many birds on site; excel year round base; new excel san facs; discounted fees must be paid in cash; pitches muddy after heavy rain; peaceful; interesting over Halloween."* €20.40   2019

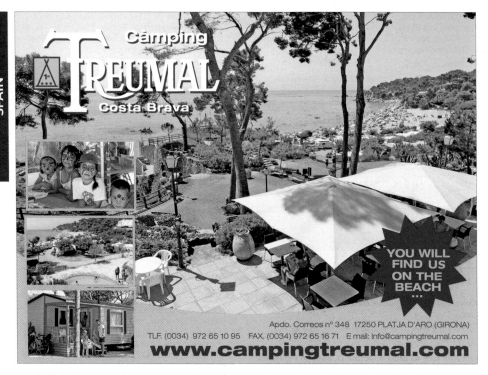

Camping TREUMAL Costa Brava

YOU WILL FIND US ON THE BEACH ...

Apdo. Correos nº 348 17250 PLATJA D'ARO (GIRONA)
TLF. (0034) 972 65 10 95   FAX. (0034) 972 65 16 71   E mail: Info@campingtreumal.com

www.campingtreumal.com

PLAYA DE ARO *3B3* (2km N Coastal) *41.83116,
3.08366* **Camping Cala Gogo,** Avda Andorra 13,
17251 Calonge (Gerona) **972-65 15 64; calagogo@
calagogo.es; www.calagogo.es**

Exit AP7 junc 6 dir Palamós/Sant Feliu. Fr Palamós
take C253 coast rd S twd Sant Antoni, site on R 2km
fr Playa de Aro, sp. 3*, Lge, pt shd, pt sl, terr, serviced
pitches; EHU (10A) inc; gas; bbq; red long stay; TV;
Eng spkn; adv bkg acc; boat hire; tennis; games area;
golf 4km; bike hire; games rm. *"Clean & recently
upgraded san facs; rest/bar with terr; no dogs Jul/Aug;
diving school; site terraced into pinewood on steep
hillside; excel family site."* **€52.00, 16 Apr-18 Sep.**
2016

PLAYA DE ARO *3B3* (2km N Coastal) *41.83666,
3.08722* **Camping Treumal,** Ctra Playa de Aro/
Palamós, C253, Km 47.5, 17250 Playa de Arro (Gerona) **972-65 10 95; info@campingtreumal.com;
www.campingtreumal.com**

Exit m'way at junc 6, 7 or 9 dir Sant Feliu de
Guixols to Playa de Aro; site is sp at km 47.5
fr C253 coast rd SW of Palamós. 1*, Lge, mkd, shd,
terr, EHU (10A) inc; gas; 25% statics; phone; Eng
spkn; adv bkg acc; ccard acc; car wash; sports facs;
games rm; tennis 1km; bike hire; golf 5km; fishing;
CKE. *"Peaceful site in pine trees; excel san facs;
manhandling poss req onto terr pitches; gd beach."*
€49.00, 31 Mar-30 Sep. **2016**

See advertisement

POLA DE SOMIEDO *1A3* (0.3km E Rural) *43.09222, -6.25222* **Camping La Pomerada de Somiedo,** 33840 Pola de Somiedo (Asturias) **985-76 34 04; csomiedo@ infonegocio.com**

♦♦♦ ⬜wd ▲ ℐ ᴹˢᴾ ✖ ⑴nr ☒nr

W fr Oviedo on A63, turn S onto AS15/AS227 to Augasmestas & Pola de Somiedo. Site adj Hotel Alba, sp fr vill. Route on steep, winding, mountain rd - suitable sm, powerful o'fits only. Sm, mkd, pt shd, EHU €4.20. "*Mountain views; nr national park.*" **€19.00, 1 Apr-31 Dec.** 2016

PONFERRADA *1B3* (16km W Rural) *42.56160, -6.74590* **Camping El Bierzo,** 24550 Villamartín de la Abadia (León) **987-56 25 15; info@campingbierzo.com; www.campingbierzo.com**

[12] ♦♦♦ ⬜wd ▲ ⅏ ℐ ᴹˢᴾ ✖ ℐ ⑴nr ⚍

Exit A6 junc 399 dir Carracedelo; after rndabt turn onto NV1 & foll sp Villamartín. Bef ent Villamartín turn L & foll site sp. 2*, Med, pt shd, EHU (3-5A) €5; phone; bus 1km; adv bkg acc; CKE. "*Attractive, rvside site in pleasant, lge, level grassed area with mature trees; gd, clean facs; friendly, helpful owner takes pride in his site; Roman & medieval attractions nr; sm rv beach adj.*" **€22.00** 2019

PONT DE SUERT *3B2* (3km N Rural) *42.43083, 0.73861* **Camping Can Roig,** Ctra Boí, Km 0.5, 25520 El Pont de Suert (Lleida) **973-69 05 02; info@ campingcanroig.com; www.campingcanroig.com**

🐕 €3.60 ♦♦♦ ⬜wd ▲ ⬛ ℐ ℐ Ⓣ ℐ ☒ ⚍ ⅏

N of Pont de Suert on N230 turn NE onto L500 dir Caldes de Boí. Site in 1km. App narr for 100m. Med, mkd, hdstg, pt shd, pt sl, EHU (5A) €5.15; gas; 5% statics; adv bkg acc; ccard acc. "*NH en rte S; beautiful valley; informal, friendly, quirky site (free range poultry); v relaxed atmosphere; helpful owner; fabulous valley & national park with thermal springs; poss scruffy (2015).*" **€27.00, 1 Mar-31 Oct.** 2015

PORT DE LA SELVA, EL *3B3* (3km W Coastal) *42.34222, 3.18333* **Camping Port de la Vall,** Ctra Port de Llançà, 17489 El Port de la Selva (Gerona) **972-38 71 86; portdelavall@terra.es**

🐕 €2.95 ♦♦♦ ⬛ ℐ ℐ Ⓣ ⑴ ☒ ⚍ 🐕shgl adj

On coast rd fr French border at Llançà take GI612 twd El Port de la Selva. Site on L, easily seen. Lge, pt shd, EHU (3-5A) €6; gas; 10% statics; phone; adv bkg acc; ccard acc. "*Easy 1/2 hr walk to harbour; gd site; sm pitches & low branches poss diff - check bef siting; san facs v clean.*" **€29.00, 1 Mar-15 Oct.** 2016

POTES *1A4* (1km W Rural) *43.15527, -4.63694* **Camping La Viorna,** Ctra Santo Toribio, Km 1, Mieses, 39570 Potes (Cantabria) **942-73 20 21; info@ campinglaviorna.com; www.campinglaviorna.com**

♦♦♦(htd) ⬜wd ▲ ⅏ ⬛ ℐ ᴹˢᴾ ✖ ℐ Ⓣ ⑴ ℐ ☒ ⅏ ⚍ ⅏

Exit N634 at junc 272 onto N621 dir Panes & Potes - narr, winding rd (passable for c'vans). Fr Potes take rd to Fuente Dé sp Espinama; in 1km turn L sp Toribio. Site on R in 1km, sp fr Potes. Do not use Sat Nav. Med, mkd, pt shd, terr, EHU (6A) €3.40 (poss rev pol); bbq; bus 1km; Eng spkn; adv bkg acc; ccard acc; bike hire; CKE. "*Lovely views; gd walks; friendly, family-run, clean, tidy site; gd pool; ideal Picos de Europa; conv cable car, 4x4 tours, trekking; mkt on Mon; festival mid-Sep v noisy; some pitches diff in wet & diff lge o'fits; excel san facs; voted 8th best camp in Spain; excel.*" **€27.70, 1 Apr-1 Nov.** 2017

POTES *1A4* (3km W Rural) *43.15742, -4.65617* **Camping La Isla-Picos de Europa,** Ctra Potes-Fuente Dé, 39586 Turieno (Cantabria) **942-73 08 96; campinglaislapicosdeeuropa@gmail.com; www.campinglaislapicosdeeuropa.com**

🐕 ♦♦♦ ⬜wd ▲ ⬛ ℐ ℐ ᴹˢᴾ ⑴ Ⓣ ⑴ ℐ ☒ ⅏ ⅏

Take N521 W fr Potes twd Espinama, site on R in 3km thro vill of Turieno (app Potes fr N). 2*, Med, mkd, shd, pt sl, EHU (6A) €4 (poss rev pol); gas; bbq; red long stay; 10% statics; phone; Eng spkn; adv bkg acc; ccard acc; horseriding; cycling; CKE. "*Delightful, family-run site; friendly, helpful owners; gd san facs; conv cable car & mountain walks (map fr recep); many trees & low branches; 4x4 touring; walking; mountain treks in area; hang-gliding; rec early am dep to avoid coaches on gorge rd; highly rec; lovely loc, gd facs.*" **€25.00, 1 Apr-15 Oct.** 2017

PUERTO DE MAZARRON *4G1* (5km NE Coastal) *37.5800, -1.1950* **Camping Los Madriles,** Ctra a la Azohía 60, Km 4.5, 30868 Isla Plana (Murcia) **968-15 21 51; info@campinglosmadriles.com; www.campinglosmadriles.com**

[12] ♦♦♦ ⬜wd ▲ ⅏ ℐ ᴹˢᴾ ✖ ⑴ Ⓣ ⑴ ☒ ⅏ ⅏(htd)

🐕shgl 500m

Fr Cartegena on N332 dir Puerto de Mazarrón. Turn L at rd junc sp La Azohía (32km). Site in 4km sp. Fr Murcia on E15/N340 dir Lorca exit junc 627 onto MU603 to Mazarrón, then foll sp. (Do not use rd fr Cartegena unless powerful tow vehicle/gd weight differential - use rte fr m'way thro Mazarrón). Lge, hdg, mkd, hdstg, pt shd, pt sl, serviced pitches; EHU (10A) €5; gas; red long stay; bus; Eng spkn; adv bkg req; ccard acc; games area; jacuzzi; CKE. "*Clean, well-run, v popular winter site; adv bkg req; some sm pitches, some with sea views; sl bet terrs; 3 days min stay high ssn; v helpful staff; excel.*" **€38.40** 2019

SPAIN

PUERTO DE SANTA MARIA, EL *2H3* (2km SW Coastal) *36.58768, -6.24092* **Camping Playa Las Dunas de San Antón,** Paseo Maritimo La Puntilla s/n, 11500 El Puerto de Santa María (Cádiz) **956-87 22 10; info@lasdunascamping.com; www.lasdunas camping.com**

12 🛊 🕯 🛉🕯 (wo) ▲ 🛪 🕹 🕹 🖪 🗸 (msp) 🕯 🍸 🗓 🗜 🖾 🗷 sand 50m

Fr N or S exit A4 at El Puerto de Sta María. Foll site sp carefully to avoid narr rds of town cent. Site 2-3km S of marina & leisure complex of Puerto Sherry. Alt, fr A4 take Rota rd & look for sp to site & Hotel Playa Las Dunas. Site better sp fr this dir & avoids town. 3*, Lge, pt shd, pt sl, EHU (10A) inc; gas; 30% statics; phone; Eng spkn; adv bkg rec; ccard acc; sports facs; CKE. *"Friendly staff; conv Cádiz & Jerez sherry region, birdwatching areas & beaches; conv ferry or catamaran to Cádiz; facs poss stretched high ssn; pitches quiet away fr rd; take care caterpillars in spring, poss dangerous to dogs; dusty site but staff water rds; gd; excel facs; busy; guarded; excel new shwr block (2016); pool adj; old elec conns."* **€26.00**   **2019**

RIAZA *1C4* (1.5km W Rural) *41.26995, -3.49750* **Camping Riaza,** Ctra de la Estación s/n, 40500 Riaza (Segovia) **921-55 05 80; info@camping-riaza.com; www.camping-riaza.com**

12 🛊 🕯 🛉🕯 (htd) (wo) ▲ 🛪 🕹 🕹 🖪 🗸 (msp) 🦋 🕯 🍸 🗓 🗜 🖾 🗷 🦭 🛋

Fr N exit A1/E5 junc 104, fr S exit 103 onto N110 N. In 12km turn R at rndabt on ent to town, site on L. Lge, hdg, unshd, EHU (10A) €4.70 (rev pol); bbq; 30% statics; phone; bus 900m; Eng spkn; adv bkg acc; games rm; games area. *"Vg site; various pitch sizes - some lge; excel san facs; easy access to/fr Santander or Bilbao; dogs free; beautiful little town."* **€31.00**   **2017**

RIBADEO *1A2* (12km N Rural/Coastal) *43.554004, -7.111085* **Rinlo Costa Camping,** Rua Campo Maria Mendez, s/n 27715 Rinlo **679-25 52 81; info@rinlo costa.es; www.rinlocosta.es**

12 🛊 🗸 🗜 🖾 🦎 🛋

Fr N634 take LU141 twrds Rinlo. Over rly bdge (0.5km) take 1st L and foll rd round for another 0.5km. Turn L and site ahead on R. Sm, EHU (6A) €4.50; bbq; cooking facs; bike hire. **€24.00**   **2018**

RIBADEO *1A2* (18km W Coastal) *43.56237, -7.20762* **Camping Gaivota,** Playa de Barreiros, 27792 Barreiros **982 12 44 51; campinggaivota@gmail.com; www.campingpobladogaivota.com**

🛊 🕯 🛉🕯 (wo) ▲ 🛪 🖪 🗸 (msp) 🦋 🕯 🍸 🗓 🗜 🗷 adj

Fr Berreiros take N634, turn L at KM 567, betRibadeo & Foz. Foll camping sp. Med, hdg, pt shd, EHU (6A); gas; bbq; twin axles; TV; 5% statics; phone. *"V well cared for; superb beaches; family run; pleasant bar & rest; excel."* **€30.00, 28 Mar-15 Oct.**   **2015**

RIBADESELLA *1A3* (3km W Rural) *43.46258, -5.08725* **Camping Ribadesella,** Sebreño s/n, 33560 Ribadesella (Asturias) **985 858293 or 985 857721; info@camping-ribadesella.com; www.camping-ribadesella.com**

🛊 €2.50 🛉🕯 (wo) ▲ 🛪 🕹 🕹 🖪 🗸 🦋 🍸 🗓 🗜 🗷 🖾
🦭 (covrd, htd) 🗷 sand 4km

W fr Ribadesella take N632. After 2km fork L up hill. Site on L after 2km. Poss diff for lge o'fits & alt rte fr Ribadesella vill to site to avoid steep uphill turn can be used. Lge, mkd, pt shd, pt sl, terr, EHU (10A) €5; gas; bbq; red long stay; Eng spkn; adv bkg acc; ccard acc; tennis; games area; games rm; CKE. *"Clean san facs; some sm pitches; attractive fishing vill; prehistoric cave paintings nrby; excel; not much shd; steps or slopes to walk to top rate facs; 35min easy downhill walk to town, shorter walk down steep lane to beach; rec; terr site; rest has cvrd terrace and lovely views."* **€36.00, 12 Apr-22 Sep.**   **2019**

> ## "I like to fill in the reports as I travel from site to site"
>
> You'll find report forms at the back of this guide, or you can fill them in online at camc.com/europereport.

RIBADESELLA *1A3* (8km W Rural/Coastal) *43.47472, -5.13416* **Camping Playa de Vega,** Vega, 33345 Ribadesella (Asturias) **985-86 04 06; info@camping playadevega.com; www.campingplayadevega.com**

🛊 🛉🕯 (wo) ▲ 🗸 🦋 🕯 🍸 🗓 🗜 🗷 sand 400m

Fr A8 exit junc 336 sp Ribadesella W, thro Bones. At rndabt cont W dir Caravia, turn R opp quarry sp Playa de Vega. Fr cent of Ribadesella (poss congestion) W on N632. Cont for 5km past turning to autovia. Turn R at sp Vega & site. 3*, Med, hdg, pt shd, terr, serviced pitches; EHU €4.15; bbq; TV; phone; bus 700m; ccard acc; CKE. *"Sh walk to vg beach thro orchards; beach rest; sm pitches not suitable lge o'fits; poss overgrown LS; immac san facs; a gem of a site; beware very narr bdge on ent rd."* **€24.50, 15 Jun-15 Sep.**   **2017**

RIBEIRA *1B2* (10km N Rural) *42.62100, -8.98600* **Camping Ría de Arosa II,** Oleiros, 15993 Santa Eugenia (Uxía) de Ribeira (La Coruña) **981- 86 59 11; rural@campingriadearosa.com; www.camping riadearosa.com**

12 🛊 €2.50 🛉🕯 (htd) (wo) ▲ 🛪 🕹 🕹 🖪 🗸 (msp) 🦋 🕯 🍸 🗓 🗜 🖾 🛋

Exit AP9 junc 93 Padrón & take N550 then AC305/VG11 to Ribeira. Then take AC550 to Oleiros to site, well sp. V lge, mkd, hdg, shd, EHU (6A) inc; gas; bbq; TV; 10% statics; phone; Eng spkn; adv bkg acc; ccard acc; fishing; tennis; games area; games rm; CKE. *"Beautiful area; helpful, friendly staff; excel; lots to do; excel pool; great facs."* **€28.50**   **2015**

ROCIO, EL *2G3* (2km N Rural) *37.14194, -6.49250* **Camping La Aldea,** Ctra del Rocío, Km 25, 21750 El Rocío,Almonte (Huelva) **959-44 26 77; info@ campinglaaldea.com; www.campinglaaldea.com**

[12] ♈ €3 ♥♥(htd) [WD] ♨ ♿ ♿ ☐ ✓ [MP] ❦ ⏲ ⊕ ♨ ☎ ⚠ ⚓ (htd)

Fr A49 turn S at junc 48 onto A483 by-passing Almonte, site sp just bef El Rocío rndabt. Fr W (Portugal) turn off at junc 60 to A484 to Almonte, then A483. 3*, Lge, hdstg, mkd, hdg, pt shd, EHU (10A) €6.50; gas; bbq; red long stay; 30% statics; phone; bus 500m; Eng spkn; adv bkg acc; ccard acc; horseriding nr; CKE. *"Well-appointed & maintained site; winter rallies; excel san facs; friendly, helpful staff; tight turns on site; most pitches have kerb or gully; van washing facs; pitches soft after rain; rd noise; easy walk to interesting town; avoid festival (in May-7 weeks after Easter) when town cr & site charges higher; poss windy; excel birdwatching nrby (lagoon 1km); beautiful site; gd pool & rest."* **€30.00** **2019**

RONDA *2H3* (1km S Rural) *36.72111, -5.17166* **Camping El Sur,** Ctra Ronda-Algeciras Km 1.5, 29400 Ronda (Málaga) **952-87 59 39; info@campingelsur.com; www.campingelsur.com**

[12] ♈ €1.70 ♥♥(htd) [WD] ♨ ♿ ♿ ☐ ✓ [MP] 🦋 ⏲ ⊕ nr ♨ ☎ ⚠ ⚓

Site on W side of A369 dir Algeciras. Do not tow thro Ronda. Med, mkd, hdstg, pt shd, sl, terr, EHU (5-10A) €4.30-5.35 (poss rev pol &/or no earth); red long stay; phone; Eng spkn; adv bkg acc; CKE. *"Gd rd fr coast with spectacular views; long haul for lge o'fits; busy family-run site in lovely setting; conv National Parks & Pileta Caves; poss diff access some pitches due trees & high kerbs; hard, rocky grnd; san facs poss stretched high ssn; easy walk to town; friendly staff; vg rest; excel."* **€27.00** **2019**

ROSES *3B3* (1km W Urban/Coastal) *42.26638, 3.16305* **Camping Joncar Mar,** Ctra Figueres s/n, 17480 Roses (Gerona) **972-25 67 02; info@camping joncarmar.com; www.campingjoncarmar.com**

[12] ♈ €2.40 ♥♥(htd) [WD] ♨ ♿ ☐ ✓ ⏲ ❦ ⊕ ☎ ⚠ ♪ ⚓
🏖 sand 150m

At Figueres take C260 W for Roses. On ent Roses turn sharp R at last rndabt at end of dual c'way. Site on both sides or rd - go to R (better) side, park & report to recep on L. 2*, Lge, pt shd, pt sl, EHU (6-10A) poss no earth; gas; red long stay; 15% statics; phone; bus 500m; Eng spkn; adv bkg acc; ccard acc; golf 15km; games rm. *"Conv walk into Roses; hotels & apartment blocks bet site & beach; poss cramped/ tight pitches; narr rds; vg value LS; new san facs 2015."* **€32.00** **2015**

ROSES *3B3* (2.5km W Coastal) *42.26638, 3.15611* **Camping Salatà,** Port Reig s/n, 17480 Roses (Gerona) **972-25 60 86; info@campingsalata.com; www.campingsalata.com**

♈ €2.80 ♥♥(htd) [WD] ♨ ♿ ♿ ☐ ✓ ⏲ ❦ ⊕ ♨ ☎ ⚠ ⚓ (htd)
🏖 sand 200m

App Roses on rd C260. On ent Roses take 1st R after Roses sp & Caprabo supmkt. Lge, mkd, hdstg, pt shd, EHU (6-10A) inc; gas; red long stay; 10% statics; phone; Eng spkn; adv bkg acc; ccard acc; CKE. *"Vg area for sub-aqua sports; vg clean facs, but not enough; dogs not acc Jul/Aug; red facs LS; pleasant walk/cycle to town; overpriced."* **€50.70, 12 Mar-31 Oct.** **2016**

SAHAGUN *1B3* (1km W Rural) *42.37188, -5.04280* **Camping Pedro Ponce,** Avda Tineo, s/n 24326 Sahagun **987 78 04 15; campingsahagun@ hotmail.com; www.villadesahagun.es**

♈ ♥♥ [WD] ♨ ♿ ♿ ☐ ✓ ⏲ ❦ ⊕ ☎ nr ♨ ♪ ⚓

Leave A231 at junc 46 onto N120. Foll sp Shagun. Site on in 1km. Lge, unshd, EHU (6A); twin axles; 60% statics; phone; bus adj; Eng spkn; ccard acc. *"Excel municipal site; modern facs; sep area for tourers; interesting town; vg."* **€17.00, 1 Mar-31 Oct.** **2015**

"We must tell the Club about that great site we found"

Get your site reports in by mid-August and we'll do our best to get your updates into the next edition.

SALAMANCA *1C3* (17km NE Rural) *41.05805, -5.54611* **Camping Olimpia,** Ctra de Gomecello, Km 3.150, 37427 Pedrosillo el Ralo (Salamanca) **923-08 08 54 or 620-46 12 07; info@campingolimpia.com; www.campingolimpia.com**

[12] ♈ €1 ♥♥(htd) [WD] ☐ ✓ ⏲ ⊕ ♨

Exit A62 junc 225 dir Pedrosillo el Ralo & La Vellés, strt over rndabt, site sp. Sm, hdg, pt shd, EHU €3; phone; bus 300m; Eng spkn; adv bkg acc; site clsd 8-16 Sep; CKE. *"Helpful, friendly & pleasant owner; really gd 2 course meal for €10 (2014); handy fr rd with little noise & easy to park; poss open w/ends only LS; excel; grass pitches; clean facs; perfect; some pitches tight."* **€20.00** **2018**

SALAMANCA *1C3* (5km E Rural) *40.97611, -5.60472*
Camping Don Quijote, Ctra Aldealengua, Km 1930,
37193 Cabrerizos (Salamanca) **923-20 90 52; info@
campingdonquijote.com; www.campingdon
quijote.com**

🛪 ♦♦ wo ▲ ♨ ⚲ 🖵 ⁄ msp 🦋 ⁂ 🍴 Ⓗ ⚓ 🛢 /🏔 ⚞ 🧖

⚓ sand 200m

**Fr Madrid or fr S cross Rv Tormes by most easterly
bdge to join inner ring rd. Foll Paseo de Canalejas
for 800m to Plaza España. Turn R onto SA804 Avda
de los Comuneros & strt on for 5km. Site ent 2km
after town boundary sp. Fr other dirs, head into
city & foll inner ring rd to Plaza España. Site well
sp fr rv & ring rd.** Med, hdstg, mkd, hdg, pt shd, EHU
(10A) inc; bbq; twin axles; 10% statics; phone; bus;
Eng spkn; adv bkg acc; ccard acc; rv fishing; CKE. *"Gd
rv walks; conv city cent; 45 mins easy cycle ride 6km
to town along rv; rv Tormes flows alongside site with
pleasant walks; friendly owner; highly rec; new excel
san facs (2016); v friendly; 12 min walk to bus stop."*
€24.00, 1 Mar-31 Oct. 2017

SALAMANCA *1C3* (7km E Urban) *40.94722, -5.6150*
Camping Regio, Ctra Ávila-Madrid, Km 4, 37900 Santa
Marta de Tormes (Salamanca) **923-13 88 88; recepcion@
campingregio.com; www.campingregio.com**

⓬ 🛪 ♦♦ wo ▲ ♨ ⚲ 🖵 ⁄ msp 🦋 ⁂ 🍴 Ⓗ ⚓ 🛢 /🏔

**Fr E on SA20/N501 outer ring rd, pass hotel/
camping sp visible on L & exit Sta Marta de Tormes,
site directly behind Hotel Regio. Foll sp to hotel.**
3*, Lge, mkd, pt shd, pt sl, EHU (10A) €3.95 (no earth);
gas; TV; 5% statics; phone; bus to Salamanca; Eng
spkn; ccard acc; car wash; bike hire; CKE. *"In LS stop at
24hr hotel recep; poss no hdstg in wet conditions; conv
en rte Portugal; refurbished facs to excel standard; site
poss untidy, & ltd security in LS; hotel pool high ssn;
hypmkt 3km; spacious pitches but some poss tight for
lge o'fits; take care lge brick markers when reversing;
hourly bus in and out of city; excel pool; vg; facs up to
gd standard & htd; highly rec."* **€23.00** 2019

SALOU *3C2* (1km S Urban/Coastal) *41.0752, 1.1176*
Camping Sangulí, Paseo Miramar-Plaza Venus, 43840
Salou (Tarragona) **977-38 16 41; mail@sanguli.es;
www.sanguli.es**

🛪 ♦♦ (htd) wo ▲ ♨ ⚲ 🖵 ⁄ msp ⁂ 🍴 Ⓗ ⚓ 🛢 /🏔 ⚞ 🧖 🖐

⚓ sand 50m

**Exit AP7/E15 junc 35. At 1st rndbt take dir to Salou
(Plaça Europa), at 2nd rndbt foll site sp.**
5*, V lge, hdstg, mkd, shd, pt sl, serviced pitches; EHU
(10A) inc; gas; bbq; red long stay; TV; 35% statics;
phone; bus; Eng spkn; adv bkg rec; ccard acc; games
area; waterslide; games rm; jacuzzi; car wash; tennis;
CKE. *"Quiet end of Salou nr Cambrils & 3km Port
Aventura; site facs recently updated/upgraded;
fitness rm; excursions; cinema; youth club; mini
club; amphitheatre; excel, well-maintained site."*
€75.00, 5 Apr-3 Nov. 2019

SAN ROQUE *2H3* (7km NE Rural) *36.25031, -5.33808*
Camping La Casita, Ctra N340, Km 126.2, 11360 San
Roque (Cádiz) **956-78 00 31**

⓬ 🛪 €2.67 ♦♦ wo ▲ ♨ ⚲ ⁄ msp Ⓗ 🛢 /🏔 ⚞ ⚓ 🧖 sand 3km

**Site sp 'Via de Servicio' parallel to AP7/E15. Access
at km 119 fr S, km 127 fr N. Site visible fr rd.**
Lge, pt shd, pt sl, terr, EHU (10A) €4.54; red long stay;
90% statics; phone; bus 100m; Eng spkn; adv bkg req;
ccard acc; horseriding; CKE. *"Shwrs solar htd - water
temp depends on weather (poss cold); san facs poss
unclean; friendly staff; conv Gibraltar & Morocco; daily
buses to La Línea & Algeciras; ferries to N Africa (secure
parking at port); golf course next to site; great rest;
poor site."* **€39.50** 2016

SAN SEBASTIAN/DONOSTIA *3A1* (/km W Rural)
43.30458, -2.04588 **Camping Igueldo,** Paseo Padre
Orkolaga 69, 20008 San Sebastián (Guipúzkoa) **943-21
45 02; info@campingigueldo.com; www.camping
igueldo.com**

⓬ ♦♦ wo ▲ ♨ ⚲ 🖵 ⁄ ⁂ 🍴 Ⓗ 🛢 /🏔 ⚓ sand 5km

**Fr W on A8, leave m'way at junc 9 twd city cent,
take 1st R & R at rndabt twd Avda de Tolosa sp
Ondarreta. At sea front turn hard L at rndabt sp to
site (Avda Satrústegui) & foll sp up steep hill 4km to
site. Fr E exit junc 8 then as above. Site sp as Garoa
Camping Bungalows. Steep app poss diff for lge
o'fits.** Lge, hdg, mkd, pt shd, terr, serviced pitches;
EHU (10A) inc; gas; red long stay; TV; phone; bus to
city adj; Eng spkn; CKE. *"Vg, clean facs; sm pitches
poss diff; spectacular views; pitches muddy when wet;
excel rest 1km (open in winter); pool 5km; frequent
bus to beautiful, interesting town; new pool (2017)."*
€37.00 2017

"I need an on-site restaurant"

We do our best to make sure site information
is correct, but it is always best to check any
must-have facilities are still available or will
be open during your visit.

SAN TIRSO DE ABRES *1A2* (0.5km N Rural) *43.41352,
-7.14141* **Amaido,** El Llano, 33774 San Tirso de Abres
**616-78 11 55; amaido@amaido.com; www.amaido.
com**

🛪 ♦♦ wo ▲ ♨ ⚲ 🖵 ⁄ msp 🛢 /🏔

**Head N on A6 twds Lugo & exit 497 for N-640 twds
Oviedo/Lugo Centro cidade. At rndabt take 4th exit
onto N-640, turn R at LU-P-6104, turn R onto Vegas,
then take 2nd L. Site at end of rd.** Med, hdg, pt shd,
terr, EHU (6A); bbq; twin axles; TV; adv bkg acc; bike
hire; games area. *"Lovely wooded site set in a circle
around facs; farm animals; vg site."*
€20.00, 10 Apr-15 Sep. 2019

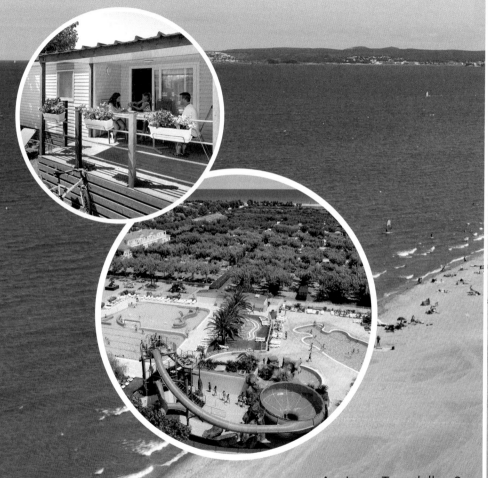

SAN VICENTE DE LA BARQUERA *1A4* (1km E Coastal) *43.38901, -4.3853* **Camping El Rosal,** Ctra de la Playa s/n, 39540 San Vicente de la Barquera (Cantabria) **942-71 01 65; info@campingelrosal.com; www.campingelrosal.com**

🚶🚻 wc ♨ ♿ 🚿 ⚊ / 🦋 ⚑ ⓣ 🍴 ⓣ 🛒 ✗ 🏖 sand adj

Fr A8 km 264, foll sp San Vicente. Turn R over bdge then 1st L (site sp) immed at end of bdge; keep L & foll sp to site. Barier height 3.1m. Med, mkd, pt shd, pt sl, terr, EHU (6A) €4.80; gas; phone; Eng spkn; adv bkg acc; ccard acc; CKE. *"Lovely site in pine wood o'looking bay; surfing beach; some modern, clean facs; helpful staff; vg rest; easy walk or cycle ride to interesting town; Sat mkt; no hot water at sinks."* **€27.00, 1 Apr-30 Sep.**   2019

SAN VICENTE DE LA BARQUERA *1A4* (6km E Coastal) *43.38529, -4.33831* **Camping Playa de Oyambre,** Finca Peña Gerra, 39540 San Vicente de la Barquera (Cantabria) **942-71 14 61; camping@oyambre.com; www.oyambre.com**

🐕 🚶🚻 wc ♨ ⚊ / MSP ⚑ 🍴 ⓣ 🛒 ✗ 🏊 🏖 800m

E70/A8 Santander-Oviedo, exit sp 264 S. Vicente de la Barquera, then N634 for 3 km to Comillas exit on the Ctra La Revilla-Comillas (CA 131) bet km posts 27 and 28. 3*, Lge, mkd, pt shd, pt sl, terr, EHU (10A) €4.55; gas; 40% statics; bus 200m; Eng spkn; adv bkg acc; ccard acc; CKE. *"V well-kept site; clean, helpful owner; quiet week days LS; gd base for N coast & Picos de Europa; 4x4 avail to tow to pitch if wet; some sm pitches & rd noise some pitches; conv Santander ferry; immac san facs; excel site; staff speak gd english; rest rec; gd base to tour N coast & Picos de Europa."* **€27.50, 4 Mar-30 Oct.**   2015

SANT JORDI *3D2* (2km SW Rural) *40.49318, 0.31806* **Camping Maestrat Park,** 12320 Sant Jordi (Castellón) **964-86 08 89 or 679-29 87 95 (mob); info@maestratpark.es; www.maestratpark.es**

12 🐕 🚶🚻 wc ♨ ♿ 🚿 ⚊ / MSP ⚑ 🍴 ⓣ 🛒 ✗ 🏊 🖐

Exit AP7 junc 42 onto CV11 to Sant Rafel del Riu. At rndabt with fuel stn take CV11 to Traiguera; then at rndabt take 1st exit onto N232 dir Vinarós & at next rndabt take 2nd exit sp Calig. Site 2km on L. Sm, hdstg, mkd, hdg, pt shd, pt sl, EHU (10-16A) €4.50; bbq; red long stay; twin axles; TV; 25% statics; phone; bus; Eng spkn; adv bkg acc; games rm; bike hire; CKE. *"Excel; club memb owner; excel for v lge o'fits."* **€25.00**   2015

SANT PERE PESCADOR *3B3* (1km SE Coastal) *42.18180, 3.10403* **Camping L'Àmfora,** Avda Josep Tarradellas 2, 17470 Sant Pere Pescador (Gerona) **972-52 05 40; info@campingamfora.com; www.campingamfora.com**

🐕 €4.95 🚶🚻 (htd) wc ♨ ♿ 🚿 ⚊ / MSP 🦋 ⚑ 🍴 ⓣ 🛒 ✗ 🖐 🚲 🏖 sand adj

Fr N exit junc 3 fr AP7 onto N11 fro Figueres/Roses. At junc with C260 foll sp Castelló d'Empúries & Roses. At Castelló turn R at rndabt sp Sant Pere Pescador then foll sp to L'Amfora. Fr S exit junc 5 fr AP7 onto GI 623/GI 624 to Sant Pere Pescador. 4*, V lge, mkd, hdg, pt shd, pt sl, serviced pitches; EHU (10A) inc; gas; bbq (charcoal, elec); red long stay; TV; 15% statics; phone; Eng spkn; adv bkg acc; fishing; horseriding 5km; bike hire; games rm; windsurfing school; tennis; waterslide; ice; CKE. *"Excel, well-run, clean site; no o'fits over 10m Apr-Sep; helpful staff; immac san facs; gd rest; private san facs avail; poss flooding on some pitches when wet; Parque Acuatico 18km."* **€60.40, 14 Apr-27 Sep, E22.**   2019

See advertisement on previous page

SANT PERE PESCADOR *3B3* (2km SE Coastal) *42.16194, 3.10888* **Camping Las Dunas,** 17470 Sant Pere Pescador (Gerona) (Postal Address: Aptdo Correos 23, 17130 L'Escala) **972-52 17 17 or 01205 366856 (UK); info@campinglasdunas.com; www.campinglasdunas.com**

🐕 €4.50 🚶🚻 wc ♨ ♿ 🚿 ⚊ / MSP 🦋 ⚑ 🍴 ⓣ 🛒 ✗ 🖐 🏊 🖐 🏖 sand adj

Exit AP7 junc 5 dir Viladamat & L'Escala; 2km bef L'Escala turn L for Sant Martí d'Empúries, turn L bef ent vill for 2km, camp sp. V lge, mkd, pt shd, pt sl, serviced pitches; EHU (6A) inc; gas; bbq; TV; 5% statics; phone; Eng spkn; adv bkg req; games area; games rm; tennis; watersports; CKE. *"Greco-Roman ruins in Empúries; gd sized pitches - extra for serviced; busy, popular site; souvenir shop; money exchange; cash machine; doctor; excel, clean facs; vg site."* **€72.50, 15 May-15 Sep.**   2019

See advertisement opposite

SANT PERE PESCADOR *3B3* (1.3km S Coastal) *42.18816, 3.10265* **Camping Las Palmeras,** Ctra de la Platja 9, 17470 Sant Pere Pescador (Gerona) **972-52 05 06; info@campinglaspalmeras.com; www.campinglaspalmeras.com**

🐕€4.50 ♀♂ ⓌⒹ ⚓ ♿ ☕ ◨ / ᴹˢᴾ 🦋 ♈ ⍦ ⑪ ⛽ 🛒 ⚠ ✏

⛷ (htd) 🏖 ⛵ sand 200m

Exit AP7 junc 3 or 4 at Figueras onto C260 dir Roses/Cadaqués rd. After 8km at Castelló d'Empúries turn S for Sant Pere Pescador & cont twd beach. Site on R of rd. 1*, Lge, mkd, shd, serviced pitches; EHU (5-16A) €3.90; gas; TV; phone; Eng spkn; adv bkg acc; games area; bike hire; games rm; tennis; CKE. "*Pleasant site; helpful, friendly staff; superb, clean san facs; cash point; gd cycle tracks; nature reserve nrby; excel.*"
€47.70, 15 Apr-5 Nov.   2016

See advertisement above

SANTA ELENA *2F4* (0.4km E Rural) *38.34305, -3.53611* **Camping Despeñaperros,** Calle Infanta Elena s/n, Junto a Autovia de Andulucia, Km 257, 23213 Santa Elena (Jaén) **953-66 41 92; info@camping despenaperros.com; www.campingdespenaperros. com**

12 🐕 ♀♂ ⓌⒹ ⚓ ♿ ☕ ◨ / ᴹˢᴾ ⍦ ♈ ⑪ 🛒 🛒 ⚠ ⛷

Leave A4/E5 at junc 257 or 259, site well sp to N side of vill nr municipal leisure complex. 3*, Med, hdstg, mkd, pt shd, serviced pitches; EHU (10A) €4.25 (poss rev pol); gas; red long stay; TV (pitch); 80% statics; phone; bus 500m; adv bkg acc; ccard acc; CKE. "*Gd winter NH in wooded location; gd size pitches but muddy if wet; gd walking area, perfect for dogs; friendly, helpful staff; clean san facs; disabled facs wc only; conv national park & m'way; gd rest; sh walk to vill & shops; site v rural; beautiful area.*" €24.00   2017

"That's changed – Should I let the Club know?"

If you find something on site that's different from the site entry, fill in a report and let us know. See camc.com/europereport.

SPAIN

SANTA MARINA DE VALDEON *1A3* (0.6km N Rural) *43.13638, -4.89472* **Camping El Cares,** El Cardo, 24915 Santa Marina de Valdeón (León) **987-74 26 76;** campingelcares@hotmail.com

🐕 €2.10 ♦♦ 🔲 wc ♨ ♿ 🔥 🚿 ⚋ 🦋 ▼ ⓗ 🛒

Fr S take N621 to Portilla de la Reina. Turn L onto LE243 to Santa Marina. Avoid vill (narr rd), go to Northern end of vill bypass. Site is sp on L. 2*, Med, pt shd, terr, EHU (5A) €3.20; 10% statics; phone; bus 1km; ccard acc; CKE. *"Lovely, scenic site high in mountains; gd base for Cares Gorge; friendly, helpful staff; gd views; tight access - not rec if towing or lge m'van."* **€26.50, 1 Jun-15 Oct.** **2016**

"I like to fill in the reports as I travel from site to site"

You'll find report forms at the back of this guide, or you can fill them in online at camc.com/europereport.

SANTA POLA *4F2* (1km NW Urban/Coastal) *38.20105, -0.56983* **Camping Bahía de Santa Pola,** Ctra de Elche s/n, Km. 11, 03130 Santa Pola (Alicante) **965-41 10 12;** campingbahia@gmail.com; www.campingbahia.com

🔲12 🐕 ♦♦ (htd) 🔲 wc ♨ ♿ 🔥 🚿 ⚋ 🦋 ⓗ 🛒 ⚏ ⚓ sand 1km

Exit A7 junc 72 dir airport, cont to N332 & turn R dir Cartagena. At rndabt take exit sp Elx/Elche onto CV865, site 100m on R. Lge, mkd, hdstg, pt shd, EHU (10A) €3; gas; red long stay; TV (pitch); 50% statics; phone; bus adj; Eng spkn; adv bkg acc; ccard acc; CKE. *"Helpful, friendly manager; well-organised site; sm pitches; recep in red building facing ent; excel san facs; site rds steep; attractive coastal cycle path."* **€25.00** **2019**

SANTAELLA *2G3* (5km N Rural) *37.62263, -4.85950* **Camping La Campiña,** La Guijarrosa-Santaella, 14547 Santaella (Córdoba) **957-31 53 03;** info@ campinglacampina.com; www.camping lacampina.com

🔲12 🐕 €2 ♦♦ 🔲 wc ♨ ♿ 🔥 🚿 ⚋ ▼ ⓗ 🛒 ⚏ ⚓

Fr A4/E5 leave at km 441 onto A386 rd dir La Rambla to Santaella for 11km, turn L onto A379 for 5km & foll sp. 2*, Sm, mkd, hdstg, pt shd, pt sl, EHU (10A) €4; gas; bbq; red long stay; TV; bus at gate to Córdoba; Eng spkn; adv bkg acc; ccard acc; CKE. *"Fine views; friendly, warm welcome; popular, family-run site; many pitches sm for lge o'fits; guided walks; poss clsd winter - phone to check; helpful & knowledgeable owner; great site."* **€29.00** **2017**

SANTANDER *1A4* (5km NE Coastal) *43.48916, -3.79361* **Camping Cabo Mayor,** Avda. del Faro s/n, 39012 Santander (Cantabria) **942-39 15 42;** info@ cabomayor.com; www.cabomayor.com

♦♦ 🔲 wc ♨ ♿ 🔥 🚿 ⚋ 🦋 ♍ ▼ ⓗ ⚏ 🛒 ⚏ ⚓ ⚓ adj

Sp thro town but not v clearly. On waterfront (turn R if arr by ferry). At lge junc do not foll quayside, take uphill rd (resort type prom) & foll sp for Faro de Cabo Mayor. Site 200m bef lighthouse on L. Lge, mkd, unshd, terr, EHU (10A) inc; gas; TV; 10% statics; phone; bus to Santander nrby; Eng spkn; CKE. *"Med to lge pitches; site popular with lge youth groups hg ssn; shwrs clsd 2230-0800; conv ferry; pitches priced by size, pleasant coastal walk to Sardinero beachs; gd NH; well organised & clean; gd facs but dated; no hot water for washing up; excel; gd welcome."* **€20.00, 27 Mar-12 Oct.** **2018**

SANTANDER *1A4* (8km W Coastal) *43.47678, -3.87303* **Camping Virgen del Mar,** Ctra Santander-Liencres, San Román-Corbán s/n, 39000 Santander (Cantabria) **942-34 24 25;** cvirdmar@ceoecant.es; www.campingvirgendelmar.com

🔲12 ♦♦ 🔲 wc ♨ ♿ 🔥 🚿 ⚋ ♍ 🦋 ▼ ⓗ 🛒 ⚏ ⚓ ⚓ sand 300m

Fr ferry turn R, then L up to football stadium, L again leads strt into San Román. If app fr W, take A67 (El Sardinero) then S20, leave at junc 2 dir Liencres, strt on. Site well sp. 2*, Lge, mkd, pt shd, EHU (4-10A) €4; red long stay; bus 500m; adv bkg acc; CKE. *"Basic facs, poss ltd hot water; some sm pitches not suitable lge o'fits; site adj cemetary; phone in LS to check site open; expensive LS; gd for ferry; recep not v friendly."* **€27.00** **2019**

SANTIAGO DE COMPOSTELA *1A2* (3.5km NE Urban) *42.88972, -8.52444* **Camping As Cancelas,** Rua do Xullo 25, 35, 15704 Santiago de Compostela (La Coruña) **981-58 02 66 or 981-58 04 76;** info@campingascancelas.com; www.camping ascancelas.com

🔲12 🐕 ♦♦ 🔲 wc ♨ ♿ 🔥 🚿 ⚋ 🦋 ♍ ▼ ⓗ 🛒 ⚏ 🪚 ⚓ ⚓

Exit AP9 junc 67 & foll sp Santiago. At rndabt with lge service stn turn L sp 'camping' & foll sp to site turning L at McDonalds. Site adj Guardia Civil barracks. NB-Do not use sat nav if app fr Lugo on N547. 2*, Lge, mkd, shd, pt sl, terr, EHU (5A) inc; gas; bbq; TV; phone; bus 100m; Eng spkn; CKE. *"Busy site-conv for pilgrims; rec arr early high ssn; some sm pitches poss diff c'vans & steep ascent; gd clean san facs, stretched when busy; gd rest; bus to city 100m fr gate avoids steep 15 min walk back fr town (LS adequate car parks in town); poss interference with car/ c'van electrics fr local transmitter, if problems report to site recep; LS recep in bar; arr in sq by Cathedral at 1100 for Thanksgiving service at 1200; helpful owner; excel site; facs v clean; wifi vg."* **€33.60** **2017**

SANTILLANA DEL MAR *1A4* (2.5km E Rural) *43.38222, -4.08305* **Camping Altamira,** Barrio Las Quintas s/n, 39330 Queveda (Cantabria) **942-84 01 81; nfo@ campingaltamira.es; www.campingaltamira.es**

⚭ ♨ ⊟ 🚿 ▽ ⓦ 🅿 ⚓

Clear sp to Santillana fr A67; site on R 3km bef vill. 2*, Med, mkd, pt shd, pt sl, terr, EHU (3A)- (5A) €2 (poss rev pol); gas; TV; 30% statics; bus 100m; Eng spkn; adv bkg req; ccard acc; horseriding; CKE. *"Pleasant site; ltd facs LS; nr Altimira cave paintings; easy access Santander ferry on m'way; gd coastal walks; open w/end only Nov-Mar - rec phone ahead; excel; san facs v clean & modern; local rests nrby."* **€22.00, 10 Mar-7 Dec.** 2019

SANTILLANA DEL MAR *1A4* (1km NW Rural) *43.39333, -4.11222* **Camping Santillana del Mar,** Ctra de Comillas s/n, 39330 Santillana del Mar (Cantabria) 942-81 82 50; **www.campingsantillana.com**

12 ⚭ ♨ ⓦ ♨ ⚿ ⚐ ⊟ 🚿 ᴹᴾ ⓌⓅ ▽ ⓘ 🅰 ⚓ ⚒ ⚓
🛁 ⚓5km

Fr W exit A8 junc 230 Santillana-Comillas, then foll sp Santillana & site on rd CA131. Fr E exit A67 junc 187 & foll sp Santillana. Turn R onto CA131, site on R up hill after vill. 3*, Lge, pt shd, sl, terr, EHU (6A) inc (poss rev pol); gas; 20% statics; phone; bus 300m; Eng spkn; horseriding; bike hire; tennis; golf 15km; CKE. *"Useful site in beautiful historic vill; hot water only in shwrs; diff access to fresh water & to mv disposal point; narr, winding access rds, projecting trees & kerbs to some pitches - not rec lge o'fits or twin axles; car wash; cash machine; poss muddy LS & pitches rutted; poss travellers; gd views; lovely walk to town; poor facs (2014); NH."* **€24.00** 2017

"We must tell the Club about that great site we found"

Get your site reports in by mid-August and we'll do our best to get your updates into the next edition.

SANTO DOMINGO DE LA CALZADA *1B4* (3.6km E Rural) *42.44083, -2.91506* **Camping Banares,** Ctra N120, Km 42.2, 26250 Santo Domingo de la Calzada **941-34 01 31; info@campingbanares.es; www.campingbanares.es**

12 ⚭ ♨ ⓦ ♨ ⚿ ⊟ 🚿 ᴹᴾ ▽ ⓘ 🅰 ⚓ ⚒ 🛁

Fr N120 Burgos-Logroño rd, turn N at Santo Domingo, foll sp Banares & site. 4*, Sm, unshd, pt sl, EHU (5-10A) €5.50; gas; 90% statics; Eng spkn; adv bkg acc; ccard acc; games area; tennis; CKE. *"Interesting, historic town; shops, bars, rests 3km; NH only."* **€32.60** 2016

SANXENXO *1B2* (4.5km SW Coastal) *42.39254, -8.84517* **Camping Playa Paxariñas,** Ctra C550, Km 2.3 Lanzada-Portonovo, 36960 Sanxenxo (Pontevedra) **986-72 30 55; info@campingpaxarinas. com; www.campingpaxarinas.com**

⚭ ⚭ ⓦ ♨ ⚿ ⚐ ⊟ 🚿 ⚑ ⓌⓅ ▽ ⓘ 🅰 ⚓ ⚓ sand adj

Fr Pontevedra W on P0308 coast rd; 3km after Sanxenxo. Site thro hotel on L at bend. Site poorly sp. Fr AP9 fr N exit junc 119 onto VRG41 & exit for Sanxenxo. Turn R at 3rd rndabt for Portonovo to site in dir O Grove. Do not turn L to port area on ent Portonovo. Lge, mkd, shd, pt sl, terr, EHU (5A) €4.75; gas; bbq; red long stay; TV; 75% statics; phone; bus adj; Eng spkn; adv bkg acc; ccard acc; CKE. *"Site in gd position; secluded beaches; views over estuary; take care high kerbs on pitches; excel san facs - ltd facs LS & poss clsd; lovely unspoilt site; plenty of shd."* **€32.00, 17 Mar-15 Oct.** 2016

SANXENXO *1B2* (3km NW Coastal) *42.41777, -8.87555* **Camping Monte Cabo,** Soutullo 174, 36990 Noalla (Pontevedra) **986-74 41 41; info@montecabo. com; www.montecabo.com**

12 ⚭ ⓦ ♨ ⚿ ⊟ 🚿 ⚑ ⓌⓅ ▽ ⓘ 🅰 ⚓ ⚓ sand 250m

Fr AP9 exit junc 119 onto upgraded VRG4.1 dir Sanxenxo. Ignore sp for Sanxenxo until rndabt sp A Toxa/La Toja, where turn L onto P308. Cont to Fontenla supmkt on R - minor rd to site just bef supmkt. Rd P308 fr AP9 junc 129 best avoided. Sm, mkd, pt shd, terr, EHU €4.25; red long stay; TV; 10% statics; phone; bus 600m; Eng spkn; adv bkg acc; ccard acc; CKE. *"Peaceful, friendly site set above sm beach (access via steep path) with views; sm pitches; beautiful coastline & interesting historical sites; vg."* **€30.00** 2017

SARRIA *1B2* (2km E Rural) *42.77625, -7.39552* **Camping Vila de Sarria,** Ctra. De Pintín, Km 1 Sarria 27600 **982 53 54 67; info@campingviladesarria.com; www.campingviladesarria.com**

⚭ ⚭ ⓦ ♨ ⚿ ⊟ 🚿 ⚿ ⓌⓅ ▽ ⓘ 🅰 ⚓nr

Leave Sarria on LU5602 twds Pintin. Site on L in 1km. Med, pt shd, pt sl, EHU; twin axles; Eng spkn; adv bkg acc; ccard acc. *"Quiet site on Camino de Santiago Rte; excel rest; v pleasant, welcoming staff; busy w/ends; vg."* **€22.50, Easter-30 Sep.** 2015

SAX *4F2* (6km NW Rural) *38.56875, -0.84913* **Camping Gwen & Michael,** Colonia de Santa Eulalia 1, 03630 Sax (Alicante) **965-47 44 19 or 7718 18 58 05(UK)**

⚭ ⚭ ⓦ ♨ ⚿ ⊟ 🚿 ⚑ ⓘ nr ⚓nr

Exit A31 at junc km 191 & foll sp for Santa Eulalia, site on R just bef vill sq. Rec phone prior to arr. Sm, hdg, hdstg, unshd, EHU (3A) €1. *"Vg CL-type site; friendly British owners; beautiful area; gd NH & touring base; c'van storage avail; 3 rest nrby."* **€15.00, 15 Mar-30 Nov.** 2016

SPAIN

SEGOVIA *1C4* (2km SE Urban) *40.93138, -4.09250*
Camping El Acueducto, Ctra de la Granja, 40004
Segovia 921-42 50 00; informacion@camping
acueducto.com; www.campingacueducto.com

🐕 ♀♀ WD ♨ ♿ ⊟ ⌀ MSP ⛱ ⵏ Ⓗ nr 🅿 ⚠ 🛶 ⛵

Turn off Segovia by-pass N110/SG20 at La Granja
exit, but head twd Segovia on DL601. Site in approx
500m off dual c'way just bef Restaurante Lago.
Lge, mkd, pt shd, pt sl, EHU (6-10A) €5; gas; bbq;
10% statics; phone; bus 150m; bike hire; CKE. *"Excel;*
helpful staff; lovely views; clean facs; gates locked
0000-0800; gd bus service; some pitches sm & diff for
lge o'fits; city a 'must' to visit; new (unhtd) facs for
women (2016); bus stop and gd spmkt 10min walk;
site muddy after rain; unfriendly new owner (2018)."
€32.50, 26 Mar-15 Oct. **2018**

SENA DE LUNA *1A3* (1km S Rural) *42.92181, -5.96153*
Camping Río Luna, Ctra de Abelgas s/n, 24145 Sena
de Luna (León) **987-59 77 14; info@campingrioluna.**
com; www.campingrioluna.com

🐕 ♀♀(htd) WD ♨ ♿ ⊟ ⌀ MSP 🦋 ⛱ ⵏ ⓪

S fr Oviedo on AP66, at junc 93 turn W onto CL626
to Sena de Luna in approx 5km. Site on L, sp.
1*, Med, pt shd, EHU (5A) €3.80; bbq; sw nr; TV;
phone; adv bkg acc; ccard acc. *"Vg, scenic site; walking,*
climbing; cent for wild boar & wolves; rural, rustic site;
hot shwrs." **€18.00, Easter & 1 May-30 Sep.** **2019**

SITGES *3C3* (2km SW Urban/Coastal) *41.23351,*
1.78111 **Camping Bungalow Park El Garrofer,** Ctra
C246A, Km 39, 08870 Sitges (Barcelona) **93 894 17**
80; info@garroferpark.com; www.garroferpark.com

🐕 €2.65 ♀♀(htd) WD ♨ ♿ ⊟ ⌀ MSP ⛱ ⵏ Ⓗ ⓪ ⊟ ⚠
⚓ 🛶 ⵏ shgl 900m

Exit 26 on the C-32 dir St. Pere de Ribes, at 1st
rndabt take 1st exit, at 2nd rndabt take 2nd exit, foll
rd C-31 to campsite. V lge, hdstg, mkd, hdg, pt shd,
serviced pitches; EHU (5-10A) €4.10 (poss rev pol);
gas; TV; 80% statics; phone; bus adj; Eng spkn; adv
bkg acc; ccard acc; games rm; tennis 800m; car wash;
site clsd 19 Dec-27 Jan to tourers; windsurfing; games
area; horseriding; bike hire; CKE. *"Great location, conv*
Barcelona, bus adj; sep area for m'vans; pleasant staff;
recep open 0800-2100; gd level site; quiet; gd old &
new facs." **€40.00, 22 Feb-15 Dec.** **2019**

SORIA *3C1* (2km SW Rural) *41.74588, -2.48456*
Camping Fuente de la Teja, Ctra Madrid-Soria,
Km 223, 42004 Soria 975-22 29 67; camping@
fuentedelateja.com; www.fuentedelateja.com

🐕 ♀♀ WD ♨ ♿ ⊟ ⌀ ⛱ ⵏ Ⓗ ⓪ ⊟ nr ⚠ 🛶

Fr new ring road SO-20 follow Madrid to S edge of
town. Take exit 8 sp Redonda then R at rndabt. 2*,
Med, mkd, pt shd, pt sl, EHU (6A) €3 (poss no earth);
gas; bbq; TV; 10% statics; phone; Eng spkn; adv bkg
acc; ccard acc; CKE. *"Vg site; excel, gd for NH; vg san*
facs; interesting town; phone ahead to check site poss
open bet Oct & Easter; hypmkt 3km; easy access to site;
pitches around 100sqm, suits o'fits upto 10m; friendly
staff; access fr 9am." **€23.30, 1 Mar-31 Oct.** **2019**

SUECA *4E2* (5km NE Coastal) *39.30354, -0.29270*
Camping Les Barraquetes, Playa de Sueca, Mareny
Barraquetes, 46410 Sueca (València) **961-76 07 23;**
info@barraquetes.com; www.barraquetes.com

🐕 ♀♀ WD ♨ ♿ ⊟ ⌀ MSP ⛱ ⵏ 🅿 ⚠ 🛶 ⚓ ⊟ ⵏ sand 350m

Exit AP7 junc 58 dir Sueca onto N332. In Sueca take
CV500 to Mareny Barraquetes. Or S fr València
on CV500 coast rd. Foll sp for Cullera & Sueca.
Site on L. Med, mkd, pt shd, EHU (10A) €5.88; gas;
bbq; red long stay; twin axles; TV; 70% statics;
phone; bus 500m; Eng spkn; ccard acc; games
area; waterslide; tennis; windsurfing school; CKE.
"Quiet, family atmosphere; conv touring base &
València; quiet beach 8 min walk; helpful staff; gd."
€33.00, 16 Jan-14 Dec. **2017**

TAPIA DE CASARIEGO *1A3* (2km SW Coastal)
43.56394, -6.95247 **Camping Playa de Tapia,** La
Reburdia, 33740 Tapia de Casariego (Asturias)
985-47 27 21

🐕 ♀♀ WD ♨ ♿ ⊟ ⌀ MSP 🦋 ⛱ ⵏ Ⓗ ⊟ ⵏ sand 1m

Fr Ribadeo pass thro vill of Serentes on N634 past
1st camping sp. Site on L at 546km post, foll sp to
site. 2*, Med, mkd, hdg, pt shd, pt sl, EHU (16A) €4.06;
gas; phone; bus 800m; Eng spkn; adv bkg acc; CKE.
"Gd access; busy, well-maintained, friendly site;
o'looking coast & harbour; poss ltd hot water; walking
dist to delightful town."
€23.00, Holy Week & 1 Jun-15 Sep. **2015**

TARAZONA *3B1* (8km SE Rural) *41.81890, -1.69230*
Camping Veruela Moncayo, Ctra Vera-Veruela,
50580 Vera de Moncayo (Zaragoza) **976 64 90 34;**
antoniogp@able.es

12 🐕 ♀♀ WD ♨ ♿ ⊟ ⌀ ⛱ ⵏ Ⓗ ⊟ ⵏ nr ⚠

Fr Zaragoza, take AP68 or N232 twd Tudela/
Logroño; after approx. 50km, turn L to join N122
(km stone 75) twd Tarazona; cont 30km & turn L
twd Vera de Moncayo; go thro town cent; site on
R; well sp. Med, hdg, pt shd, pt sl, EHU; gas;
adv bkg acc; bike hire; CKE. *"Quiet site adj monastery;*
friendly owner; gd." **€26.00** **2017**

TARIFA *2H3* (10km NW Coastal) *36.06908, 5.68036*
Camping Valdevaqueros, Ctra N340 km 75,5 11380
Tarifa 34 956 684 174; info@campingvaldevaqueros.
com; www.campingvaldevaqueros.com

12 🐕 ♀♀ WD ♨ ⌀ ⛱ ⵏ Ⓗ ⊟ ⚓ 🛶 ⊟ ⵏ sandy 1km

Campsite is sp 9km fr Tarifa on the N340 twds
Cadiz. Lge, pt shd, pt sl, EHU (6A); TV; 50% statics;
phone; Eng spkn; adv bkg rec; games area; bike hire.
"Excel site; watersports nrby." **€34.00** **2019**

TARRAGONA *3C3* (0.6km NE Urban/Coastal) *40.88707, 0.80630* **Camping Nautic,** Calle Libertat s/n, 43860 L'Ametlla de Mar Tarragona 34 977 456 110; info@campingnautic.com; www.camping nautic.com

🏕 🚐🐕 wc 🚿♨️♿🚽❌✉️🛒🍴🍺🍽️🛒🏪⛲🏊🛥️🎣

Fr N340 exit at km 1113 sp L'Ametlla de Mar (or A7 exit 39). Over rlwy bdge, foll rd to L. Turn R after park and TO on R, foll signs to campsite. Lge, hdstg, pt shd, terr, EHU; TV; 25% statics; phone; bus 500m, train 700m; Eng spkn; adv bkg acc; games area; CCI. *"Vg site; tennis court; 5 mins to attractive town with rest & sm supmkt; lge Mercadona outsite town; site on different levels."* €40.00, 6 Apr-3 Nov.   2019

TARRAGONA *3C3* (5km NE Coastal) *41.13019, 1.31170* **Camping Las Palmeras,** N340, Km 1168, 43080 Tarragona **977-20 80 81;** laspalmeras@las palmeras.com; www.laspalmeras.com

🏕 🚐🐕 wc 🚿♨️♿🚽❌✉️🍴🍺🍽️🛒🏪⛲🏊🛥️🛥️ 🎣 sand adj

Exit AP7 at junc 32 (sp Altafulla). After about 5km on N340 twd Tarragona take sp L turn at crest of hill. Site sp. 1*, V lge, mkd, pt shd, EHU (6A) inc; gas; red long stay; 10% statics; phone; ccard acc; games rm; tennis; games area; CKE. *"Gd beach; ideal for families; poss mosquito prob; many sporting facs; gd, clean san facs; friendly, helpful staff; naturist beach 1km; supmkt 5km; excel site."* €45.00, 2 Apr-12 Oct.   2019

TARRAGONA *3C3* (12km E Coastal) *41.1324, 1.3604* **Camping-Caravaning Tamarit Park,** Playa Tamarit, Ctra N340, Km 1172, 43008 Playa Tamarit (Tarragona) **977-65 01 28;** tamaritpark@tamarit.com; www.tamarit.com

🏕 €4 🚐🐕(htd) wc 🚿♨️♿🚽❌✉️🍴🍺🍽️🛒🏪⛲🏊🎣🛥️(htd) 🛒🎣 shgl adj

Fr A7/E15 exit junc 32 sp Altafulla/Torredembarra, at rndabt join N340 by-pass sp Tarragona. At rndabt foll sp Altafulla, turn sharp R to cross rlwy bdge to site in 1.2km, sp. V lge, hdstg, hdg, shd, pt sl, serviced pitches; EHU (10A) inc; gas; bbq; red long stay; TV; 30% statics; phone; Eng spkn; adv bkg rec; ccard acc; games area; watersports; tennis; CKE. *"Well-maintained, secure site with family atmosphere; excel beach; superb pool; private bthrms avail; best site in area but poss noisy at night & w/end; variable pitch prices; beachside pitches avail; cash machine; car wash; take care overhanging trees; Altafulla sh walk along beach worth visit; excel."* €65.00, 14 Mar-16 Oct.
                                      2016

TOLEDO *1D4* (3.5km W Rural) *39.86530, -4.04714* **Camping El Greco,** Ctra Pueblo Montalban, Km.0.7, 45004 Toledo **925-22 00 90;** info@camping elgreco.es; www.campingelgreco.es

12 🏕 🚐🐕(htd) wc 🚿♿🚽❌✉️🍴🍺🍽️🛒🏪⛲🏊🛥️

Site on CM4000 between CM40 ring road & Puenta de la Cava bridge. Fr E foll yellow sp. Fr W look for 5 flagpoles on L next to Cirgarral Del Santoangel Custodio. 3*, Med, hdg, mkd, hdstg, pl shd, pt sl, EHU (6-10A) inc (poss rev pol); gas; bbq; phone; bus to town, train to Madrid fr town; Eng spkn; ccard acc; games area; CKE. *"Clean, tidy, well-maintained; all pitches on gravel; easy parking on o'skts - adj Puerta de San Martín rec - or bus; some pitches poss tight; san facs clean; lovely, scenic situation; excel rest; friendly, helpful owners; vg; dusty; gd rest; site poss neglected during LS; gd pool, closes fr 15 Sept; cheap bar; nice, neat site; mv service pnt basic."* €31.00   2018

SPAIN

TORDESILLAS *1C3* (2km SSW Urban) *41.49584, -5.00494* **Kawan Village El Astral,** Camino de Pollos 8, 47100 Tordesillas (Valladolid) **983-77 09 53; info@ campingelastral.es; www.campingelastral.com**

12 🐕 €2.35 ♦♦ (htd) 🅦 ♨ ♿ 🖳 🖉 ⓜ 🦋 ♛ 🍴 ⑭ ♨ 🛒 ⚓ ⛱

Fr NE on A62/E80 thro town turn L at rndabt over rv & immed after bdge turn R dir Salamanca & almost immed R again into narr gravel track (bef Parador) & foll rd to site; foll camping sp & Parador. Poorly sp. Fr A6 exit sp Tordesillas & take A62. Cross bdge out of town & foll site sp. Med, hdg, mkd, hdstg, pt shd, EHU (5A-10A) €3.60-5 (rev pol); gas; TV; 10% statics; phone; Eng spkn; ccard acc; tennis; bike hire; rv fishing; site open w/end Mar & Oct; CKE. *"V helpful owners & staff; easy walk to interesting town; pleasant site by rv; vg, modern, clean san facs & excel facs; popular NH; excel site in every way, facs superb; various size pitches; worth a visit; conv o'night on rte to S of Spain/Portugal; pull thro pitches avail; excel."* **€26.00, E03.** **2019**

TORLA *3B2* (1.5km N Rural) *42.63948, -0.10948* **Camping Ordesa,** Ctra de Ordesa s/n, 22376 Torla (Huesca) **974-11 77 21; camping@campingordesa.es; www.campingordesa.es**

🐕 €3 ♦♦ 🅦 ♨ ♨ 🖳 🖉 🦋 ♛ ⑭ 🛒 nr ⚓ ⛱

Fr Ainsa on N260 twd Torla. Pass Torla turn R onto A135 (Valle de Ordesa twd Ordesa National Park). Site 2km N of Torla, adj Hotel Ordesa. Med, pt shd, serviced pitches; EHU (6A) €5.50; 10% statics; phone; bus 1km; Eng spkn; adv bkg rec; ccard acc; tennis; CKE. *"V scenic; recep in adj Hotel Ordesa; excel rest; helpful staff; facs poss stretched w/end; long, narr pitches & lge trees on access rd poss diff lge o'fits; ltd facs LS; no access to National Park by car Jul/Aug, shuttlebus fr Torla."* **€22.60, 28 Mar-30 Sep.** **2016**

TORLA *3B2* (1km NE Rural) *42.63181, -0.10685* **Camping Rió Ara,** Ctra Ordesa s/n, 22376 Torla (Huesca) **974-48 62 48; campingrioara@ordesa.net; www.campingrioara.com**

🐕 ♦♦ 🅦 ♨ ♨ ♿ 🖳 🖉 ⓜ ♛ 🍴 ⑭ nr 🛒 ⚓

Leave N260/A135 on bend approx 2km N of Broto sp Torla & Ordesa National Park. Drive thro Torla; as leaving vill turn R sp Rió Ara. Steep, narr rd down to & across narr bdge (worth it). Sm, pt shd, pt sl, EHU (6A) €4.25; bbq; TV; bus 500m; adv bkg acc; CKE. *"Attractive, well-kept, family-run site; mainly tents; conv for Torla; bus to Ordesa National Park (high ssn); not rec for lge o'fits due to steep app; gd walking & birdwatching; excel; fantastic views; wonderful area.""Facs dated but functional and clean; 20m walk to Torla."* **€24.00, 1 Apr-30 Sep.** **2015**

TORRE DEL MAR *2H4* (1.6km S Coastal) *36.7342, -4.1003* **Camping Torre del Mar,** Paseo Maritimo s/n, 29740 Torre del Mar (Málaga) **952-54 02 24; info@ campingtorredelmar.com; www.campingtorre delmar.com**

12 ♦♦ 🅦 ♨ ♿ 🖳 🖉 ⓜ 🦋 🍴 nr ⑭ nr 🛒 ⚓ ⛱ ⚓

⛱ shgl 50m

Fr N340 coast rd, at rndabt at W end of town with 'correos' on corner turn twds sea sp Faro, Torre del Mar. At rndabt with lighthouse adj turn R, then 2nd R, site adj big hotel, ent bet lge stone pillars (no name sp). 2*, Lge, hdg, hdstg, mkd, shd, serviced pitches; EHU (16A) €4.40 (long lead req); gas; red long stay; TV (pitch); 39% statics; phone; tennis; CKE. *"Tidy, clean, friendly, well-run site; some sm pitches; site rds tight; gd, clean san facs; popular LS, constant hot water; poorly laid out; poss flooding in parts of site; conv for town."* **€39.00** **2016**

TORRE DEL MAR *2H4* (7km W Coastal) *36.71967, -4.16471* **Camping Valle Niza Playa,** Ctra N340, km 264, 1 29792 Valle Niza/Malaga **952-51 31 81; info@ campingvalleniza.es; www.campingvalleniza.es**

12 🐕 ♦♦ 🅦 ♨ ♨ 🖳 🖉 ♛ 🍴 ⑭ 🛒 ⚓ ⛱ ⛱shgl

A7 Malaga-Motril exit 265 Cajiz Costa; at T-junc L onto N340 Coast rd twd Torre Del Mar. Site in 1km. 1*, Med, mkd, pt shd, EHU (6-10A); bbq; twin axles; TV; 50% statics; bus 0.3km; adv bkg acc; ccard acc; games area. *"Gdn ctr adj; poor beach across rd; gd."* **€33.00** **2017**

TORREVIEJA *4F2* (7km SW Rural) *37.97500, -0.75111* **Camping Florantilles,** Ctra San Miguel de Salinas-Torrevieja, 03193 San Miguel de Salinas (Alicante) **965-72 04 56; camping@campingflorantilles.com; www.campingflorantilles.com**

12 ♦♦ 🅦 ♨ ♿ 🖳 🖉 ⓜ 🍴 ♨ 🛒 ⚓ ⛱ 🚿 ⛱sand 5km

Exit AP7 junc 758 onto CV95, sp Orihuela, Torrevieja Sud. Turn R at rndabt & after 300m turn R again, site immed on L. Or if travelling on N332 S past Alicante airport twd Torrevieja. Leave Torrevieja by-pass sp Torrevieja, San Miguel. Turn R onto CV95 & foll for 3km thro urbanisation 'Los Balcones', then cont for 500m, under by-pass, round rndabt & up hill, site sp on R. Lge, hdg, mkd, hdstg, pt shd, terr, EHU (10A) inc; gas; bbq; TV; 20% statics; adv bkg acc; ccard acc; golf nr; horseriding 10km; games rm; CKE. *"Popular, British owned site; fitness studio/keep fit classes; workshops: calligraphy, card making, drawing/painting, reiki, sound therapy etc; basic Spanish classes; 3 golf courses nrby; no o'fits over 10m; recep clsd 1330-1630; walking club; friendly staff; many long-stay visitors & all year c'vans; suitable mature couples; own transport ess; gd cyling, both flat & hilly; conv hot spa baths at Fortuna & salt lakes."* **€30.00, E11.** **2017**

TORROELLA DE MONTGRI *3B3* (6km SE Coastal) *42.01111, 3.18833* **Camping El Delfin Verde,** Ctra Torroella de Montgrí-Palafrugell, Km 4, 17257 Torroella de Montgrí (Gerona) **972-75 84 54;** info@ eldelfinverde.com; www.eldelfinverde.com

🏕 🚁 €4 🛉🛉 wo 🕭 ♨ 🚿 🔲 ♦ MSP 🦋 ⛲ 🍽 🄌 🛒 🛂 ⛛ 🏊 ⛵

🌴 *sand adj*

Fr N leave A7 at junc 5 dir L'Escala. At Viladamat turn R onto C31 sp La Bisbal. After a few km turn L twd Torroella de Montgrí. At rndabt foll sp for Pals (also sp El Delfin Verde). At the flags turn L sp Els Mas Pinell. Foll site sp for 5km. 4*, V lge, mkd, pt shd, pt sl, EHU (6A) inc; bbq; TV; 40% statics; ccard acc; games rm; horseriding 4km; windsurfing; fishing; tennis; bike hire; CKE. *"Superb, gd value site; winter storage; excel pool; wide range of facs; sportsgrnd; hairdresser; disco; no o'fits over 8m high ssn; dogs not acc high ssn; money exchange; clean, modern san facs; all water de-salinated fr fresh water production plant; bottled water rec for drinking & cooking; mkt Mon."*
€58.00, 17 May-20 Sep. 2017

TORROX COSTA *2H4* (2km NNW Urban) *36.73944, -3.94972* **Camping El Pino,** Urbanización Torrox Park s/n, 29793 Torrox Costa (Málaga) **952-53 00 06;** info@campingelpino.com; www.campingelpino.com

12 🏕 🚁 €2.50 🛉🛉 wo 🕭 ♨ 🚿 🔲 ♦ 🍽 🄌 ⛛ 🛂 ⛛ 🏊

🌴 *sand 800m*

Exit A7 at km 285, turn S at 1st rndabt, turn L at 2nd rndabt & foll sp Torrox Costa N340; in 1.5km at rndabt turn R to Torrox Costa, then L onto rndabt sp Nerja, site well sp in 4km. App rd steep with S bends. Fr N340 fr Torrox Costa foll sp Torrox Park, site sp. Lge, mkd, shd, terr, EHU €3.80 (long lead req); gas; bbq; red long stay; 35% statics; phone; Eng spkn; games area; golf 8km; car wash; CKE. *"Gd size pitches but high kerbs; narr ent/exit; gd hill walks; conv Malaga; Nerja caves, Ronda; gd touring base; noise fr rd and bar; san facs adequate."*
€18.00 2019

See advertisement

TOSSA DE MAR *3B3* (3km SW Coastal) *41.71509, 2.90672* **Camping Cala Llevado,** Ctra Tossa-Lloret, Km 3, 17320 Tossa de Mar (Gerona) **972-34 03 14;** info@calallevado.com; www.calallevado.com

🛉🛉 wo 🕭 ♨ 🚿 🔲 ♦ MSP 🦋 ⛲ 🍽 🄌 🛒 🛂 ⛛ 🏊 🏖

🌴 *shgl adj*

Exit AP7 junc 9 dir Lloret. In Lloret take GI 682 dir Tossa de Mar. Site well sp. 4*, V lge, mkd, shd, terr, EHU (5-10A) €3.50; gas; TV; 10% statics; phone; Eng spkn; adv bkg acc; waterskiing; tennis; windsurfing; games area; boat trips; sports facs; fishing; CKE.
€29.00, Holy Week & 1 May-30 Sep. 2016

UNQUERA *1A4* (5km W Rural) *43.3750, -4.56416* **Camping Colombres (formerly El Mirador de Llavandes),** Vegas Grandes, 33590 Colombres (Asturias) **985-41 22 44;** info@campingcolombres.com; www.campingcolombres.com

🏕 🛉🛉 ♨ 🚿 🔲 ♦ 🦋 ⛲ 🍽 🄌 🛒 🛂 ⛛ 🏊 🛒 🌴 *sand 2km*

Fr N634 12km W of San Vicente de la Barquera turn at km 283/284 dir Noriega, site in 1.3km. Med, mkd, pt shd, terr, EHU (6A); gas; bbq; twin axles; TV; Eng spkn; adv bkg rec; ccard acc; games area. *"Peaceful setting; excel for touring Picos; new owners, new amenities, new pool(2015); vg site; mkd cycle rtes; patrolled grnds."* **€30.00, 23 Mar-20 Sep.** 2015

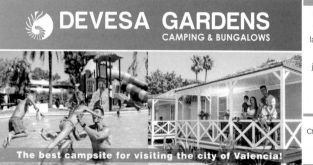
VALENCIA *4E2* (16km S Rural) *39.32302, -0.30940* **Camping Devesa Gardens**, Ctra El Saler, Km 13, 46012 València **961-61 11 36; contacto@devesagardens.com; www.devesagardens.com**

12 ♦♦(htd) ⓌⒹ ⚓ ⚙ ⛟ ⌿ ᴹˢᴾ ✺ ⓨ ⑪ ⎙ ⚞ ⚒ ⚓ 700m

S fr València on CV500, site well sp on R 4km S of El Saler. Med, hdstg, mkd, pt shd, EHU (7-15A) €5; gas; bbq; 70% statics; phone; bus to València; adv bkg acc; ccard acc; horseriding; tennis. *"Friendly, helpful staff; site has own zoo (clsd LS); lake canoeing; excel; san facs being refurb (2017); lovely pool area; easy access to tourist areas."* **€35.00** 2017

See advertisement above

VALLE DE CABUERNIGA *1A4* (1km E Rural) *43.22800, -4.28900* **Camping El Molino de Cabuérniga**, Sopeña, 39510 Cabuérniga (Cantabria) **942-70 62 59; info@campingcabuerniga.com; www.campingcabuerniga.com**

12 ✺ €1.50 ♦♦ ⚓ ⛟ ⌿ ✺ ⑪ ⓨ ⎙ ⚞

Sopeña is 55 km. SW of Santander. Fr A8 (Santander - Oviedo) take 249 exit and join N634 to Cabezón de la Sal. Turn SW on CA180 twds Reinosa for 11 km. to Sopeña (site sp to L). Turn into vill (car req - low bldgs), cont bearing R foll sp to site. Med, shd, EHU (6A) check earth; gas; phone; bus 500m; adv bkg acc; ccard acc; tennis; fishing; CKE. *"Excel site & facs on edge of vill; no shops in vicinity, but gd location, rds to site narr in places; lovely; open, level site with trees & well mkd pitches; lovely stone bldgs; mkd walks to nrby vill."* **€29.00** 2019

VEJER DE LA FRONTERA *2H3* (10km S Coastal) *36.20084, -6.03506* **Camping Pinar San José,** Ctra de Vejer-Caños de Meca, Km 10.2, Zahora 17, 11159 Barbate (Cadiz) **956-43 70 30; info@campingpinarsanjose.com; www.campingpinarsanjose.com**

12 ✺ €2 ♦♦ ⓌⒹ ⚓ ⚙ ⛟ ⌿ ᴹˢᴾ ✺ ⓨ ⑪ ⎙ ⚞ ⚒ ⚓
✺ sand 700m

Fr A48/N340 exit junc 36 onto A314 to Barbate, then foll dir Los Caños de Meca. Turn R at seashore rd dir Zahora. Site on L, 2km beyond town. Med, mkd, shd, EHU inc; TV (pitch); 10% statics; adv bkg acc; games area; tennis. *"Excel, modern facs."* **€64.00** 2019

See advertisement below

VELEZ MALAGA *2G4* (16km NNW Rural) *36.87383, -4.18527* **Camping Rural Presa la Vinuela**, Carretera A-356, Km 30, 29712 La Viñuela Málaga **952-55 45 62; campingpresalavinuela@hotmail.com; www.campinglavinuela.es**

12 ✺ €1.10 ♦♦ ⓌⒹ ⚓ ⛟ ⌿ ⑪ ⓨ ⑪ ⚞ ⚒

Site is on A356 N of Velez Malaga adjoining the W shore of la Vinuela lake. Fr junc with A402, foll sp to Colmenar/Los Romanes. Stay on A356(don't turn off into Los Romanes). Site is on R approx 2.5km after turn for Los Romanes, next to rest El Pantano. Sm, mkd, hdstg, hdg, pt shd, terr, EHU (5A); TV; 20% statics; Eng spkn; adv bkg acc; games area; games rm. *"Excel site."* **€26.00** 2019

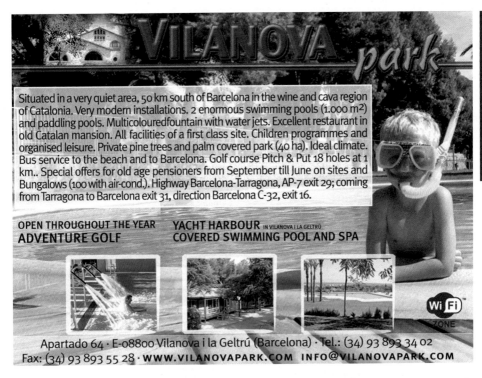
VILANOVA I LA GELTRU *3C3* (3km NW Urban) *41.23190, 1.69075* **Camping Vilanova Park,** Ctra Arboç, Km 2.5, 08800 Vilanova i la Geltru (Barcelona) **938-93 34 02;** info@vilanovapark.com or reservas@vilanovapark.com; www.vilanovapark.com
🔟 🐕 €12.50 ♦♦(htd) 🆆🅾 ♨ 👶 ♿ 🍴 ∥ 🆖 🍵 ▽ ⑪ 🎮 🏊 🚿 🅿 ⚠ 🌊(covrd, htd) 🏖 🏖 sand 3km

Fr N on AP7 exit junc 29 onto C15 dir Vilanova; then take C31 dir Cubelles. Leave at 153km exit dir Vilanova Oeste/L'Arboç to site. Fr W on C32/A16 take Vilanova-Sant Pere de Ribes exit. Take C31 & at 153km exit take BV2115 dir L'Arboc to site. Fr AP7 W leave at exit 31 onto the C32 (A16); take exit 16 (Vilanova-L'Arboc exit) onto BV2115 to site. Parked cars may block loop & obscure site sp. V lge, hdstg, mkd, hdg, pt shd, terr, serviced pitches; EHU (10A) inc (poss rev pol); gas; bbq (elec, gas); sw nr; red long stay; TV; 50% statics; phone; bus directly fr campsite to Barcelona; Eng spkn; adv bkg req; ccard acc; horseriding 500m; games rm; bike hire; sauna; fishing; tennis; golf 1km; CKE. *"Gd for children; excel san facs; gd rest & bar; gd winter facs; jacuzzi; spa; fitness cent; helpful staff; gd security; some sm pitches with diff access due trees or ramps; conv bus/train Barcelona, Tarragona, Port Aventura & coast; mkt Sat; excel site; superb."* **€63.00, E08.**
2019

See advertisement

VILLAFRANCA *3B1* (1.5km S Rural) *42.26333, -1.73861* **Camping Bardenas,** Ctra NA-660 PK 13.4, 31330 Villafranca **34 94 88 46 191;** info@campingbardenas.com; www.campingbardenas.com
🔟 ♦♦(htd) 🆆🅾 ♨ 👶 ♿ 🍴 ⑪ 🎮 🏊

Fr N leave AP15 at Junc 29 onto NA660 sp Villafranca. Site on R 1.5km S of town. Med, hdstg, unshd, bbq; 30% statics; ccard acc; games rm; CCI. *"Gd site for winter stopover en rte to S Spain; facs ltd in severe weather; excel rest."* **€27.00**
2019

VILLAFRANCA DE CORDOBA *2F4* (1km W Rural) *37.95333, -4.54710* **Camping La Albolafia,** Camino de la Vega s/n, 14420 Villafranca de Córdoba (Córdoba) **957-19 08 35;** informacion@campingalbolafia.com; www.campingalbolafia.com
🐕 €2.80 ♦♦ 🆆🅾 ♨ 👶 ♿ ∥ 🦋 🍵 ▽ ⑪ 🎮 🏊 ⚠ 🌊

Exit A4/E5 junc 377, cross rv & at rndabt turn L & foll sp to site in 2km. Beware humps in app rd. Med, hdg, mkd, hdstg, pt shd, EHU (10A) inc (long lead poss req); bbq; twin axles; TV; 10% statics; phone; bus to Córdoba 500m; Eng spkn; CKE. *"V pleasant, well-run, friendly, clean site; watersports park nrby; bar & rest clsd end May; ok for stopover."* **€27.00, 15 Feb-9 Dec.**
2017

SPAIN

VILLAMANAN *1B3* (6km SE Rural) *42.29527, -5.53777*
Camping Pico Verde, Ctra Mayorga-Astorga, Km 27.6,
24200 Valencia de Don Juan (León) **987-75 05 25;**
campingpicoverde@gmail.com; http://www.verial.es/
campingpicoverde/

🏕 🏕️ 🕴 🛁 & 🖫 🗑 ✀ ⊕ 🖫 ◭ 🏊 (covrd) 🖾

Fr N630 S, turn E at km 32.2 onto C621 sp **Valencia
de Don Juan. Site in 4km on R.** 3*, Med, mkd, EHU
(6A) inc; 25% statics; tennis; CKE. *"Friendly, helpful
staff; conv León; picturesque vill; sw caps to be worn in
pool; phone ahead to check site open if travelling close
to opening/closing dates."* **€20.00, 15 Jun-8 Sep.**
2019

VILLARGORDO DEL CABRIEL *4E1* (3km NW Rural)
39.5525, -1.47444 **Kiko Park Rural,** Ctra Embalse de
Contreras, Km 3, 46317 Villargordo del Cabriel
(València) **962-13 90 82;** kikoparkrural@kikopark.com;
www.kikopark.com/rural

12 🏕 🖫€0.80 🕴 🖫 🛁 & 🖫 🖫 MP 🍷 ⊕ 🖫 🖫 🏊

A3/E901 València-Madrid, exit junc 255 to
Villargordo del Cabriel, foll sp to site. Med, mkd,
hdstg, pt shd, terr, serviced pitches; EHU (6A) €3.70;
gas; sw nr; red long stay; TV; 10% statics; Eng spkn;
adv bkg rec; ccard acc; canoeing; horseriding; white
water rafting; fishing; bike hire; watersports; CKE.
*"Beautiful location; superb, well-run, peaceful site; lge
pitches; gd walking; vg rest; many activities; helpful, v
friendly family run site; gd hdstg; excel."* **€33.00**
2015

"There aren't many sites open at this time of year"

If you're travelling outside peak season
remember to call ahead to check site opening
dates – even if the entry says 'open all year'.

VINAROS *3D2* (5km N Coastal) *40.49363, 0.48504*
Camping Vinarós, Ctra N340, Km 1054, 12500
Vinarós (Castellón) **964-40 24 24;** info@camping
vinaros.com; www.campingvinaros.com

12 🏕 🖫€3 🕴 (htd) 🖫 🛁 🛁 & 🖫 🖫 MP ✀ 🍷 ⊕ nr 🖫 🖫 nr
◭ 🏊 🖫 shgl 1km

Fr N exit AP7 junc 42 onto N238 dir Vinarós.
**Straight on at first 2 rndabt, at 3rd rndabt turn L
(3rd exit) dir Tarragona. Site on R at Km1054.**
Lge, hdstg, mkd, hdg, pt shd, serviced pitches; EHU
(6A) inc; gas; red long stay; 15% statics; phone; bus
adj; Eng spkn; adv bkg rec; ccard acc; CKE. *"Excel gd
value, busy, well-run site; many long-stay winter
residents; spacious pitches; vg clean, modern san facs;
elec volts poss v low in evening; gd rest; friendly,
helpful staff; rec use bottled water; currency exchange;
Peñiscola Castle & Morello worth a visit; easy cycle to
town; ok stopover."* **€13.00** 2017

VINUELA *2G4* (7.5km NW Rural) *36.87383, -4.18527*
Camping Presa La Viñuela, Ctra A356, km 30 29712
Viñuela **952-55 45 62;** campingpresalavinuela@
hotmail.com; www.campinglavinuela.es

🏕 🖫€1.10 🕴 🖫 🛁 🖫 🖫 ✀ 🍷 🍷 ⊕ 🖫 🏊

Site on A356 N of Velez Malaga adjoining the W
shore of la Vinuela lake. Fr junc with A402, foll sp
to Colmenar & Los Romanes. Stay on A356 (don't
turn off into Los Romanes). Site is on R approx
2.5km after the turn for Los Romanes, next to El
Pantano rest. Sm, mkd, hdstg, shd, terr, EHU (5A);
TV; 20% statics; Eng spkn; adv bkg acc; games rm;
games area. *"Excel site; fab views."*
€21.00, 1 Jan-30 Sep. 2019

VINUESA *3B1* (2km N Rural) *41.92647, -2.76285*
Camping Cobijo, Ctra Laguna Negra, Km 2, 42150
Vinuesa (Soria) **975-37 83 31;** recepcion@camping
cobijo.com; www.campingcobijo.com

🏕 🏕️ 🕴 🖫 🛁 🛁 & 🖫 🖫 ✀ 🍷 ⊕ 🖫 🖫 ◭ 🏊

Travelling W fr Soria to Burgos, at Abejar R on
SO840. by-pass Abejar cont to Vinuesa. Well sp
fr there. Lge, pt shd, pt sl, EHU (3-6A) €4-5.70 (long
lead poss req); gas; bbq; 10% statics; phone; Eng
spkn; ccard acc; bike hire; CKE. *"Friendly staff; clean,
attractive site; some pitches in wooded area poss diff
lge o'fits; special elec connector supplied (deposit);
ltd bar & rest LS, excel rests in town; gd walks."*
€28.00, 1 Apr-1 Nov. 2017

VITORIA/GASTEIZ *3B1* (5.5km SW Rural) *42.83114,
-2.72248* **Camping Ibaya,** Nacional 102, Km 346.5,
Zuazo de Vitoria 01195 Vitoria/Gasteiz (Alava)
945-14 76 20; info@campingibaia.com; www.camping
ibaia.com

12 🏕 🕴 🖫 🛁 🖫 🍷 🍷 ⊕ nr 🖫 🖫 ◭

Fr A1 take exit 343 sp N102/A3302. At rndabt foll sp
N102 Vitoria/Gasteiz. At next rndabt take 3rd exit &
immed turn L twd filling stn. Site ent on R in 100m,
sp. Sm, mkd, hdstg, pt shd, pt sl, EHU (5A) €5.40; gas;
bbq; 10% statics; phone; Eng spkn; CKE. *"NH only; gd,
modern san facs; phone ahead to check open LS; fair
site."* **€29.50** 2016

ZARAGOZA *3C1* (6km W Urban) *41.63766, -0.94227*
Camping Ciudad de Zaragoza, Calle San Juan
Bautista de la Salle s/n, 50012 Zaragoza **876-24 14 95;**
info@campingzaragoza.com; www.camping
zaragoza.com

12 🏕 🖫€3.75 🕴 (htd) 🖫 🛁 🛁 & 🖫 🖫 MP 🍷 🍷 ⊕ 🖫 🖫 ◭ 🏊

Fr western ring rd Z40 go E on N11A Av Manuel
Rodriguez Ayuso. Pass one rndabt then R onto C
San Juan Batista de la Salle to 2nd rndabt, u-turn
to find site ent on R in 150m. 4*, Lge, hdstg, mkd,
pt shd, pt sl, EHU (10A) €5.75; bbq; twin axles; TV;
50% statics; Eng spkn; adv bkg acc; games area;
tennis. *"Modern san facs; poss travellers; unattractive
and tired, but conv site in suburbs; gd sh stay; poss
noisy (campers & daytime aircraft); gd food at bar;
helpful staff; gd NH from Bilbao ferry."* **€35.00** 2019

ZARAUTZ *3A1 (3km NE Coastal) 43.28958, -2.14603*
Gran Camping Zarautz, Monte Talaimendi s/n,
20800 Zarautz (Guipúzkoa) **943-83 12 38; info@**
grancampingzarautz.com; www.grancamping
zarautz.com

12 🐾 ♦♦(htd) 🐝 🏊 ⚓ ♿ ▣ ⊘ 🅜 ⦾ ⧖ ⑪ 🛒 ⧄ ⌂ 1km

**Exit A8 junc 11 Zarautz, strt on at 1st & 2nd rndabt
after toll & foll site sp. On N634 fr San Sebastián to
Zarautz, R at rndabt. On N634 fr Bilbao to Zarautz
L at rndabt.** Lge, hdstg, mkd, hdg, pt shd, pt sl, terr,
EHU (6-10A) inc; gas; bbq; TV; 50% statics; phone;
train/bus to Bilbao & San Sebastian; Eng spkn; adv
bkg acc; ccard acc; golf 1km; games rm; CKE. *"Site
on cliff o'looking bay; excel beach, gd base for coast
& mountains; helpful, friendly staff; some pitches sm
with steep access & o'looked fr terr above; sans facs
upgraded but poor standard and insufficient when
cr; excel rest; pitches poss muddy; NH for Bilbao
ferry; rec arr early to secure pitch; v steep walk to
beach (part naturist); gd for NH; excel train service
to San Sebastián; gd shop on site; ACSI discount."*
€31.00 2017

ZARAUTZ *3A1 (8km E Coastal) 43.27777, -2.12305*
Camping Orio Kanpina, 20810 Orio (Guipúzkoa)
943-83 48 01; info@oriokanpina.com; www.orio
kanpina.com

♦♦ 🐝 🏊 ⚓ ♿ ▣ ⊘ 🅜 🦋 ⦾ ⧖ ⑪ nr 📶 🛒 ⧄ 🛶 🖐

🌴 sand adj

**Fr E on A8 exit junc 33 & at rndabt foll sp Orio,
Kanpin & Playa. Site on R. Or to avoid town cent
(rec) cross bdge & foll N634 for 1km, turn L at sp
Orio & camping, turn R at rndabt to site.** Lge, mkd, pt
shd, pt sl, EHU (5A) inc; gas; 50% statics; phone; Eng
spkn; adv bkg acc; ccard acc; car wash; tennis; CKE.
*"Busy, well maintained site; flats now built bet site
& beach & new marina adj - now no sea views; walks;
gd facs; friendly staff; useful NH bef leaving Spain;
interesting sm town."* **€36.00, 1 Mar-12 Nov.** 2017

Map I

© Collins Bartholomew Ltd 2020

Legend:
- Motorways
- Major roads
- Main Roads

Site legend:
- ● All year site(s)
- ● Seasonal site(s)
- ○ No sites listed
- 200m +
- 0–200m

PORTUGAL

MOROCCO

Map 2

FRANCE

Map 3

MEDITERRANEAN SEA

MINORCA

MAJORCA

ANDORRA LA VELLA

see inset on Map 4

Marseille
Montpellier
Béziers
Narbonne
Toulouse
Pamiers
St-Gaudens
Tarbes
Pau
Biarritz
Irún
DONOSTIA/SAN SEBASTIÁN
Mundaka
Lekeitio
Deba
Zarautz
Arbizu
A15
A1
A8
AP1
Etxarri-Aranatz
VITORIA/Aranatz
GASTEIZ
Nájera
AP68
A12
N232
NIII
VINUESA
SORIA
N234
N122
TARAZONA
N121
N121
AP15
N13
Mendigorria
Lumbier
PAMPLONA/IRUÑA
Sangüesa
Hecho
Isaba
Ochagavía
Auritz
N240
N330
Jaca
Ayerbe
Biescas
Broto
Torla
Sabiñánigo
Ainsa
Bielsa
Alquézar
HUESCA
A22
A23
Bossost
Espot
Pont de Suert
N230
Balaguer
LERIDA/LLEIDA
AP2
N11
Caspe
N232
N211
N240
ZARAGOZA
A23
Calatayud
Nuévalos
A15
A2
Albarracín
TERUEL
N330
N420
A23
N211
N420
Cuenca
A40
N320
Sacedón
N204
Viver
A23
Navajas
Moncofa
Benicàssim
Oropesa
Alcossebre
Peñiscola
Benicarló
Vinaròs
Alcànar
Deltebre
Morella
Sant Jordi
Calig
N232
Arnes
L'Ametlla de Mar
L'Hospitalet de l'Infant
Salou
A2
N240
Montblanc
AP7
A27
N420
N11

160

SPAIN

Map 4

© Collins Bartholomew Ltd 2020

161

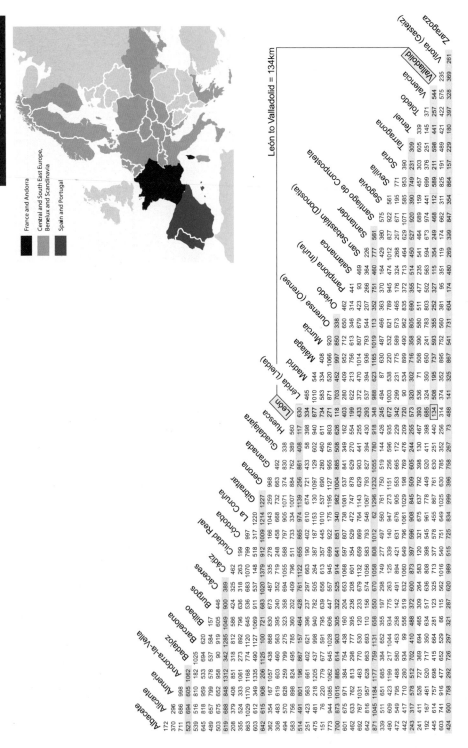

SPAIN

France and Andorra
Central and South East Europe, Benelux and Scandinavia
Spain and Portugal

León to Valladolid = 134km

Site Report Form

If campsite is already listed, complete only those sections of the form where changes apply or alternatively use the Abbreviated Site Report form on the following pages.

Sites not reported on for 5 years may be deleted from the guide

Year of guide used	20.........	Is site listed?	Listed on page no.	Unlisted	Date of visit	........./........./.........

A – CAMPSITE NAME AND LOCATION

Country		Name of town/village site listed under *(see Sites Location Maps)*			

Distance & direction from centre of town site is listed under *(in a straight line)*	...................km	eg N, NE, S, SW	Urban	Rural	Coastal

Site open all year?	Y / N	Period site is open *(if not all year)*	................./................. to ..../.................

Site name		Naturist site	Y / N

Site address	

Telephone		Fax	
E-mail		Website	

B – CAMPSITE CHARGES

Charge for outfit + 2 adults in local currency	PRICE	

C – DIRECTIONS

Brief, specific directions to site (in km) *To convert miles to kilometres multiply by 8 and divide by 5 or use Conversion Table in guide*	
GPS	Latitude...*(eg 12.34567)* Longitude...*(eg 1.23456 or -1.23456)*

D – SITE INFORMATION

Dogs allowed	DOGS	Y / N	Price per night .... *(if allowed)*	
Facilities for disabled				
Public Transport within 5km	BUS / TRAM / TRAIN	Adj		Nearby
Reduction long stay	RED LONG STAY	Credit Card accepted		CCARD ACC
Advance bookings accepted/recommended/required		ADV BKG ACC / REC / REQ		
Camping Key Europe or Camping Card International accepted in lieu of passport		CKE/CCI		

E – SITE DESCRIPTION

SITE size ie number of pitches	Small Max 50	SM	Medium 51-150	MED	Large 151-500	LGE	Very large 500+	V LGE	Unchanged
Pitch features if **NOT** open-plan/grassy	HDG PITCH	Hedged	HDG PITCH	Marked or numbered	MKD PITCH	Hardstanding or gravel	HDSTG	Unchanged
If site is **NOT** level, is it	PT SL	Part sloping	PT SL	Sloping	SL	Terraced	TERR	Unchanged
Is site shaded?		SHD	Shaded	SHD	Part shaded	PT SHD	Unshaded	UNSHD	Unchanged
ELECTRIC HOOK UP *if not included in price above*	EL PNTS		Price................................		Amps....................	
% Static caravans / mobile homes / chalets / cottages / fixed tents on site			................% STATICS	
Serviced Pitched	Y / N	Twin axles caravans allowed?	TWIN AXLES Y / N

You can also complete forms online: camc.com/europereport

E – SITE DESCRIPTION CONTINUED...

Phone on site	PHONE			Wifi Internet	WIFI
Television	TV RM		TV CAB / SAT	Playground	PLAYGRND
Entertainment in high season	ENTMNT			English spoken	ENG SPKN
Motorhome Service Point	Y / N				

F – CATERING

Bar	BAR	On site	or	Within 2km
Restaurant	REST	On site	or	Within 2km
Shop(s)	SHOP(S)	On site	or	Within 2km
Snack bar / take-away	SNACKS	On site	Y / N	
Cooking facilities	COOKING FACS	On site	Y / N	
Supplies of bottled gas on site	GAS	Y / N		
Barbecue allowed	BBQ	Charcoal	Gas	Elec	Sep area

G – SANITARY FACILITIES

WC	Heated	HTD WC	Continental	CONT	Own San recommended	OWN SAN REC
Chemical disposal point		CHEM DISP				
Hot shower(s)	SHWR(S)	Inc in site fee?	Y / N			
Child / baby facilities (bathroom)		FAM BTHRM		Launderette / Washing Machine		LNDRY

H – OTHER INFORMATION

Swimming pool	POOL	HEATED	COVERED	INDOOR	PADDLING POOL
Beach	BEACH	Adj	or ....km	Sand	Shingle
Alternative swimming (lake)	SW	Adj	or ....km	Sand	Shingle
Games /sports area / Games room	GAMES AREA		GAMES ROOM		

I – ADDITIONAL REMARKS AND/OR ITEMS OF INTEREST

Tourist attractions, unusual features or other facilities, eg waterslide, tennis, cycle hire, watersports, horseriding, separate car park, walking distance to shops etc	YOUR OPINION OF THE SITE:
	EXCEL
	VERY GOOD
	GOOD
	FAIR | POOR
	NIGHT HALT ONLY
Your comments & opinions may be used in future editions of the guide, if you do not wish them to be used please tick	

J – MEMBER DETAILS

ARE YOU A:	Caravanner		Motorhomer		Trailer-tenter?	
NAME:			MEMBERSHIP NO:			
			POST CODE:			
DO YOU NEED MORE BLANK SITE REPORT FORMS?			YES		NO	

Please use a separate form for each campsite and do not send receipts. Owing to the large number of site reports received, it is not possible to enter into correspondence. Please return completed form to:

**The Editor, Overseas Touring Guides, East Grinstead House
East Grinstead, West Sussex RH19 1UA**

Please note that due to changes in the rules regarding freepost we are no longer able to provide a freepost address for the return of Site Report Forms. You can still supply your site reports free online by visiting camc.com/europereport. We apologise for any inconvenience this may cause.

Site Report Form

If campsite is already listed, complete only those sections of the form where changes apply
or alternatively use the Abbreviated Site Report form on the following pages.

Sites not reported on for 5 years may be deleted from the guide

Year of guide used	20..........	Is site listed?	Listed on page no............	Unlisted	Date of visit	......../........./.........

A – CAMPSITE NAME AND LOCATION

Country		Name of town/village site listed under *(see Sites Location Maps)*				
Distance & direction from centre of town site is listed under *(in a straight line)*		....................km	eg N, NE, S, SW	Urban	Rural	Coastal
Site open all year?	Y / N	Period site is open *(if not all year)*	.................../.................. to ..../.................			
Site name				Naturist site		Y / N
Site address						
Telephone		Fax				
E-mail		Website				

B – CAMPSITE CHARGES

Charge for outfit + 2 adults in local currency	PRICE	

C – DIRECTIONS

Brief, specific directions to site (in km) *To convert miles to kilometres multiply by 8 and divide by 5 or use Conversion Table in guide*	
GPS	Latitude...(eg 12.34567) Longitude..(eg 1.23456 or -1.23456)

D – SITE INFORMATION

Dogs allowed	DOGS	Y / N	Price per night .... *(if allowed)*	
Facilities for disabled				
Public Transport within 5km	BUS / TRAM / TRAIN	Adj	Nearby	
Reduction long stay	RED LONG STAY	Credit Card accepted	CCARD ACC	
Advance bookings accepted/recommended/required		ADV BKG ACC / REC / REQ		
Camping Key Europe or Camping Card International accepted in lieu of passport			CKE/CCI	

E – SITE DESCRIPTION

SITE size ie number of pitches	Small Max 50	SM	Medium 51-150	MED	Large 151-500	LGE	Very large 500+	V LGE	Unchanged
Pitch features if **NOT** open plan/grassy		HDG PITCH	Hedged	HDG PITCH	Marked or numbered	MKD PITCH	Hardstanding or gravel	HDSTG	Unchanged
If site is **NOT** level, is it		PT SL	Part sloping	PT SL	Sloping	SL	Terraced	TERR	Unchanged
Is site shaded?		SHD	Shaded	SHD	Part shaded	PT SHD	Unshaded	UNSHD	Unchanged
ELECTRIC HOOK UP *if not included in price above*		EL PNTS			Price................			Amps......................	
% Static caravans / mobile homes / chalets / cottages / fixed tents on site								.................% STATICS	
Serviced Pitched		Y / N			Twin axles caravans allowed?			TWIN AXLES Y / N	

You can also complete forms online: camc.com/europereport

CUT ALONG DOTTED LINE

E – SITE DESCRIPTION CONTINUED…

Phone on site	PHONE		Wifi Internet	WIFI
Television	TV RM	TV CAB / SAT	Playground	PLAYGRND
Entertainment in high season	ENTMNT		English spoken	ENG SPKN
Motorhome Service Point	Y / N			

F – CATERING

Bar	BAR	On site	or	Within 2km
Restaurant	REST	On site	or	Within 2km
Shop(s)	SHOP(S)	On site	or	Within 2km
Snack bar / take-away	SNACKS	On site	Y / N	
Cooking facilities	COOKING FACS	On site	Y / N	
Supplies of bottled gas on site	GAS	Y / N		
Barbecue allowed	BBQ	Charcoal	Gas	Elec	Sep area

G – SANITARY FACILITIES

WC		Heated	HTD WC	Continental	CONT	Own San recommended	OWN SAN REC
Chemical disposal point			CHEM DISP			
Hot shower(s)		SHWR(S)	Inc in site fee?	Y / N		
Child / baby facilities (bathroom)			FAM BTHRM	Launderette / Washing Machine	LNDRY	

H – OTHER INFORMATION

Swimming pool	POOL	HEATED	COVERED	INDOOR	PADDLING POOL
Beach	BEACH	Adj	or ....km	Sand	Shingle
Alternative swimming (lake)	SW	Adj	or ....km	Sand	Shingle
Games /sports area / Games room	GAMES AREA		GAMES ROOM		

I – ADDITIONAL REMARKS AND/OR ITEMS OF INTEREST

Tourist attractions, unusual features or other facilities, eg waterslide, tennis, cycle hire, watersports, horseriding, separate car park, walking distance to shops etc	YOUR OPINION OF THE SITE:
	EXCEL
	VERY GOOD
	GOOD
	FAIR / POOR
	NIGHT HALT ONLY

Your comments & opinions may be used in future editions of the guide, if you do not wish them to be used please tick ....

J – MEMBER DETAILS

ARE YOU A:	Caravanner		Motorhomer		Trailer-tenter?	
NAME:			MEMBERSHIP NO:		
			POST CODE:		
DO YOU NEED MORE BLANK SITE REPORT FORMS?		YES		NO	

Please use a separate form for each campsite and do not send receipts. Owing to the large number of site reports received, it is not possible to enter into correspondence. Please return completed form to:

**The Editor, Overseas Touring Guides, East Grinstead House
East Grinstead, West Sussex RH19 1UA**

Please note that due to changes in the rules regarding freepost we are no longer able to provide a freepost address for the return of Site Report Forms. You can still supply your site reports free online by visiting camc.com/europereport. We apologise for any inconvenience this may cause.

Site Report Form

If campsite is already listed, complete only those sections of the form where changes apply or alternatively use the Abbreviated Site Report form on the following pages.

Sites not reported on for 5 years may be deleted from the guide

Year of guide used	20..........	Is site listed?	Listed on page no............	Unlisted	Date of visit	........./........./.........

A – CAMPSITE NAME AND LOCATION

Country		Name of town/village site listed under *(see Sites Location Maps)*					
Distance & direction from centre of town site is listed under *(in a straight line)*		....................km	eg N, NE, S, SW		Urban	Rural	Coastal
Site open all year?	Y / N	Period site is open *(if not all year)*	.................../.................. to ..../..................				
Site name					Naturist site	Y / N	
Site address							
Telephone			Fax				
E-mail			Website				

B – CAMPSITE CHARGES

Charge for outfit + 2 adults in local currency	PRICE	

C – DIRECTIONS

Brief, specific directions to site (in km) *To convert miles to kilometres multiply by 8 and divide by 5 or use Conversion Table in guide*	
GPS	Latitude..(eg 12.34567) Longitude..(eg 1.23456 or -1.23456)

D – SITE INFORMATION

Dogs allowed	DOGS	Y / N	Price per night .... *(if allowed)*	
Facilities for disabled				
Public Transport within 5km	BUS / TRAM / TRAIN	Adj		Nearby
Reduction long stay	RED LONG STAY	Credit Card accepted		CCARD ACC
Advance bookings accepted/recommended/required		ADV BKG ACC / REC / REQ		
Camping Key Europe or Camping Card International accepted in lieu of passport			CKE/CCI	

E – SITE DESCRIPTION

SITE size ie number of pitches	Small Max 50	SM	Medium 51-150	MED	Large 151-500	LGE	Very large 500+	V LGE	Unchanged
Pitch features if NOT open-plan/grassy		HDG PITCH	Hedged	HDG PITCH	Marked or numbered	MKD PITCH	Hardstanding or gravel	HDSTG	Unchanged
If site is NOT level, is it		PT SL	Part sloping	PT SL	Sloping	SL	Terraced	TERR	Unchanged
Is site shaded?		SHD	Shaded	SHD	Part shaded	PT SHD	Unshaded	UNSHD	Unchanged
ELECTRIC HOOK UP *if not included in price above*		EL PNTS		Price...............................			Amps.....................		
% Static caravans / mobile homes / chalets / cottages / fixed tents on site							................% STATICS		
Serviced Pitched		Y / N		Twin axles caravans allowed?			TWIN AXLES Y / N		

You can also complete forms online: camc.com/europereport

CUT ALONG DOTTED LINE

E – SITE DESCRIPTION CONTINUED…

Phone on site	PHONE		Wifi Internet	WIFI
Television	TV RM	TV CAB / SAT	Playground	PLAYGRND
Entertainment in high season	ENTMNT		English spoken	ENG SPKN
Motorhome Service Point	Y / N			

F – CATERING

Bar	BAR	On site	or	Within 2km		
Restaurant	REST	On site	or	Within 2km		
Shop(s)	SHOP(S)	On site	or	Within 2km		
Snack bar / take-away	SNACKS	On site	Y / N			
Cooking facilities	COOKING FACS	On site	Y / N			
Supplies of bottled gas on site	GAS	Y / N				
Barbecue allowed	BBQ	Charcoal	Gas	Elec	Sep area	

G – SANITARY FACILITIES

WC	Heated	HTD WC	Continental	CONT	Own San recommended	OWN SAN REC
Chemical disposal point		CHEM DISP				
Hot shower(s)	SHWR(S)	Inc in site fee?	Y / N			
Child / baby facilities (bathroom)		FAM BTHRM		Launderette / Washing Machine	LNDRY	

H – OTHER INFORMATION

Swimming pool	POOL	HEATED	COVERED	INDOOR	PADDLING POOL	
Beach	BEACH	Adj	or ....km	Sand	Shingle	
Alternative swimming (lake)	SW	Adj	or ....km	Sand	Shingle	
Games /sports area / Games room	GAMES AREA		GAMES ROOM			

I – ADDITIONAL REMARKS AND/OR ITEMS OF INTEREST

Tourist attractions, unusual features or other facilities, eg waterslide, tennis, cycle hire, watersports, horseriding, separate car park, walking distance to shops etc	YOUR OPINION OF THE SITE:	
	EXCEL	
	VERY GOOD	
	GOOD	
	FAIR	POOR
	NIGHT HALT ONLY	
Your comments & opinions may be used in future editions of the guide, if you do not wish them to be used please tick		

J – MEMBER DETAILS

ARE YOU A:	Caravanner		Motorhomer		Trailer-tenter?	
NAME:			MEMBERSHIP NO:			
			POST CODE:			
DO YOU NEED MORE BLANK SITE REPORT FORMS?		YES			NO	

Please use a separate form for each campsite and do not send receipts. Owing to the large number of site reports received, it is not possible to enter into correspondence. Please return completed form to:

The Editor, Overseas Touring Guides, East Grinstead House
East Grinstead, West Sussex RH19 1UA

Please note that due to changes in the rules regarding freepost we are no longer able to provide a freepost address for the return of Site Report Forms. You can still supply your site reports free online by visiting camc.com/europereport. We apologise for any inconvenience this may cause.

Abbreviated Site Report Form

Use this abbreviated Site Report Form if you have visited a number of sites and there are no changes (or only small changes) to their entries in the guide. If reporting on a new site, or reporting several changes, please use the full version of the report form. If advising prices, these should be for an outfit, and 2 adults for one night's stay. **Please indicate high or low season prices and whether electricity is included.**

Remember, if you don't tell us about sites you have visited, they may eventually be deleted from the guide.

Year of guide used	20..........	Page No.	....	Name of town/village site listed under		
Site Name					Date of visit	......./......./........
GPS	Latitude...(eg 12.34567) Longitude...(eg 1.23456 or -1.23456)					

Site is in: Andorra / Austria / Belgium / Croatia / Czech Republic / Denmark / Finland / France / Germany / Greece / Hungary / Italy / Luxembourg / Netherlands / Norway / Poland / Portugal / Slovakia / Slovenia / Spain / Sweden / Switzerland

Comments:

Charge for outfit + 2 adults in local currency	High Season	Low Season	Elec inc in price?		Y / N	............amps
			Price of elec (if not inc)			............amps

Year of guide used	20..........	Page No.	....	Name of town/village site listed under		
Site Name					Date of visit	......./......./........
GPS	Latitude...(eg 12.34567) Longitude...(eg 1.23456 or -1.23456)					

Site is in: Andorra / Austria / Belgium / Croatia / Czech Republic / Denmark / Finland / France / Germany / Greece / Hungary / Italy / Luxembourg / Netherlands / Norway / Poland / Portugal / Slovakia / Slovenia / Spain / Sweden / Switzerland

Comments:

Charge for outfit + 2 adults in local currency	High Season	Low Season	Elec inc in price?		Y / N	............amps
			Price of elec (if not inc)			............amps

Year of guide used	20..........	Page No.	....	Name of town/village site listed under		
Site Name					Date of visit	......./......./........
GPS	Latitude...(eg 12.34567) Longitude...(eg 1.23456 or -1.23456)					

Site is in: Andorra / Austria / Belgium / Croatia / Czech Republic / Denmark / Finland / France / Germany / Greece / Hungary / Italy / Luxembourg / Netherlands / Norway / Poland / Portugal / Slovakia / Slovenia / Spain / Sweden / Switzerland

Comments:

Charge for car, caravan & 2 adults in local currency	High Season	Low Season	Elec inc in price?		Y / N	............amps
			Price of elec (if not inc)			............amps

Please fill in your details and send to the address on the reverse of this form.
You can also complete forms online: camc.com/europereport

CUT ALONG DOTTED LINE

Year of guide used	20..........	Page No.	....	Name of town/village site listed under	
Site Name				Date of visit	......./......./.......
GPS	Latitude.................................(eg 12.34567) Longitude...............................(eg 1.23456 or -1.23456)				

Site is in: Andorra / Austria / Belgium / Croatia / Czech Republic / Denmark / Finland / France / Germany / Greece / Hungary / Italy / Luxembourg / Netherlands / Norway / Poland / Portugal / Slovakia / Slovenia / Spain / Sweden / Switzerland

Comments:

Charge for outfit + 2 adults in local currency	High Season	Low Season	Elec inc in price?	Y / N	.............amps
			Price of elec (if not inc)		.............amps

Year of guide used	20..........	Page No.	....	Name of town/village site listed under	
Site Name				Date of visit	......./......./.......
GPS	Latitude.................................(eg 12.34567) Longitude...............................(eg 1.23456 or -1.23456)				

Site is in: Andorra / Austria / Belgium / Croatia / Czech Republic / Denmark / Finland / France / Germany / Greece / Hungary / Italy / Luxembourg / Netherlands / Norway / Poland / Portugal / Slovakia / Slovenia / Spain / Sweden / Switzerland

Comments:

Charge for outfit + 2 adults in local currency	High Season	Low Season	Elec inc in price?	Y / N	.............amps
			Price of elec (if not inc)		.............amps

Year of guide used	20..........	Page No.	....	Name of town/village site listed under	
Site Name				Date of visit	......./......./.......
GPS	Latitude.................................(eg 12.34567) Longitude...............................(eg 1.23456 or -1.23456)				

Site is in: Andorra / Austria / Belgium / Croatia / Czech Republic / Denmark / Finland / France / Germany / Greece / Hungary / Italy / Luxembourg / Netherlands / Norway / Poland / Portugal / Slovakia / Slovenia / Spain / Sweden / Switzerland

Comments:

Charge for outfit + 2 adults in local currency	High Season	Low Season	Elec inc in price?	Y / N	.............amps
			Price of elec (if not inc)		.............amps

Your comments & opinions may be used in future editions of the guide, if you do not wish them to be used please tick ....

Name ....

Membership No. ....

Post Code ....

Are you a Caravanner / Motorhomer / Trailer-Tenter?

Do you need more blank Site Report forms?   YES / NO

Please return completed forms to:
The Editor – Overseas Touring Guides
East Grinstead House
East Grinstead
West Sussex
RH19 1FH
Please note that due to changes in the rules regarding freepost we are no longer able to provide a freepost address for the return of Site Report Forms. You can still supply your site reports free online by visiting camc.com/europereport. We apologise for any inconvenience this may cause.

You can also complete forms online: camc.com/europereport

Abbreviated Site Report Form

Use this abbreviated Site Report Form if you have visited a number of sites and there are no changes (or only small changes) to their entries in the guide. If reporting on a new site, or reporting several changes, please use the full version of the report form. If advising prices, these should be for an outfit, and 2 adults for one night's stay. **Please indicate high or low season prices and whether electricity is included.**

Remember, if you don't tell us about sites you have visited, they may eventually be deleted from the guide.

Year of guide used	20.........	Page No.	....	Name of town/village site listed under	

Site Name				Date of visit	.... /....... /........

| GPS | Latitude...................................*(eg 12.34567)* Longitude..*(eg 1.23456 or -1.23456)* | | | | |

Site is in: Andorra / Austria / Belgium / Croatia / Czech Republic / Denmark / Finland / France / Germany / Greece / Hungary / Italy / Luxembourg / Netherlands / Norway / Poland / Portugal / Slovakia / Slovenia / Spain / Sweden / Switzerland

Comments:

Charge for outfit + 2 adults in local currency	High Season	Low Season	Elec inc in price?		Y / N	.............amps
			Price of elec (if not inc)			.............amps

Year of guide used	20.........	Page No.	....	Name of town/village site listed under	

Site Name				Date of visit	.... /....... /........

| GPS | Latitude...................................*(eg 12.34567)* Longitude..*(eg 1.23456 or -1.23456)* | | | | |

Site is in: Andorra / Austria / Belgium / Croatia / Czech Republic / Denmark / Finland / France / Germany / Greece / Hungary / Italy / Luxembourg / Netherlands / Norway / Poland / Portugal / Slovakia / Slovenia / Spain / Sweden / Switzerland

Comments:

Charge for outfit + 2 adults in local currency	High Season	Low Season	Elec inc in price?		Y / N	.............amps
			Price of elec (if not inc)			.............amps

Year of guide used	20.........	Page No.	....	Name of town/village site listed under	

Site Name				Date of visit	.... /....... /........

| GPS | Latitude...................................*(eg 12.34567)* Longitude..*(eg 1.23456 or -1.23456)* | | | | |

Site is in: Andorra / Austria / Belgium / Croatia / Czech Republic / Denmark / Finland / France / Germany / Greece / Hungary / Italy / Luxembourg / Netherlands / Norway / Poland / Portugal / Slovakia / Slovenia / Spain / Sweden / Switzerland

Comments:

Charge for car, caravan & 2 adults in local currency	High Season	Low Season	Elec inc in price?		Y / N	.............amps
			Price of elec (if not inc)			.............amps

Please fill in your details and send to the address on the reverse of this form.
You can also complete forms online: camc.com/europereport

CUT ALONG DOTTED LINE

Year of guide used	20..........	Page No.	....	Name of town/village site listed under	

Site Name				Date of visit	......./......./........

GPS Latitude...(eg 12.34567) Longitude...(eg 1.23456 or -1.23456)

Site is in: Andorra / Austria / Belgium / Croatia / Czech Republic / Denmark / Finland / France / Germany / Greece / Hungary / Italy / Luxembourg / Netherlands / Norway / Poland / Portugal / Slovakia / Slovenia / Spain / Sweden / Switzerland

Comments:

Charge for outfit + 2 adults in local currency	High Season	Low Season	Elec inc in price?	Y / N	............amps
			Price of elec (if not inc)		............amps

Year of guide used	20..........	Page No.	....	Name of town/village site listed under	

Site Name				Date of visit	......./......./........

GPS Latitude...(eg 12.34567) Longitude...(eg 1.23456 or -1.23456)

Site is in: Andorra / Austria / Belgium / Croatia / Czech Republic / Denmark / Finland / France / Germany / Greece / Hungary / Italy / Luxembourg / Netherlands / Norway / Poland / Portugal / Slovakia / Slovenia / Spain / Sweden / Switzerland

Comments:

Charge for outfit + 2 adults in local currency	High Season	Low Season	Elec inc in price?	Y / N	............amps
			Price of elec (if not inc)		............amps

Year of guide used	20..........	Page No.	....	Name of town/village site listed under	

Site Name				Date of visit	......./......./........

GPS Latitude...(eg 12.34567) Longitude...(eg 1.23456 or -1.23456)

Site is in: Andorra / Austria / Belgium / Croatia / Czech Republic / Denmark / Finland / France / Germany / Greece / Hungary / Italy / Luxembourg / Netherlands / Norway / Poland / Portugal / Slovakia / Slovenia / Spain / Sweden / Switzerland

Comments:

Charge for outfit + 2 adults in local currency	High Season	Low Season	Elec inc in price?	Y / N	............amps
			Price of elec (if not inc)		............amps

Your comments & opinions may be used in future editions of the guide, if you do not wish them to be used please tick ....

Name ....

Membership No. ....

Post Code ....

Are you a Caravanner / Motorhomer / Trailer-Tenter?

Do you need more blank Site Report forms?   YES / NO

Please return completed forms to:
The Editor – Overseas Touring Guides
East Grinstead House
East Grinstead
West Sussex
RH19 1FH
Please note that due to changes in the rules regarding freepost we are no longer able to provide a freepost address for the return of Site Report Forms. You can still supply your site reports free online by visiting camc.com/europereport. We apologise for any inconvenience this may cause.

You can also complete forms online: camc.com/europereport

Abbreviated Site Report Form

Use this abbreviated Site Report Form if you have visited a number of sites and there are no changes (or only small changes) to their entries in the guide. If reporting on a new site, or reporting several changes, please use the full version of the report form. If advising prices, these should be for an outfit, and 2 adults for one night's stay. **Please indicate high or low season prices and whether electricity is included.**

Remember, if you don't tell us about sites you have visited, they may eventually be deleted from the guide.

Year of guide used 20..........		Page No.		Name of town/village site listed under		
Site Name					Date of visit	......./......./.......
GPS	Latitude..(eg 12.34567) Longitude..(eg 1.23456 or -1.23456)					

Site is in: Andorra / Austria / Belgium / Croatia / Czech Republic / Denmark / Finland / France / Germany / Greece / Hungary / Italy / Luxembourg / Netherlands / Norway / Poland / Portugal / Slovakia / Slovenia / Spain / Sweden / Switzerland

Comments:

Charge for outfit + 2 adults in local currency	High Season	Low Season	Elec inc in price?	Y / N	...........amps
			Price of elec (if not inc)		...........amps

Year of guide used 20..........		Page No.		Name of town/village site listed under		
Site Name					Date of visit	......./......./.......
GPS	Latitude..(eg 12.34567) Longitude..(eg 1.23456 or -1.23456)					

Site is in: Andorra / Austria / Belgium / Croatia / Czech Republic / Denmark / Finland / France / Germany / Greece / Hungary / Italy / Luxembourg / Netherlands / Norway / Poland / Portugal / Slovakia / Slovenia / Spain / Sweden / Switzerland

Comments:

Charge for outfit + 2 adults in local currency	High Season	Low Season	Elec inc in price?	Y / N	...........amps
			Price of elec (if not inc)		...........amps

Year of guide used 20..........		Page No.		Name of town/village site listed under		
Site Name					Date of visit	......./......./.......
GPS	Latitude..(eg 12.34567) Longitude..(eg 1.23456 or -1.23456)					

Site is in: Andorra / Austria / Belgium / Croatia / Czech Republic / Denmark / Finland / France / Germany / Greece / Hungary / Italy / Luxembourg / Netherlands / Norway / Poland / Portugal / Slovakia / Slovenia / Spain / Sweden / Switzerland

Comments:

Charge for car, caravan & 2 adults in local currency	High Season	Low Season	Elec inc in price?	Y / N	...........amps
			Price of elec (if not inc)		...........amps

Please fill in your details and send to the address on the reverse of this form.
You can also complete forms online: camc.com/europereport

CUT ALONG DOTTED LINE

Year of guide used	20..........	Page No.	....	Name of town/village site listed under	
Site Name				Date of visit	......./......./.......
GPS	Latitude...(eg 12.34567) Longitude...(eg 1.23456 or -1.23456)				

Site is in: Andorra / Austria / Belgium / Croatia / Czech Republic / Denmark / Finland / France / Germany / Greece / Hungary / Italy / Luxembourg / Netherlands / Norway / Poland / Portugal / Slovakia / Slovenia / Spain / Sweden / Switzerland

Comments:

Charge for outfit + 2 adults in local currency	High Season	Low Season	Elec inc in price?	Y / N	............amps
			Price of elec (if not inc)		............amps

Year of guide used	20..........	Page No.	....	Name of town/village site listed under	
Site Name				Date of visit	......./......./.......
GPS	Latitude...(eg 12.34567) Longitude...(eg 1.23456 or -1.23456)				

Site is in: Andorra / Austria / Belgium / Croatia / Czech Republic / Denmark / Finland / France / Germany / Greece / Hungary / Italy / Luxembourg / Netherlands / Norway / Poland / Portugal / Slovakia / Slovenia / Spain / Sweden / Switzerland

Comments:

Charge for outfit + 2 adults in local currency	High Season	Low Season	Elec inc in price?	Y / N	............amps
			Price of elec (if not inc)		............amps

Year of guide used	20..........	Page No.	....	Name of town/village site listed under	
Site Name				Date of visit	......./......./.......
GPS	Latitude...(eg 12.34567) Longitude...(eg 1.23456 or -1.23456)				

Site is in: Andorra / Austria / Belgium / Croatia / Czech Republic / Denmark / Finland / France / Germany / Greece / Hungary / Italy / Luxembourg / Netherlands / Norway / Poland / Portugal / Slovakia / Slovenia / Spain / Sweden / Switzerland

Comments:

Charge for outfit + 2 adults in local currency	High Season	Low Season	Elec inc in price?	Y / N	............amps
			Price of elec (if not inc)		............amps

Your comments & opinions may be used in future editions of the guide, if you do not wish them to be used please tick ....

Name ....

Membership No. ....

Post Code ....

Are you a Caravanner / Motorhomer / Trailer-Tenter?

Do you need more blank Site Report forms?   YES / NO

Please return completed forms to:
The Editor – Overseas Touring Guides
East Grinstead House
East Grinstead
West Sussex
RH19 1FH
Please note that due to changes in the rules regarding freepost we are no longer able to provide a freepost address for the return of Site Report Forms. You can still supply your site reports free online by visiting camc.com/europereport. We apologise for any inconvenience this may cause.

Index

Index

PEFC Certified

This product is
from sustainably
managed forests and
controlled sources

PEFC

PEFC/16-33-254   www.pefc.org